ADVANCE PRAISE FOR THE BOOK

'Sam Pitroda tells a heart-warming and uplifting story of his ascent in the world—a success story that inspires optimism and reward for persistence and hard work.'

VINT CERF, INTERNET PIONEER AND
CHIEF INTERNET EVANGELIST AT GOOGLE

'*Dreaming Big* is an all-night read—suspenseful, dramatic and fascinating. It is also a valuable education on how to get "impossible" things done. Sam Pitroda has made yet another contribution to the world of technology but also to an understanding of the complexities of Indian culture.'

MARTIN COOPER, FATHER OF THE MOBILE PHONE

'Sam's heart-warming journey reads like the story of India and its people. His life is an example of big dreams and even bigger determination. This book will inspire millions to achieve the maximum against all odds.'

MUKESH AMBANI, CHAIRMAN, RELIANCE INDUSTRIES

'A remarkable life story of an extraordinary technocrat and visionary, which travels between two seemingly contrasting journeys—successful technology entrepreneurship in the US and a pioneering role in India's connectivity revolution.'

SUNIL BHARTI MITTAL, FOUNDER-CHAIRMAN AND
GROUP CEO, BHARTI ENTERPRISES

'Connectivity fittingly stands at the centre of Sam Pitroda's autobiography, *Dreaming Big*. It permeates his contributions to technology and telecommunications, especially for the people of India. It is profoundly evident in the importance of being connected to family and friends. Sam's life and his life's work make for an inspired story. It reaffirms the belief that big dreams are indeed possible and that one person can make a difference.'

AJAY BANGA, CEO, MASTERCARD

'Sam Pitroda is a most charismatic and motivational figure. He has overcome many odds and accomplished much in India and the US. His autobiography will be an inspiration to all. But this is not just an account of the past, it is also a peep into the future.'

JAIRAM RAMESH, FORMER CABINET MINISTER OF
ENVIRONMENT AND RURAL DEVELOPMENT

'A fascinating autobiography of a man who changed the course of his country through passion, purpose and determination.'

KIRAN MAZUMDAR-SHAW, CHAIRPERSON, BIOCON

'This is an astonishing and heart-warming story of someone from the most humble beginnings, who has left his amazing imprint on India and the world. I have always admired Sam, his passion, his energy, his tenacity in the face of adversity, and his ability to dream big and implement his vision. His autobiography captures the transformation agent and visionary he is!'

NANDAN NILEKANI, CO-FOUNDER, INFOSYS,
AND FOUNDING CHAIRMAN, UIDAI (AADHAAR)

DREAMING BIG

DREAMING BIG

BIG

My Journey to Connect India

SAM PITRODA
WITH DAVID CHANOFF

PORTFOLIO
PENGUIN

PORTFOLIO
Published by the Penguin Group
Penguin Books India Pvt. Ltd, 7th Floor, Infinity Tower C, DLF Cyber City,
Gurgaon 122 002, Haryana, India
Penguin Group (USA) Inc., 375 Hudson Street, New York, New York 10014, USA
Penguin Group (Canada), 90 Eglinton Avenue East, Suite 700, Toronto,
Ontario, M4P 2Y3, Canada
Penguin Books Ltd, 80 Strand, London WC2R 0RL, England
Penguin Ireland, 25 St Stephen's Green, Dublin 2, Ireland (a division of
Penguin Books Ltd)
Penguin Group (Australia), 707 Collins Street, Melbourne, Victoria 3008, Australia
Penguin Group (NZ), 67 Apollo Drive, Rosedale, Auckland 0632, New Zealand
Penguin Books (South Africa) (Pty) Ltd, Block D, Rosebank Office Park,
181 Jan Smuts Avenue, Parktown North, Johannesburg 2193, South Africa

Penguin Books Ltd, Registered Offices: 80 Strand, London WC2R 0RL, England

First published in Portfolio by Penguin Books India 2015

Text and photographs copyright © Sam Pitroda 2015

10 9 8 7 6 5 4 3 2 1

ISBN 9780670085675

For sale in the Indian Subcontinent only

Typeset in Adobe Garamond by Manipal Digital Systems, Manipal
Printed at Replika Press Pvt. Ltd, India

A PENGUIN RANDOM HOUSE COMPANY

To
Anu, for being a partner in my journey for the past fifty-three years
and
Aria, for continuing my journey into the future

Contents

Acknowledgements   xi

Part I: Family, Foundation, Fundamentals   1

1. Parents and Childhood   3
2. School and College   15
3. To America   33
4. Love and Work   55
5. Learning to Lead   73
6. Dreaming Big   91

Part II: Dreams, Democracy, Development   109

7. Indigenous Development: C-DOT   111
8. Path to Development   131
9. Technology Missions   149
10. Telecom Commission   167
11. Defeat and Distraction   195

Part III: Rebuilding, Redefining, Reflecting   217

12. Personal Challenge   219
13. Knowledge   235
14. Digital India   255
15. Innovation   269
16. At the Crossroads   301
17. Aria   321

Acknowledgements

My biography was published in 1992, just after my heart attack in 1991. At the time, I had thought that if I lived to be seventy years of age, I would write my autobiography to tell my story in my own words. And now here I am at seventy-three, with this book in my hand, *Dreaming Big: My Journey to Connect India*, inspired by the birth of my granddaughter, Aria. My journey from a little tribal town in Orissa to Chicago, and then Delhi, to help connect India with telephones, technology, knowledge, information and innovation, has been interesting, exciting, adventurous, exhilarating, challenging, daunting and rewarding. On the one hand, it has been a long and lonely journey, while on the other, a large number of people have participated and contributed generously to who I am and what I have been able to accomplish. I am thankful to each and every one of them individually and collectively.

First, I would like to thank my late parents, Gangaram and Shanta, for raising me and filling my childhood, and that of my siblings', with their great love, care and sacrifice. I also want to thank my brothers, Manek and Pinu, my sisters, the late Manjula, Shushi, Pushpa, Jashu and Indira. My thanks are also extended to my father-in-law, Haribhai, who celebrated his hundredth birthday just this July, and my brother-in-law, Yash. This book would not have been possible without the love, support and encouragement of my wife, Anu, our son, Salil, daughter, Rajal and, daughter-in-law, Arpita. In particular, I am thankful to Rajal for her careful read of my manuscript and her significant revisions.

David Chanoff deserves special thanks for co-authoring and working with me for a year on this book. He travelled to Chicago and to India and visited places in Gujarat and Orissa described in the book in order to get a first-hand impression and a real feel of my past and present.

I am very lucky to have a group of old friends who have always encouraged me to continue my work in India for the last thirty years, including the late Dr Prakash Desai, Dr Divyesh Mehta, Dr Dinker Trivedi, Dr Piyush Vyas, Dr Shiban Ganju, Dr Dilip Desai, Mehul Desai, Dr Bhupen Trivedi, Dr Bharat Thakkar, Dinesh Trivedi, Rajiv Desai and Dr Hashmukhlal. I am thankful to them all for keeping me on course.

My most important friend of all was Rajiv Gandhi, who provided a way for me to discover my life's work and meaning. I am thankful to him for his leadership and vision.

My publisher, Penguin India, has been exceptional. I convey my gratitude to them for their expertise, time and energy in polishing the manuscript and managing the process from conceptualization to completion. I would like to thank Rachita Raj for her amazing editing, Vedanti Sikka for the cover design, Radhika Marwah for the overall management and, finally, Chiki Sarkar for initiating the process. I would also like to thank Amelia Neumann-Samek in my office for coordinating and keeping track of the multiple drafts and revisions of the manuscript.

Again, there are many others who have helped in this process and otherwise—and I hope I will get to thank them in person one day.

Now, I know what it takes to write an autobiography. There is so much to say and share that there is never enough space, time and words to include every important part of one's journey. It is never complete. There are no destinations. The journey just continues. I hope the reader gets a glimpse of my ongoing journey through this book.

Part I

Family, Foundation, Fundamentals

1

Parents and Childhood

The little boy and his friend squatted in the dust at the edge of the small crowd, listening intently to the strangers. The strangers were visiting relatives in the village of Tikar, located on the fringes of the Kutch salt desert. They were talking about a wondrous 'thing' they had seen, referring to it as an *aag gaadi*. The two boys tried with all their might to imagine the object, and though the strangers were speaking in clear Gujarati, their perception of the thing stayed maddeningly outside their grasp. They were told the aag gaadi was huge and black, that it had fire inside it, that smoke poured out from its nostrils, and that it moved by itself, as though by magic. It was powerful beyond imagination, as powerful as a god. Behind it trailed many bogies, though the boys had no idea what 'bogies' meant. All the strangers said was that there were people inside the bogies. The boys looked at each other, thinking the exact same thought. This was a thing they *had* to see with their own eyes.

The next morning at eight o'clock the boys left their homes for school, just as they always did. But instead of heading for the little, white thatch-roofed building, where they both studied in the third grade, they met at the beginning of the salt pans near the river, just beyond the last houses. The strangers had said the aag gaadi visited the town of Halvad, seven miles to the south of Tikar. Not only had the boys never been there, they had never even been beyond the millet fields dotting the outskirts of the village. But they were adventurous boys, and they were consumed with wanting to see the thing—so consumed that they ran the entire seven miles to the place.

When the boys got to Halvad, they asked the people around, 'Where is the aag gaadi?'

Some people told them to go to the 'station'. That was the place where the aag gaadi was going to come. So they went to the station and waited, speculating about what the thing was going to be like. 'Maybe it is like a giant water buffalo,' said one of the boys. 'Maybe it is like four bullocks pulling a huge cart,' said the other.

As they looked away from the station into the distance they saw something coming towards them. It looked little at first, not much more than a dot, but as it came closer, it grew bigger and bigger until it was almost upon them. A huge black thing with smoke billowing out of its top, running on its own, with nothing pulling it. They stood there, staring at it, mesmerized. Then, suddenly, the thing let out a terrifying shriek, which sent the boys bolting off towards the town. They had never heard such a horrible sound. No one had told them the aag gaadi made a noise like that.

It was only when it stopped making the noise that the boys stopped running. Warily, they made their way back to the station, not knowing what might happen next. Then they saw the bogies. Peeking inside, they saw people sitting on benches. What a thing! The boys had no chairs in their houses, no benches; they and everyone they knew squatted on the ground. And here the thing had people sitting on benches inside it!

Afterwards, they ran back to Tikar, but they didn't go back to school, something which they were punished for later on. But seeing the aag gaadi was worth it. Now they had their own stories to tell.

One of those eight-year-old boys was Gangaram Pitroda, my father, born in January 1916. In our home, in the evening, my brothers and sisters and I would sit around him, the youngest on his lap, listening intently as he told us wonderful stories—tales about the train that he and his friend had seen all that time ago, about how our mother and he travelled a thousand miles across India from Gujarat to Orissa when they were young, undertaking some of the journey by train, some on a camel's back, stories about how he made a living making nails after they started living in Titilagarh, a village about 1500 kilometres south-east of Tikar, and stories about working in the forest near Titilagarh where he cut and hauled trees, where he had seen tigers with shining yellow eyes.

When I was older I put the stories together. Our family's ancestors had been carpenters and blacksmiths—*vishwakarma*s. Our family name, Pitroda, came from *pitr*, meaning 'brass', a metal they'd used to work. Our caste was called *luhar–suthar*, meaning 'blacksmiths and carpenters', and was positioned down near the lowest rung in the hierarchy of Hindu castes. My grandfather, Kalyanji Pitroda, was a farmer, as were all the men of Tikar, but he also worked as a smith, sharpening the knives and agricultural tools of his neighbours.

My grandfather had four children, my father, Gangaram, was the youngest. My father never knew his mother; she had died when he was still very young. His father, Kalyanji, worked all the time, leaving his house before dawn to go to the fields. A widower with four young children to raise, he longed for someone to take care of them and the household while he was out in the fields or doing his blacksmithing. It so happened that shortly after our grandmother died, an older male cousin of our grandfather also died, leaving behind a wife and four children. Just as Kalyanji needed someone to care for his children, his cousin's widow needed someone to bring in money for food. In the Indian family system, the wife of an older relative is called *bhabhi*. She's considered a second mother to her younger relations and their children.

So my grandfather and his bhabhi decided to jointly raise their children—four of hers and four of his. Though they lived together they didn't marry. A bhabhi is something like a mother to you, so they respected this relationship.

Bhabhi managed the household, feeding everybody and raising the children while Kalyanji worked. And his work was never-ending. As the children came of age, they had to be married off, and each wedding was an expense that an impoverished farmer-blacksmith living on the edge of the Kutch desert could not afford. As a result, Kalyanji was forced to borrow money, several hundred rupees. 'He worked many years to pay off the interest and principal all on his loans,' our father told us. 'It was only some hundreds of rupees, but hundreds of rupees in Tikar might as well have been 10,000 rupees. Your grandfather spent his life trying to free himself from debt.'

My mother was born in a village near Tikar, in June 1918, but her older brother had settled with his family in the Gujarati city of Baroda. With her brother in Baroda, my mother, Shanta, was sent there to study, where she remained till the fourth grade. The Maharaja of Baroda was a progressive man for his time and had established schools for girls as well as boys. So even though my mother came from the same kind of poverty-stricken place as my father, she had been exposed to city life, which made her more sophisticated than a boy who had been outside his village only once—back when he and his friend had skipped school to see a common train.

Not many years after Gangaram and Shanta left school, their parents arranged for the two of them to be married. Gangaram was fifteen then, and Shanta was thirteen. Gangaram was destined to be a farmer, like his father and every other male in Tikar, but fate intervened in the shape of a drought that scorched Gujarat's farmland and withered its crops. One of Gangaram's cousins had left the village some time before, after an acquaintance had arranged a job for him in the state of Orissa, on the other side of the Indian subcontinent. Gangaram's relative now wrote to him that he and his wife were happily settled in their new home. The other news was that his employer had a job for Gangaram too; they were building a railroad in Orissa and the crew could use another labourer.

With Tikar's farmers struggling to stay alive, my parents decided that they would go, even though Orissa was so far away from their families and even though the people there spoke Oriya, a language they did not understand. My father was sixteen when they left Gujarat, my mother was fourteen.

In Orissa, Gangaram began work as a labourer on the new railway. His pay was 20 rupees a month. Even on this pittance he had been able to rent from his employer a tiny hovel, where he and my mother set up house and began having babies—first, my sister Manjula, then my brother Manek, then me.

The story my father told was that when I was born in 1942, his 20-rupees-a-month salary was simply too little to scrape by on, so he gathered his courage and went to his employer. 'I have a third child now,' he said. 'I need to have a little more money.' But as it is with such

things, his employer was not sympathetic. The answ
my father, a young man full of pride, perhaps not thi
clearly, grew angry and quit his job, not realizing how
be to find another job in a little place like Titilagarh.

So there he was—three children and a wife to feed, and out of
work. The family's prospects looked grim, but then one of his friends
had an idea. 'You're a big, strong guy,' he said—my father was six
feet tall and robust—'you should make nails. The railway needs nails.
Besides, there's a war going on [it was 1942]. They [the British] need a
lot of nails. Why don't you go into the nail-making business?'

That sounded like a good idea to Gangaram. His father was a
smith, his forefathers had worked with metal for more generations than
could be counted. Why couldn't he make nails? Of course, he'd need
money for start-up costs, a wire cutter, a hammer and a coil of wire.
But Shanta had some jewellery she had been given as wedding gifts,
and she was amenable to selling them. So they mortgaged the jewellery,
and my father started in his new profession.

It wasn't difficult for him, working metal was in his blood. He
learned on the job how to cut the wire and hammer the ends of the cut
pieces into sharpened points. And soon he was doing it, making nails.

When he had made enough nails to fill a wooden bucket, he put
the bucket on his head and walked to the British administrative outpost
a couple of miles outside of Titiligarh. But there he ran into a problem.
The British officials there spoke neither Gujarati nor Oriya. Perhaps
they spoke a few words of Hindi, but he surely did not. Nor did he
speak any English. Without a negotiating language, my father simply
put the bucket down, pointed at it and held out his hand—the universal
gesture for 'give me money'. As his friend had said they would, the
British gave him some money, which he had no choice but to accept
since he wasn't able to communicate with them and ask for more.

And that was how my father did business with the British for as
long as he was in the nail-making profession. He would put out his
hand and mutely accept whatever they chose to put into it. Every
time he trudged to the British he felt humiliated. And he swore to
himself that even if it was the last thing he ever did, he would see to it
that his children learned English; he might have been humiliated, but
he wouldn't let them face the same. The British had the money and
the power, and you had to be able to speak their language.

If anything, my mother was even more determined to educate us than our father was. She had been to school in the big city. She had seen what education meant. Even though she had had to leave school after the fourth grade, she had a sense of the power that education brought with it.

With no schools in Titilagarh, my parents found a private teacher and began sending my sister Manjula, their firstborn, and my older brother, Manek, to him. At the age of three I would see them get dressed every morning and head off to the teacher's house to study. The family story was that I was so envious of all this and made such a scene every morning that my parents decided to let me go and study too at that age.

My father wanted us to learn English, but that was not one of our teacher's main languages. Instead, we were taught in Hindi, the main language of the provinces and people of northern India. Our teacher was a gentle man, teaching us to read and write with his little son, Krishna, sitting on his lap. At night the three of us would read our lessons in the light of the kerosene lantern in our bedroom.

The dwelling where I was born was tiny, but then my father began making a little money, enough to build a house near the train tracks—three small rooms, a kitchen, a veranda. All of the kids, eight of us eventually, slept in one room on mats. When morning came we'd roll the mats up and put them away, then unroll them at night. During the summer, when our dad's older brother's eight children stayed with us, everyone's mats would be crowded into the room. Sleeping was wall-to-wall then. All of us playing together made the house a chaotic circus. Our parents also slept on mats in their own room, although they later bought a wooden bed-frame with string webbing and a thin straw mattress.

When my father expanded from the nail business into the lumber business, we had enough to acquire a water buffalo and a cow, both of whom lived in our backyard. We had outdoor toilets with holes that our family and all the immediate neighbours used. There was a well in our courtyard for drinking water. We'd draw our water from there, for bathing, cooking, drinking. My mother would cook all the staples of an Indian vegetarian meal—roti, rice, vegetables, the same every day, and with lots of spices, cumin, coriander and turmeric.

Not everyone in Titilagarh was a vegetarian though. Right across the street from us, twenty feet away, lived a Muslim family. They had eight children too. We were three brothers and five sisters, and they were five brothers and three sisters. This family kept chickens that lived in the yard next to their house. As kids we would watch those chickens, and from time to time a chicken or two would go missing. Eventually, we figured out that the missing chickens were being eaten by the family—a curious thing for us, eating something that was alive.

The nearby Santhal tribal people weren't vegetarian either. They lived in the forest some miles away, where they hunted with bows and arrows, grew their own crops, and even spoke their own language, which sounded so different to us. Two of the tribal women worked in our house, helping our mother cook, clean and look after the eight of us. One of them was called Budhwari, meaning one 'born on a Wednesday', and the other was known as Tara, meaning 'star'. All the Titilagarh women we ever saw wore saris, but Budhwari and Tara wore sarongs with nothing on top, which would have been shocking otherwise, but seemed perfectly normal to them. Budhwari and Tara were more than mothers to us. They fed us, took care of us and held us when we cried. If our mother got mad at us, they took our side. They were devoted to us. All of our family's children loved them dearly, and their memories, love and affection stayed with us as we grew older, left home and raised our own families. My respect for tribal people essentially comes from my experiences with Budhwari and Tara in Orissa.

In spite of there not being a medical clinic or doctor in the town, we still managed to stay relatively healthy, even though the water we fetched from our well was far from clean. We didn't know the concept of purifying water by boiling it; instead, we strained the well water through a piece of cloth, our idea of filtering. Sometimes there would be little fish floating in the piece of cloth. Others in the village suffered a good deal more than we did. Many, children especially, had worms in their stomachs. I once saw kids who had worms coming out of their mouths, a hair-raising sight.

Our main remedies for most sicknesses were herbal plants and opium. If one of us was hurt from something, our mother would grind up some plants, or place a drop of opium on our tongues. That was almost always enough to put a child to sleep. It was a routine thing in our house. Referred to as *afeem*, opium was sold in the market right next door to us. Mother would give me money and say, 'Go get afeem'.

The vendor would put a small measure of it on a leaf and wrap it up for me to take home.

Titilagarh was surrounded by mountains and deep forests, and was flanked by two ponds, one on either side of the village. At any time of the day one would see people bathing in the ponds, women scrubbing clothes, people washing their buffalos. That was about as exciting as things got in Titilagarh. As a little child I'd sit in front of our house with my brother Manek and watch people go by. A cow might wander down the street, or a water buffalo, or someone would pedal by on a bicycle. My friends and I played with sticks, stones and ropes. We would mould things out of mud and roll a rusted bicycle-rim down the street. Sometimes, we tied a rag around the rim and set it on fire. One of us would stand next to the rim to keep it upright and the rest would run and jump through the burning ring. Somebody among my friends had heard that this is what they did in the circus. If my mother saw us, she'd scream, 'Don't do that!' But we did it anyway.

Our big game involved the railway tracks that ran across the main street, no more than a few hundred feet from our front door. We'd take a penny and put it on the track. The engine would thunder over it, flatten it completely and eject it somewhere. Then we would all go searching for the squashed coin, overjoyed at being the first to find it. As my father's lumber business prospered, he bought us a big radio, with two knobs—a wonder. We couldn't get any reception on the radio since there were no towers or stations in range, but along with my brothers and sisters I would sit in front of it, listening to the hypnotic *peeeeeee* that whistled above the background static. These were the simple pleasures of life we grew up with. We had no toys, but we were blessed with interactions where we learned from our environment by watching, listening and experiencing people, animals and birds.

I was too young to be aware of the political passions that swirled around the movement to liberate India from British colonial rule. But my parents read the newspaper, so they were aware of what was going on. Mahatma Gandhi—Gandhiji—was our great role model and hero, someone everyone looked up to and worshipped. But though I do not remember the events surrounding Independence in 1947, I do remember Gandhi's death the following year. I was six years old at the time, sitting outside my house, when my dad came home and said, 'Gandhiji has been shot dead.' My mother let out a cry: 'Ram, Ram!'

Everyone in the house was made to take a bath, the same process as if someone in the family had died.

By one of the village ponds a big mountain loomed, on top of which sat a temple to Lord Shiva. The temple was one of the pillars around which life in Titilagarh revolved. People would go there regularly for prayer, to celebrate festivals and enjoy parties of all sorts. For us kids, though, visiting the temple was mainly just a fun outing, a chance to climb the mountain and play while the adults did whatever they were doing. Lower down the slopes was another temple, built into a deep cave whose inner reaches, we heard, tunnelled on for miles through hard rock and emerged in a secret place miles away. Since people prayed in the cave temple too we weren't able to explore it, but the mystery of the secret tunnel riveted our imaginations. Somehow, though, the prayers and rituals didn't engage me. My dad wasn't very religious, and it could be that I simply absorbed his lack of interest in that side of life.

The fact that I didn't feel drawn to Shiva or any of the other deities, though, didn't stop me from enjoying the religious festivals that swept through Titilagarh on a regular basis, catching everyone up in their pomp and excitement. A huge occasion for all was the festival of the Ratha Yatra, for example, where the great god Jagannath, Lord of the Universe, was taken out of his temple in a giant chariot pulled by hundreds of devotees, with a priest dressed as a street sweeper humbly sweeping around the chariot, rendering service to the god.

Jagannath himself, meaning the main idols representing him, lived in a huge temple in the city of Puri in Orissa. The main Jagannath festival was held there, but every town in Orissa celebrated its own smaller version. In Titilagarh the entire village came together, the townspeople hauling with ropes our own great chariot with the idols inside. The chariot was massive, and the villagers spent several months building and decorating it.

The communities that comprised the village each celebrated their specific festivals, and the devotees of the different gods took special pride in their specific processions and activities. It was during these festivities that all the village folk would come together to enjoy the holiday foods and be with each other. There were festival days when we would have feasts, one when we ate only leftover food, another when people fasted; there was a festival for Krishna, the incarnation of Lord Vishnu, preserver of the universe; in another—Holi—people showered each other with coloured water and powders in celebration of the beginning of spring, when the vibrant colours of nature come back to life

Living among Titilagarh's Hindus were a number of Muslim families, including our immediate neighbours and others. Jain families were there too, and a few Sikh families as well. The community encompassed the local Oriyas, Marwaris, Gujaratis, Punjabis, Biharis and the tribals from the mountains. The tribal people were nearby and, of course, people of various castes lived in the village. But in Titilagarh, harmony reigned, and I think part of that was due to all the festivals that brought the communities together. They encouraged tolerance and helped relieve whatever tensions might have been brewing beneath the surface. Once, many years later, I was visiting the Soviet Union (as it was called then), and one of the ministers told me, 'Mr Pitroda, we are extremely impressed with India. We are impressed by how you hold so many different communities together without guns. You have so many different peoples and languages. We too have many different peoples, but if we put down our guns, our whole country would collapse.'

Festivals aside, Titilagarh may not have had much in the way of entertainment, but strange things were witnessed, and people with marvellous and apparently magical properties walked among us. There was, for example, a man called Kitchkitcho, who fell into a kind of frenzied trance every year on the same day. When the fit took him, he'd walk through the village shaking uncontrollably, under the influence of invisible forces, jerking this way and that as if being pulled apart by spirits.

It was in that state that Kitchkitcho would make his way from one house to another. On such days, families who could afford it would kill a goat, severing its head, when he came to their door. He would then take the decapitated head and suck the blood right out of the oozing neck. After he had drunk the blood the mother of the household would hand him the family's baby. (With the high birth rate, chances were always good that there would be a baby in the house.) Kitchkitcho would shake and jerk around with the baby, then he'd throw the baby up in the air, catch it, then give it back to the parents. This was thought to be auspicious, a blessing from someone possessed by the gods. Then he would head to the next house, trailed by the crowd of men, women and children that always gathered behind him.

There was another Titilagarh man who also suffered from possession. He too would wander the village in a shaking fit. The only way to bring him out of his frenzy was to give him a pot of boiling tea, right off the stove. He would take it and drink the whole thing, then slowly come back to his normal self, just as if he were coming back from some other world. That was another thing we couldn't understand. How could a person drink something boiling hot and have no reaction? As children we wondered about it, and I am still amazed to this day. There was no explanation for it. It seemed magical, another of the crazy things around us.

When my father was in the nail business he had a little stall where he did his work and hired smiths from the neighbouring villages to help him. But the lumber business took him into the forests days away from Titilagarh. He would hitch our bullock up to a covered cart, and with a driver he'd head off into the forest for a month or two of cutting trees and hauling wood. When I saw him getting ready to go, I would grab on to his legs and hold on, crying my heart out because I knew he would be gone for so long and also because I knew the forest was a dangerous place, full of tigers. I never saw tigers in our village, but from time to time we would hear that one had prowled down the street of our neighbouring town, looking hungrily for something to eat. Once in a while someone who ventured into the forest would be taken by a tiger. Sometimes, bloody remains would be found, at other times the person simply disappeared off the face of the earth. The villagers hunted tigers, killed them and dragged them back. Like many others in Titilagarh, over time we acquired a tiger skin or two. We made rugs and gloves out of them. We wore tiger belts and tiger-skin shoes.

For his lumber business, our father took with him a big knife attached to a long stick, although he knew it would be a flimsy defence against a tiger. Once, he was asleep inside the bullock cart while heading out to his work site with his driver, when his kerosene lamp swung at the back of the cart in the darkness. Waking up, he saw two bright eyes—a tiger was following close behind. 'I looked at the tiger,' he told us. 'His eyes were bright yellow. There was nothing I could do. I started saying, "Ram, Ram, Ram," praying that he wouldn't kill me. The tiger followed us for a while, then disappeared into the jungle.'

After he had been in the forest for what seemed like forever we would finally get news from a returning forest worker that our father would be returning home that week. All of us would become very excited. 'Dad is coming home, Dad is coming home!' we'd sing. We'd wait outside for him to appear, lining up in order of height, from big to small. At night we'd see an approaching bullock cart with a lantern swinging in the back, but it would turn out to be someone else, and we'd be terribly disappointed. So we'd wait and, after three or four days, he would finally appear.

As he was hard-working and astute, my father's lumber business flourished over time. With more money in his pocket he expanded our house and bought two or three more bicycles. Eventually, he acquired a cheap jeep to replace our bullock cart. By the time I was seven or eight he had established a lumberyard in town. He even built a small sawmill so that he could sell finished wood to his customers in the cities.

Through all of this, our mother and he never took their eyes off the progress we were making with our teacher. By the time my brother Manek was eleven and I eight we were outgrowing what our teacher was able to teach us; besides, he taught his lessons in Hindi and our parents wanted us to learn in Gujarati and English. 'You two need to go to school in Gujarat,' they told us. By chance, my father had a friend in the province who knew of a boarding school, and soon we learned we had been admitted to study there.

Neither Manek nor I were ready to leave home. The prospect of travelling across the country by ourselves and living with strangers was deeply unsettling as neither of us had ever been out of Titilagarh. As our mother packed our belongings into a metal trunk, tears streamed down both our faces. Mother herself was sobbing loudly as she folded clothes and tucked them into the trunk. She could hardly stand to part with us. We were so young to be leaving for a place where we would have to wash our own clothes, do our own dishes, make our own beds, and we wouldn't be allowed to eat what we wanted or do the things we always did, where we would be under the strict discipline of people we did not know. Sending us away tore at her heart. But our father and she had made up their minds. It was all for our future. Nothing was more important than giving children a good education, and my parents understood that it was empowering, defining and essential to our long-term growth and prosperity. Sending Manek and me a thousand miles away to Gujarat for education at the tender ages of eleven and eight, respectively, was the single-most important decision our parents made that changed the destiny of our family and our future generations.

2

School and College

I had seen the train go by my house a thousand times, but I had never imagined what it would be like to leave home riding away in it—a possibility too remote to enter my mind. But when the day came, our parents, some of our brothers and sisters and several distant relatives came to see us off at the Titilagarh train station. 'Crowded' is not the word to describe the train cars. People lay on the roofs, they clung to the sides like monkeys. There seemed no way in the world we could get on board. But our relatives found an open window where the passengers inside seemed packed a little less densely. There, they picked us up, Manek first, then me, and jammed us through the window, followed by the trunk our mom had packed so lovingly.

From Titilagarh the train chugged to Raipur. From Raipur it carried us to Nagpur and onwards to Bhusaval, Surat, Baroda and, finally, to Anand. Three days altogether, a thousand miles across India. Sometimes, the rush of people surging around at the different stops would separate us. Manek would find himself in one place, I in another. We wouldn't be able to see each other, which frightened me.

What if we lost each other? What would I do then? Occasionally, by some stroke of luck, a seat would open up near us and we'd jump to grab it. But most of the way we stood, sometimes wedged in so tightly that I could catch a nap standing upright.

I remember being amazed to see some passengers squeezing themselves on to the train with animals, wooden cages filled with cackling chickens and, once or twice, even a bleating goat. One traveller standing next to me had a basket of dried fish on his head. When the train lurched around a curve the basket overturned, showering me with fish. By then I was past caring. The coal-burning engine filled the air over the wagons with black soot and, after three days, Manek and I had both turned the colour of charcoal. Our hair was thick with coal dust—which had also coated our skin—and our clothes were caked in grime.

Mom had packed food for us: puris, fried potatoes, vegetables, pickles and a can of water. Sometimes, when the train stopped at stations, we would buy chickpeas from the vendors who marched alongside the stationary wagons, hawking their wares. I cannot now remember how we went to the bathroom; I think mostly we just held it in.

After what seemed like several eternities, the train pulled into Anand station, where we managed to push our way through the compartments and get off with our trunk. We found our way to the bus station for the last leg of our journey. We were on our way to the little town of Vidyanagar, home of the Sharda Mandir boarding school.

From the street the boarding school looked okay—a long, white one-storey building, a portico and hundreds of shoes lined up outside doorways stretching the length of the covered walkway. But as we stepped up beneath the columns we were filled with anxiety. This strange place was to be our new home for the next few years; our comfortable lives, the lives we had always known, were about to change in uncertain, perhaps worrisome, ways. One of the teachers greeted us as we walked up to the office door, dragging our trunk. He took us to a different building in the back, across a dusty courtyard, a dormitory and long hallways with small rooms for the 200 or so students. Manek and I were placed in one room along with two others. We had hardly got to know our room-mates when classes began. We informed our parents about our well-being by post, which normally took about five days to reach the recipient.

I was starting fifth grade, Manek the sixth. The language of instruction at the school was Gujarati, our family language, which we had learned to read and write at home, so that posed no problem. The teachers were almost all helpful and caring. One of them, Sumanbhai, was a Gandhian from Mumbai who had made teaching in a small village his life's work. He was an innovative teacher, and since Manek and I were from so far away, with no family around and no one coming to visit us, he took us under his wing, bringing us to his home, feeding us and making us feel like family. Sumanbhai got us interested in things we had never thought about or encountered in Titilagarh. He encouraged us to participate in plays, and in our music ensemble I began to learn the tabla, and Manek the flute.

Our fellow students were from all over the country. They brought with them little habits and customs from their home towns. They did odd, interesting things. One of our neighbours was Upendra, a sincere, pleasant boy, seemingly normal. Except that he did something strange with a frog he kept in his room. Every evening at five, as soon as he came back from class, he'd take two wires, plug them in and give the frog an electric shock. The frog would jump, and Upendra would measure the jump and log it in his book. He did this every day, and each day at five a bunch of us would crowd into his room to see how the frog was doing that day, how far he would jump. *12 September: 42 inches. 13 September: 39 inches.* We were all keeping track.

All these kids were looking for things to do. And that included me as well. I had found that I could do the yoga headstand pose, the *salamba*. Then I found I could do the *urdhva*, the backbend pose. So I would do that. Then for some reason Manek decided that I should practise this thing on a platform of some sort. We'd take a table, put four normal soda bottles on it, a chair on top of the bottles, four more bottles on top and, finally, another little table. Then I'd slowly and carefully climb up on the chair and on to the table. Once on the table, I'd do the salamba. After that I'd bend backwards into the urdhva, with Manek standing around to catch me in case things started to topple.

Sharda Mandir had been established near Sardar Vallabhbhai Patel's village. Patel, together with Gandhi and Nehru, had been one of the fathers of India's liberation. Each morning would begin with prayers, then exercise, then bathing. Cleanliness was important. Discipline and self-control were important. Our teachers wore the Gandhian dhoti. The atmosphere was suffused with Gandhian teachings.

The emphasis at Sharda Mandir was on living a moral life, being honest in everything, and never lying, stealing or doing anything disruptive to the community, and taking responsibility for ourselves. But being young boys, we sometimes found it difficult to adhere to the strict discipline. Not stealing didn't mean, for instance, that we didn't go raiding the surrounding mango orchards, or sneak into the berry farms to pick and eat the delicious little red berries and big green berries that were grown in the area. This was especially delightful since our food was strictly regulated. We were prohibited from having anything that was not on the school menu, including, for example, lemons, which we personally thought might enhance our vegetarian diet, and which, by chance, were grown on the nearby big family farm of one of our classmates—which is probably what brought lemons to our minds in the first place.

'Maybe you could bring us some lemons,' we suggested to our friend at one point, figuring we could cut them up, sneak them into the dining hall and surreptitiously squeeze lemon juice on our vegetables.

'Sure,' said our friend. 'No problem. Keep your window open tomorrow.'

So we did. I thought he would be dropping just a few lemons off. But when we walked into our room after school we found it awash with lemons. He must have enlisted the help of half a dozen students to bring the bags of lemons from the farm and pour them into our room through the open window. The place smelled like a lemon orchard. This would be a big problem if the teachers caught us. What in the world were we going to do with so many lemons?

Then somebody said, 'Why don't we squeeze them and put the juice into little medicine bottles?' What an idea! We collected a number of little bottles some of the boys had that had contained their medications, and started an industrial-scale operation, squeezing lemons and filling bottles. The following day, a dozen kids showed up in the dining hall carrying concealed 'medicine' bottles. They'd open them when the teachers weren't looking and drip lemon juice on to their peas, rice and beans—an anti-authoritarian triumph of epic proportions!

The moral regimen at school didn't prevent this kind of mild defiance indulged in occasionally by the students. It was imaginative.

The Gandhians taught self-reliance and creativity, which we practised. We also used creative self-reliance to thwart the room inspections carried out by the teachers. After dinner we were supposed to study quietly in our rooms, but we would, in fact, mainly goof off and play games. Somebody had noticed that the walls between the rooms were just one-brick thick. Not only that, we found that if you worked at it, you could even loosen and remove a brick, which everyone in our hall did, hanging shirts or pants over the gaps to hide them. When a teacher showed up for inspection, hushed whispers travelled like lightning down the hall from room to room through the peepholes: 'Teacher is coming! Teacher is coming!' The inspectors thought we were the best behaved, most studious group of boys they had ever seen.

These kinds of things were hardly criminal activities; but in fact there was a real criminal at large in the town of Vidyanagar, the famous chief of a gang of robbers and murderers, a dacoit, the Indian equivalent of a mob boss. None of us had ever seen him, but he fascinated us all. He had guns and knives and did things that held our imaginations in thrall.

I don't think the strict Gandhian moral code we lived under whetted our appetite for our obsession with this dacoit and his criminality. Famous bandit chiefs have always exerted a hold over India's imagination—the same way Mafia bosses do in America; and boys like us were the least likely to ignore the presence of such a person living so close by.

The school's devotion to absolute honesty, though, did result in a tragedy that horrified me and the many other boys who witnessed it. The matter concerned a twelve-year-old classmate of ours by the name of Zaver. I didn't know him very well even though he lived in the room next to ours. I wasn't sure where he came from or what his background was. But everyone knew about his hobby of collecting burned-out light bulbs. If a bulb went out in someone's room, he would promptly go and collect it. He had found a way to fill used bulbs with coloured water, and he would string these into garlands in a way that seemed decorative, even beautiful.

Zaver had made five or six of these garlands before one of the teachers discovered them and harshly took him to task. 'This is stealing!' he admonished. 'You cannot be a dishonest person, taking things that don't belong to you. You should not be doing this!'

Zaver didn't understand. It had never occurred to him that he might be doing something wrong, and here he was accused of stealing and chastised as a thief. Zaver was so deeply humiliated by this accusation that there seemed only one way out for him. He decided to kill himself.

There was a railway track not too far from the school, and early in the morning, before the train came, Zaver went there and lay down on it, stretching his neck across the track. The early morning train came not long after and severed his head.

At seven o'clock each morning all the boys assembled outside for exercise time. With a teacher leading, we did jumping jacks, squats, stretches and other gymnastic moves. One of our classmates who was more athletic and fitness-oriented than the rest of us used to get up even earlier to run for fifteen or twenty minutes, then come back in time to join the rest of the group.

That morning we were all in the yard, rubbing the sleep out of our eyes and getting ready to begin exercising, when this boy ran towards us, gripping something in his hand. It took a moment for us to grasp that the thing he was holding was Zaver's head. Everyone started shouting, 'Look, look, look! What's happened?' We stared, dumbfounded, in shock. 'Why do you have Zaver's head? Have you killed Zaver?'

'I was running near the tracks,' our friend gasped, continuing, 'I saw Zaver's body, also his head. The train must have run over him. I thought nobody would believe me, so I brought his head back.' And that was the end of the gory and heartbreaking incident.

～

We were at school for five months before the first vacations came upon us. The train back to Titilagarh was just as crowded as it had been during our initial journey, but the trip seemed less of an adventure. We were more sophisticated now. We had been to the other side of the country, made friends with fellow students from all over, familiarized ourselves with their different languages and habits, and acquired knowledge about things we had never heard of or even thought of before.

The train rolled into Titilagarh's little station at 10.30 in the night, but there they were—our family members waving a welcome lantern at us. What a wonderful feeling to be home. We walked down with our bags from the railway station straight to our house, where Mom had a delicious meal ready. Everybody was happy and crying, especially her. There her children were, home at last from so far away, where they had no family to help them, where she suspected they probably weren't being fed properly, where they had to do their own laundry, wash their own dishes, clean their own room. She was suffering from the knowledge of it all. Of course, we hadn't been suffering in any way. We were learning to take care of ourselves and becoming confident that we could do it. We were growing up. But it was a great happiness to be at home with everyone, where we could have a break from the five months of Gandhian self-reliance that had been drilled into us, where we didn't have to get up at 5.30 every morning to exercise or say our prayers, where we felt enveloped in love—where we were free.

Manek and I studied at the Sharda Mandir school until I was thirteen and he sixteen. We learned the subjects on the curriculum—the math and science, languages and history. But it wasn't all academics, we absorbed the Gandhian life philosophy of honouring the work done with your hands, of understanding the importance of the dignity of labour, of self-reliance, self-discipline, of respect for yourself and others, of never telling an untruth, of simplicity. Over time these principles got ingrained into our psyches. Gandhi himself had died a number of years earlier, but his teachings were alive and pervaded throughout India, and nowhere more so than in our school.

After five years, though, it was time to move on, to someplace that would give us a broader exposure than the cocoon of a Gandhian boarding school in a small village. Our mother had gone to primary school in Baroda, one of the biggest cities in Gujarat, the city where her older brother had settled down. Our uncle still lived in Baroda, so it seemed logical for us to find schools there, a place with some family around, for help and even moral support. Manek enrolled in a local high-school; I opted for a technical school where machinery, carpentry, plumbing and electrical work were taught. I liked that. And being the son of a metal worker and woodsman, I thought it was a good thing for me to do. I was, after all, a hereditary suthar, someone who should know how to work with his hands.

The high-school course was two years long, the same as the technical school. But when we finished in those places, we were thirsty for still more education.

In Baroda there was a well-known institution of higher learning, the Maharaja Sayajirao University, established by the progressive King Gaekwad. We were poor, but we had good grades. Manek and I both enrolled there, in the science faculty, which we had heard something about. The university was home to other colleges as well, teaching the arts, humanities, engineering—but, sadly, nobody had told us about these, as we had no one to guide or mentor us. No one in our extended family had ever been to university, and many, if not most, of our aunts and uncles could neither read nor write.

By this time we had taken a small two-room apartment with one of our cousins, Vajubhai, who had also come from Titilagarh to Baroda to study. Manek and I had been living together our entire lives, having been away from home for years now. We had always been close—inseparable, in fact. We wore the same clothes, liked the same movies and music, and ate the same food. Every day we rode to school together on our sole bicycle, Manek pedalling, me riding pillion, holding our books. We were more than brothers—we were each others' best friends and closest confidants.

The major subjects I studied were physics, mathematics and chemistry. Chemistry I wasn't fond of, but physics and mathematics I found captivating. I might not have been an especially attentive student before, but now I was surely enthralled. Mathematical series, especially, opened up a new world of thought—the Jacobian series, the Taylor series and the trigonometric series. I was completely taken in, delving in deeper and deeper as my studies progressed. Math seemed to me the very foundation of life. Our mathematics professors kept me on the edge of my seat. Numbers, I noticed, made things happen, made the world go round. The concept of zero, for example—what a powerful concept it is; you go up to some point, put a zero, then you start all over again; here in front of us was the origin of decimal notation. With just this little idea of zero, you can link up all the things in the world; you can go up to millions and billions. You can't do that without the notion of zero, a concept I was thrilled to learn had first been formulated by Indian mathematicians.

The same went for physics too. Physics was an extension of mathematics, the application of math in the real world. You could sit at your desk with paper and a pencil and determine exactly at what point a car driving at a certain speed would tip over going around a curve of a certain radius. In your head you could see the laws that governed how objects interact, how they move, collide, speed up and slow down. I read about Isaac Newton, Niels Bohr, Werner Heisenberg, Enrico Fermi and, above all, Albert Einstein.

I was awestruck by these people who seemed to make things happen simply by thinking about them. I had learned to revere Gandhi, now I learned to revere Einstein. One influenced great global events by his actions, the other explained the mysticism of our universe with his thinking.

They fascinated me. Gandhi, marching to Dandi to protest the salt tax, fasting to bring about change and reconciliation, and changing the course of history by projecting his immense moral force. Einstein, on the other hand, sitting there with paper and pencil, creating an entirely new science, with no equipment, no instruments, no computers. Nothing. He just visualized it, sitting there and saying to himself, 'Ah, these things go like this, those like that. Particles, waves, energy, velocity.' Ah. Changing the whole direction of the world and humanity. Gandhi became my role model for truth, simplicity, love, sacrifice, character and ethics. And Einstein became my role model for scientific thinking, imagination and innovations.

Sharda Mandir taught us discipline, tolerance, morals and character. At Maharaja Sayajirao University my intellectual life opened up. And, if anything, my social world opened up even more—or at least it seemed more important to me. I participated in plays, played cricket and debated boisterously. *In the interest of a healthy cooperative movement, the pace of sound growth should be forced through state aid.* That was the topic written on the slip of paper I drew at one of the debate contests. I was supposed to deliver a ten-minute extemporaneous argument in favour of the topic. But what did it mean? I had no idea. I panicked. Then I thought, just take it a phrase at a time. *A healthy cooperative movement.* Explain what that might be. *The pace of growth.* Now explain that. You had to be able to think on your feet. I quickly learned on my feet.

I acted in plays, in Gujarati and Hindi dramas, memorizing speeches and participating in acting competitions. I was also part of a travelling drama troupe. This experience showed me that I wasn't nervous about performing in front of crowds, and I found acting to be an excellent way to improve one's memory, what with learning the dialogues and all.

Manek and I had known and become used to kids from far away at our boarding school. But the mix at the university was so much broader, more interesting and wealthier. Many of our fellow students were rich, urban kids. They drove to school on their own motorbikes while we were still riding double on our bicycle. We truly began to see another side of life here. The possibilities seemed endless, and doors were opening up to vistas we hadn't imagined.

At least that was the way it seemed to me. Manek, though, was taking a different path. Despite his inherent intelligence, he wasn't doing too well in his studies and, after our second year in college, he decided to go back to Titilagarh to help our father out with his business, which was going through a difficult period at the time.

Given our father's problems, I realized I was going to have to start making money on my own. One obvious way of doing so was by tutoring. I was a second-year student now, and good at physics and math—why couldn't I teach first-year students? I started off with just one tutee, but by the end of the year I had accumulated five pupils, who would all come by my apartment at night. In the second year I had gone up to fifteen students, and as I moved further ahead, I began teaching more and more students with advanced capabilities.

My acting career helped me again as I learned to be a good communicator. Teaching also forced me to clarify my own thoughts. I often needed to answer questions I hadn't thought of myself, so I learned to work at it and understand issues more thoroughly as I went along. I enjoyed teaching. The students would come over and sit in front of my blackboard. They called me 'sir'. I felt good inside. My self-esteem went up. I was young, I was teaching college kids, I was respected. I was only charging a small fee, but the money multiplied quickly.

Then my dad announced that my younger brother, Pinu, was ready to come to Baroda to study. 'I'm sending him,' he said. 'He'll go to school there. It is your responsibility to take care of him.' So Pinu came to live with us. Later, my younger sister, Sushi, also came to study. That was a big thing for my parents to do, sending a thirteen-year-old girl a thousand miles away. So I became the head of the Pitroda gang in Baroda. I felt more like a father to them than a brother.

Sushi was a teenager. I was concerned about her studies and her well-being, but one thing I wasn't worried about was boys. Like all Indian girls at that time, Sushi was raised to marry the person our parents chose for her. Other boys would never be allowed to enter the picture.

Sons too were expected to marry whomever their parents chose, and not long after Manek returned home, my parents selected a girl they thought would be right for him. He didn't know her, he had never met her. 'Why don't *you* go see her,' he told me. 'If you like her, I'll marry her.' I went and met her, liked her, and Manek married her in a simple ceremony that took place in her home so as to avoid the usual wedding expenses that would otherwise befall her dad. Immediately, Manek sent his wife to Baroda to take care of his younger siblings.

On account of living by ourselves from an early age, we learned to survive on our own. We acquired new skills, took risks, thought out of the box and solved our own problems. We weren't burdened by traditional/cultural baggage and taboos. We decided what is right and what is wrong on the basis of ethics, values and honesty, without being affected by prejudices and social pressures. We had no elders to please or parents' orders to follow. We knew that we were loved by our family, and that they would support us in our educational endeavours. We set our own guidelines, managed our own schedules, finances, studies and social interactions. We were essentially living the life of an entrepreneur with autonomy, freedom and flexibility. Early in life we realized that one has to *take* responsibility for things—it is not going to be assigned to you by somebody. This kind of freedom for children in the 1950s was unusual; however, it was essential for our education to be in Gujarat, away from home.

Some time after Manek was married I received a message from a close mutual friend of ours, Kirit Vaidya. Kirit was coming to Baroda to meet his to-be wife's family. Would I mind accompanying him when he went to visit them?

At the appointed time I went on my bicycle to the address I had been given. As I walked into the house I saw this beautiful, young girl who was drying her hair, which she must have just washed. Her hair was a lustrous black, and it flowed down her back. Her face was lovely, with fine, delicate features. She saw me and smiled shyly. That night I wrote in my diary: 'Today I met the girl I'm going to marry.'

The girl I had seen was the younger sister of Kirit's fiancée. Her name was Anjana—Anjana Chhaya. She was a first-year student at the university.

As Kirit's wedding approached, I had tea several times with his future father-in-law, a high-level government officer in the Indian Administrative Service, who had been posted in Baroda to acquire land for a government refinery. I even met the rest of the family. They were all extremely friendly—I was their future son-in-law's friend. It turned out that they were Nagar Brahmins, occupying the absolute pinnacle on the caste ladder, higher even than regular Brahmins. How this might work in the scheme of things considering I was a suthar interested in marrying their daughter, I didn't know. But I wasn't concerned yet. I was going to keep my marriage intentions strictly to myself.

The family had just moved to Baroda, so they didn't know their way around the city. I did, though, so I was able to help them with all the wedding planning, which also gave me a chance to see Anjana. As time went on I became more and more friendly with the family. They were hard-core Brahmins, but any superiority or other caste-based feelings they may have had, they did not impose on me, as I didn't sense any kind of disrespect from them. I was, by this time, going in for my master's in physics. I was into drama and debating. I had even been elected the student representative, something akin to the president of the student body. I was known at the university, where Anjana—'Anu' to me—was just starting out as a freshman.

As my friendship with the family grew, I began to spend more and more time with them all. Among other things, I designed and helped build a sofa set for their living room, drawing on the woodworking skills I had learned at the technical school. All of this gave me the chance to see Anu and get to know her better. Although she was only a first-year student, she was already a big hit on campus. She was amazing—so beautiful that everyone noticed her. Boys stopped and stared when she walked by; they whistled at her and talked about her. I still didn't let her know anything about how I felt, but the fact was that I was smitten. I was at the family's house so much that I was missing classes, something that my professors eventually noticed. 'What's going on with you?' one of them asked me. 'You're not coming to class. You're not doing your experiments. You're always goofing off. Keep this up and you'll never pass. There's no way you'll get your degree.' I had been warned.

A turning point in our relationship came when Anu's father, a collector, was transferred again, and the family had to move, first to Surat, then to the city of Godhra, sixty or seventy miles from Baroda. With her family away, Anu moved into the university dormitory. In those days, a female student staying by herself in the dorm needed either a family member or an appointed local guardian to be responsible for her.

I was by now a good friend of the family as well as an old friend of their son-in-law, Kirit. They knew about my Gandhian boarding-school background. They had even heard about a campus incident where a couple of male students had made some vulgar remarks to a female student while I had been in the vicinity, looking at a school bulletin-board.

Turning around, the girl, thinking I was the culprit, had begun screaming at me. 'How can you say something like that to me? Don't you have a mother? A sister?'

I had no idea what she was talking about. I had a moustache at the time, and was just looking at her nonplussed, distractedly stroking my moustache, which angered her even more, inevitably drawing a crowd of curious students who collected to see what was happening. Everyone was looking at the girl and me. She was screaming. I was saying nothing, numb, and in a state of shock, wondering what was going on and how this altercation had begun. Meanwhile, the original culprits, the boys who had made the remarks, had coolly walked away and were nowhere in sight.

As this scene was unfolding, the then university dean, Dr M.N. Bhatt, came by. 'What's going on here?' he said.

'Sir, someone did something to this girl, I'm not sure what. But it wasn't me. I was just standing here when she began yelling at me.'

'You.' The dean turned to the girl. 'You're an arts student. You don't even belong in this part of campus. I know this boy. I believe him. If he says he didn't do it, he didn't do it.'

The dean trusted me. The family trusted me. I was the obvious choice for taking responsibility for Anu once her family left. And that is how I came to be appointed her official local guardian.

By this time, I had two younger sisters and a brother living with me in our apartment. Anu began spending a great deal of time with us, teaching my siblings, playing games with them and generally taking care of them on and off. With her family gone, we became her family, at least her substitute family. If she wanted to stay late or even sleep over, that was okay. I was her guardian. I could write her a note.

More than a year had passed since we had met, but I still hadn't said anything to her about my feelings. But finally I just couldn't hold it in. It was time. One night she was at our apartment studying with my brother and sisters, all of us sitting around the dining table. When the others weren't looking, I wrote a note and passed it to her. 'I am in love with you,' I wrote. 'Will you marry me?'

Anu read the note, but said nothing. Instead, she glanced at my brother and sisters, whose heads were bent down over their books. Then she passed a note back to me. It was a single word. 'Yes.'

Now we started seeing each other as boyfriend and girlfriend. I'd borrow a motorcycle and take Anu for bike rides. We'd proudly walk hand in hand, find some secluded spot where we could share an intimate moment and kiss, or we'd go to a friend's apartment near the university. We even went away for a weekend together to a hotel in Ahmedabad, Gujarat's capital city. We were—in each others' eyes, at least—bonded together, even though neither of our families had an inkling yet of any of it.

It sounds strange to say this, fifty years later, but though we were together all the time, though we even spent a weekend at a hotel, we had never had sex. Doing what we were doing was by itself a total violation of what was acceptable to society at the time. Sex seemed something just too far over the boundary lines of morality and not in accordance with how we were brought up. Also, by this time, I had almost completed my master's in science and was planning to continue my studies in America. 'Who knows what might happen to me over there,' I told Anu. 'What if I die there? What would happen to you then?'

Finally, I just could not keep this secret from her parents any longer. I had no idea how this was going to play out. I was their family friend. They had appointed me Anu's guardian. They trusted me implicitly. And here I was telling them that I wanted to *marry* their daughter? And then, of course, on top of that, I was a suthar . . . wanting to marry their Nagar Brahmin daughter.

But I had to do it sometime. I mustered up all my courage. I took a bus to Godhra, found my way to their house, knocked on the door and walked in. The next thing I knew their dog came running at me and bit me on the hand. By the time their servant had pulled him away, I was in too much turmoil to say a word to them. I just didn't have the guts.

But I did tell my family. My dad was happy about it. I had found a girl I loved—that was enough for him. My mother, on the other hand, was most definitely not pleased. She may have given up on me and my ways by that time, but this was hardly tolerable. She thought that if I married outside our caste she would have a big problem finding husbands for my sisters.

By this time I had accumulated quite a lot of savings from all the tutoring I was doing. I was thinking about going to America to study—the holy grail for Indian students. I was also thinking that maybe when I came back I would start my own company. My father was a businessman, maybe I was suited for that field as well. I loved physics, especially the electronics side. Perhaps I could start some kind of electronics company. The possibilities were endless.

With that idyllic future in mind, I looked for and found over an acre of land that was within my budget and made an offer, which the owner accepted. But when I was ready to close the deal I found that I needed to buy a transaction stamp, which I hadn't known about and hadn't factored into my expenses, which meant I was 2000 rupees short. Not only that, I was locked in. If I couldn't pay up immediately, I'd lose the land and my money.

In desperation, I went to a school friend of mine whose father owned a dairy shop and asked if I could borrow the outstanding amount. He didn't hesitate. 'Sure,' he said. 'No problem.' But my friend's father wouldn't hear of it. It was the religious holiday of Dhan Teras. 'Don't you know you can't lend anyone money now?' his father countered. This started a big father–son argument, which was only settled when my friend thrust the money into my hands.

With the extra 2000 I signed the deed of sale and became a landowner. In a demonstration of irrational self-assuredness, I put up a sign that read 'Pitroda Electronics'. I had a vision in my head of the factory I would build in my imagined future.

All of this, however, meant that I didn't have a penny to my name, in addition to being 2000 rupees in debt. That wouldn't have mattered, particularly if I was going to stay in India. Despite my professors' predictions of failure and doom, I passed my master's exam with first-class honours. I could have stepped into an instructor's job in the physics department, earned the money, paid my debts and pursued my career.

But golden America beckoned. One day I had seen a newspaper headline: 'President John F. Kennedy Will Send a Man to the Moon'. The next thought that came into my head was: I need to go to America. That's the place! Look at what they're doing—they're sending men to the moon!

I talked to Manek about it, and he was keen that I go. We were so close that we saw ourselves in each other. Manek hadn't been able to finish his studies, but he couldn't have been happier that I had done it—the first in our family. I think he saw his own dreams in me. And going to America? Everyone dreamed of going to America. It was exciting and alluring. America meant freedom and opportunity. America meant prosperity.

I read about colleges at the US consulate and applied to the University of Oregon, where I was accepted. But one of my classmates Bhupen Trivedi had heard about the Illinois Institute of Technology. He already had a scholarship to do his PhD there. 'It's supposed to be a very good school,' he told me. So I thought, why not go with Bhupen? (Neither of us had heard about places like MIT or Caltech at the time.) So I applied there, and got accepted too.

To actually go there, of course, required money, which—after buying land for my future factory and being in debt to my friend—I didn't have. When I looked at the situation closely, I figured that I would need 3000 rupees to buy a ticket. The first semester's tuition instalment at the Illinois Institute was 3300 rupees. I'd need around 7000 rupees to cover the whole thing: travel plus school.

With high hopes, I applied to the Orissa provincial government for a scholarship. I was told they didn't offer any. But they said they could give me an educational loan of 600 dollars. Following this, I tutored students like crazy to make extra money and managed to put together the equivalent of 400 dollars. This was enough to get me to Chicago and pay my tuition. I'd have no money to live on, but Bhupen's scholarship was going to provide a monthly stipend and we were close friends. 'Don't worry,' said Bhupen. 'It should be enough for the both of us.'

We were registered for the second semester, starting in January 1965. Since we had plenty of time to get to Chicago, Bhupen and I decided that we ought to travel slowly and experience the world along the way. We could take a boat from Bombay (as it was known at the time) to Genoa in Italy. From there we could go by train through Paris, then cross the English Channel to England. From London we'd fly to New York, and go by bus to Chicago. We found a boat to Italy that stopped first at Karachi, then Aden, then Egypt. A former female classmate of mine was then based in London. I wrote to her that we were arriving and she wrote back inviting us to stay with her for four or five days. Everything was in place. We bought our tickets and got ready to go.

Bhupen's family accompanied us to Bombay, the port of departure from where our boat was leaving. My parents and my sisters came to bid us farewell too. As did Anu, whose parents still knew nothing about our marriage plans. We had decided that I would settle down first and find a way to earn a living as well as go to school. Then I would send for her and we would get married. Of course, we'd have to tell her parents first, which could potentially create a big problem. But I had the confidence of youth. Somehow, we'd be able to work this out with them. We had no doubt.

Our boat left from the great Gateway of India on Bombay's south harbour, a monumental arched structure the British had built as a fitting arrival and departure point for viceroys and generals. As Bhupen and I stepped on to the gangway and turned to wave goodbye, our entire leave-taking party was bathed in tears—Bhupen's family, my parents and sisters, and Anu. It was a sad sight, all our loved ones standing there, weeping, on the dock. But Bhupen and I were exhilarated. We were about to start the adventure of our lives.

As we climbed the gangway I saw somebody I thought I knew a few steps ahead of us.

'Mahen,' I said, 'is that you?'

'Yes?' he said, turning.

It was Mahen Tamakuwala, a classmate of mine from boarding school.

When we got on board we found there was a bunch of other Indian students going to America and England, maybe ten of us all together, a little Indian gang. As the boat's engines rumbled and we began to slide out of the harbour and into the Arabian Sea, we stood at the railing together and watched the Gateway slowly recede, then disappear. Suddenly, it seemed to me as if I had lost my entire life. Somehow, the earth had shifted. Everything was gone, back there, below the horizon, my family, my friends, my connections, my roots, my love—especially my love—all of it lost. We were alone on a vast, empty sea. I felt a surge of emotions. Tears welled up in my eyes, but I blinked them away. I knew the others might see me. If they saw me cry, I knew I'd be finished.

Watching Bombay slip away beyond the horizon, I had felt a pang of loss. As I stood at the ship's railing staring into the blackness, something much deeper hit me. For the first time in my life I found myself thinking about India itself—my home, the place I loved, which I had always taken so completely for granted. India contained so much, so many languages and cultures and peoples, all mixed together. India housed mystics and snake charmers, gods and goddesses. It had music and dancing, its own colours, sounds, smells and the taste of spices. I had never valued them. I had never valued any of it.

I thought: Look at the things you could do in my country. You could grow up in a distant village like I had. From a place like Titilagarh you could rise up and go to school. You could learn Hindi, Oriya, Gujarati and English. You could study at a university at almost no cost. I had never considered any of that properly. I had never considered it at all.

I had left that world, for good, it seemed to me then. Not just Anu and my parents and sisters and brothers, but my country—my land. It was gone, vanished back there in the blackness. *Now I cannot hear them, see them, touch them or even talk to them. They have become my past.* I felt a love for India unlike anything I had ever felt before. I felt so heartsick that for a moment I wondered if I would survive my foray abroad. I thought of how Gandhi, Nehru and the other leaders must have felt when they left India. I know they learnt to appreciate India even more when they went overseas. I swore that I would never forget. I would cherish my memories, no matter what happened. *I will come back, some day, to value all that I have never valued, and cherish all that I have never cherished.* I felt abandoned, utterly alone, filled with longing for all that I had parted with so carelessly, without a thought for the immensity and magnificence of the world that I was leaving.

3

To America

With India out of sight we were momentarily at a loss for what to do. Then we saw some of our fellow passengers with glasses of beer in their hands. The ship's bar was open. 'Look,' somebody said, 'why don't we try it?' I had never had beer before in my life. I was sure none of the others had either. But there the bar was, and the beer didn't even cost anything. On this ship passengers were given free beer during the first hour of a new voyage.

We approached the bar tentatively, even shyly. We ordered beers, except for a couple of students who didn't want to risk it.

'Sure,' said the bartender. 'What kind?'

We looked around. 'Whatever that guy's having,' I said, motioning towards one of our fellow passengers.

A moment later we had beer glasses in our hands. I raised mine and took a sip of the most bitter, horrible thing I'd ever tasted. I glanced around. The looks on the faces of the rest of our newly minted beer drinkers said everything. 'What should we do?' someone whispered. 'We can't just throw it out. We'll look insane.'

'Let's go over to the railing,' I whispered back. 'Pour out a little at a time. Pretend you're drinking, but pour it out little by little. No one will see what we're doing.' All of us proceeded to follow this direction. And it was clear that none of us was going to be heading back to the bar anytime soon!

Our next encounter with new things didn't go well either. We had all been billeted in cramped cabins, housing four bunk-beds each along with a tiny attached bathroom. Things there weren't exactly as we had expected them to be. Where was the hole to squat over? And where was the bucket of water to clean yourself with?

This was worrisome. How were we supposed to go to the toilet here? We discussed it together, but no one had a clue. Fortunately, before the problem became urgent a porter came by. We showed him the bathroom, with its strange porcelain contraption. 'What is this thing?' we asked. 'And what is this roll of paper doing here?'

He explained it to us. Interesting—though he didn't explain where the paper was supposed to go until he came by to clean up the next day. We weren't around when he came, so he helpfully left us a note. 'The paper goes in the bowl. Not in the wastebasket.' Okay, we thought, the bowl. The bowl—surely that meant the sink? It took us another day to straighten that point out, by which time we felt that we had been accustoming ourselves to these foreign ways pretty well.

As the days passed, though, I was caught up in the novelty of the world I was discovering. I was smack in the middle of the white man. Except for the ten or eleven of us, almost all the other passengers were European. I had never seen so many of them together in one place. And these white people were always on the deck, sunbathing, drinking beer, sipping cocktails. They'd shoot birds from the deck, as if they were out hunting somewhere. I'd never seen such sights. At night there were dances, with the men and women holding each other. I sat there and watched, thinking that I could never, ever have held a woman that way, even if one had asked me to.

I realized I had to adapt. I decided I wasn't going to eat with my hands any more. I was going to sit properly. I couldn't behave like I did in the village; I had to behave the way the people around me behaved. Our fellow passengers would put their napkins on their laps, so I did the same. After dinner there was a dessert of cheese. What was this thing—cheese? We had never seen it. Cheese, a few grapes and crackers. People picked at them delicately. It was some kind of a white-person ritual; they all did it. Did it mean something? I didn't know.

I was leaving my old habits behind. I thought: How must Gandhi have felt, leaving India on a boat for a different world? Our vessel was sophisticated at least. On our boat there was no discrimination. To our fellow passengers we were just students. Nice kids. The older women talked to us, they treated us with warmth and sympathy— Oh, poor children, going so far away from home. It wasn't like this in Gandhi's time. We weren't brown people to be looked down upon, condescended to, despised.

I thought about Gandhi, as I often did when something significant was happening to me. The boarding school had put him inside my head permanently. Okay, I thought, *You have to change, so change. But not your fundamentals. You can be like Gandhi. Don't worry about your wants. You should stay simple, stay pure. You can change, but you can stay the same too. No matter how far you go.*

~

Our ship stopped for a day in Karachi, where we had dinner with a Parsi family one of the boys' parents knew. The next stop was the port city of Aden in Yemen, still a British colony back then. Mahen wanted to buy a watch there. Someone had told him that the best ones came from the Swiss watchmaker Favre-Leuba—unavailable in India, but apparently obtainable for sale in the Aden marketplace. So off we went to the market where we marvelled at the profusion of goods, the variety of shirts, pants, jackets, scarves, leather goods, luggage, watches. How rich this place must be, we thought.

In my heart I was missing my mother and father, my brothers and sisters, Anu—especially Anu. But my head was saying, *Listen, that's over. You won't be seeing them for a long, long time. You're on your own in this foreign universe. You have to be strong. You've decided to explore the world? You've decided to have adventures? Good! Now is your time to do it. The only thing you need is change—within and without.*

Our next stop was Egypt. The ship was going through the canal, but passengers had the option to either stay on board or go by bus to the tourist sights and meet the ship at the far end.

We took the bus. We were especially excited to see the Pyramids and the Great Sphinx in Giza. Everything was on such a monumental scale that it seemed other-worldly. We had seen camels in India, but there was still something exotic and strange about the Egyptian animals. The people we met, the guides and others, were extremely friendly. That was true of Cairo also, though the street scenes there seemed more familiar. 'Look at this chaos,' said Bhupen. A crush of cars and rickshaws and people jammed the streets. 'It looks like India.' People were screaming and shouting, jostling us, harassing us to buy things. The pungent smell of spices and street food filled the air.

As part of the tour, our guide took us to the university where we noticed the presence of many beautiful girls. All those girls, most, in those days, without headscarves, their hair flowing freely, their skirts shorter than what we were used to seeing, captivated us. We stared after them. 'Why are we going all the way to America?' Bhupen said. 'This would have been closer to home, it even feels like home. Look at those girls. Maybe we should have come here instead.'

Back on the ship, our next stop was Naples, with a side trip to Pompeii. This was our first exposure to a European country. Naples was fabulous; it opened our eyes completely. Great buildings, and—after Cairo—everything seemed so clean, as if it had just been washed yesterday. So *this* is civilization, we thought. And then Pompeii, with its erotic frescoes had our eyes wide open like saucers.

I think none of us had quite recovered from Pompeii when we got back to the ship and found that one of our fellow passengers, an Italian woman, was looking for us. We had got to know this lady during the trip. She had taken it upon herself to be kind to us—explaining things, showing us what foods were what, giving us fruit, offering us bottles of water—but she overdid it. We could feel there was something a little strange going on, as though she maybe wanted something from us, though we couldn't imagine what that could be. Finally, it seemed as if she was going to reveal her real motives.

'I need to talk to you,' she told me.

'Okay,' I said.

'Look, our last stop is Genoa. I have ten suitcases. There are ten of you. Do you think each one of you could carry one of my bags through customs for me? It would mean a lot. You're in transit out of Italy, so they won't be checking you. They won't ask you anything. What do you think? Could you carry them?'

She had obviously done this before. She had it all worked out, how we'd get the bags through, and how she'd meet us at the train station and get them from us. She had boarded the boat in Hong Kong, her luggage packed full of whatever it was she was smuggling. I would have bet anything that she had previously also found Indian students like us who had boarded the ship in Bombay. Like us, they must have been young, innocent and thankful for somebody who was happy to make friends with them and explain how things worked.

I called a meeting with our gang. Everybody said, 'We can't do that. It's smuggling. We'll get caught. We'll be in jail.'

I said, 'Look, nothing's going to happen to us. We're in transit, so there's no customs check. We can take her bags along with ours. Worst case—if you get nervous you can just leave the bag somewhere. Come on, we have to take the risk. We are on a journey to take risks. You can't *not* accept this. It's interesting, right? It's a challenge. It's an adventure.'

In the end, they gave in. We each took one bag. At the terminal there were two lines, one for people staying in Italy, one for those in transit. We got in the transit line, which moved quickly past a customs policeman who was surveying the people who passed by him with a distinct lack of interest, stopping no one and asking no questions.

In a minute we were out on the street with all the bags, breathing deep sighs of relief. Cabs were waiting for us, part of the travel package. We piled the luggage in and headed off to the Genoa train station, where we found our train platform and stood around, waiting nervously for the ship lady to arrive, trying hard to look as though we weren't watching the two blue-uniformed policemen who were strolling through the station.

Finally, she arrived, bringing a couple of porters to get the bags. 'Here,' she said, 'gifts for you.' She handed us two bottles of wine and some wrapped sandwiches. A minute later she had taken the bags and was gone. We had accomplished the mission! We were victors!

We opened the sandwiches. 'What's this?' I asked Bhupen.

'It's ham,' he said. 'Pig meat. We can't eat this stuff.'

We tossed the ham out and ate the bread. The wine bottles we dumped into a trash can. But we felt good. This was still a win. We took a risk and succeeded. It felt like maybe we could adapt to this new world after all.

~

We took a train from Genoa to London and found ourselves on a ferry in the English Channel in the middle of winter on a violent sea. Our boat trip across the Arabian Sea had been on water as smooth as glass under sunny skies. Our passage through the Mediterranean had been calm and uneventful. But the English Channel was raging. Huge waves battered the ferry. The wind howled. Our boat pitched this way and that, flinging things around, first to one side, then the other. Everywhere we looked, people were vomiting. It wasn't long before we joined them. Everything was filthy, as if the ship hadn't been cleaned after the last crossing—or ever. The only saving grace was that in a few hours we had reached Dover and our misery finally ended.

From Dover we took a train to Victoria Station, where our group split up. With England's large Indian population, almost everyone had friends or relatives who were expecting them.

In the chill London winter Bhupen and I headed off to the house of my friend Vinodini Patel, who had invited us to stay with her. We had been told that the UK was cold and that Chicago would be even colder, but we hadn't understood properly. 'Cold' to us meant an extra sweater. But 'cold in London' meant something different. Cold in London was a wet chill and a sharp wind that cut through to our bones.

When we reached Vinodini's house we were in for a bit of a surprise. We rang the doorbell, but no one answered. We rang again—nothing. The house was locked tight. It was eleven in the morning. It dawned on us that she and her husband must be at work, which we hadn't considered. We stood there at her doorstep, each holding a suitcase. They'll probably be back at five, we thought. What could we do? On the sidewalk just down her house was a red telephone booth. Bhupen and I crowded ourselves into it, with our bags, and managed to pull the door shut. There was no heat, except for whatever our bodies were generating themselves, which wasn't much. But at least we were out of the wind.

Over the next six hours a fair number of people came by to make calls, giving us odd looks and knocking on the glass. Whenever someone would come, Bhupen and I would get out with our suitcases. When they had finished their call, we'd get back in.

Finally, a little after five, to our vast relief we saw a light come on in Vinodini's apartment. By now we were frozen stiff, but we were so happy to get some real warmth that the ordeal faded quickly from our minds. Vinodini seemed as happy to see us as we were to see her. She showed us our rooms, and immediately began cooking. When we were ready to go to sleep, she gave us each a red rubber bag filled with hot water.

'Vinodini,' I said, 'what is this? What is the idea behind it?'

'This is for the cold,' she said. 'So you'll feel a little warmer.'

'That's funny, you sleep with a bag of hot water?'

'Yes,' she said. 'It's very English.'

The next day she said, 'Look, I need to get you both topcoats. You can't be without winter coats here.' So our first stop was a store to buy coats, which felt very warm and comfortable, especially after our experience in the phone booth.

We spent the next couple of days in London getting oriented to a Western lifestyle. We loved London. The double-decker buses, the bobbies with their funny hats, the mounted soldiers outside Whitehall in their splendid uniforms. London was beautiful and clean. Now we understood that maybe Naples wasn't quite as perfect as we had thought. Everybody we saw seemed to be carrying umbrellas, even though it wasn't raining. And people just didn't talk to each other. Instead, they said, 'Excuse me,' and 'I'm sorry,' and 'Please,' and 'Thank you.'

Even more impressive was the sense of orderliness all around. Everyone was doing whatever they were doing, the vendors, shoppers, sightseers. But it wasn't at all chaotic; there was no mass confusion, the noise level didn't break your eardrums. Everything seemed to be working. I was observing all this closely. We all were. A system with order, I thought. What a way to live!

We took it all in, thinking we needed to get used to this world. One couldn't just go up and talk to people like we did at home. You'd have to say, 'Please, excuse me, I'm sorry,' first. We needed to learn this.

After three days in London we went to Heathrow Airport, where we met the three or four others who were going to America to study. None of us had flown before; we'd only seen planes from a distance. But by this time we considered ourselves sophisticates. We refused to be shocked when the BOAC jet roared down the runway, took off into the air and flew us across the Atlantic. Destination: New York City.

The only problem was that there was a snowstorm raging in New York, and so we were diverted to Montreal, where the airline put us up overnight at the Sheraton Hotel. None of us had ever been in a hotel anywhere near this luxurious. In my room I found a television set, which got me especially excited.

I knew about televisions. I had studied electronics and understood how they worked. Vinodini had one in her house, but I had been too nervous to touch it. But here I had one all to myself that I was free to fiddle with. I looked at the vertical, the horizontal, I counted the dots. I went into the back of the set and looked at the tube. I was like a monkey with a toy. Then I went to find the others, excited to tell them about it. So excited that I locked myself out. I pulled the door close behind me and it locked by itself—what a fascinating concept. In India if you wanted to lock a door you had to manually close the latch. I thought, *What an interesting idea. You do this, the internal thing goes in. You turn it that way, the internal thing comes out. You close it, it locks. Fascinating. What genius design.*

But I had been locked out. In fact, by this time the others had managed to lock themselves out too.

We went downstairs. The person at the desk said, 'It's not a problem, I'll give you another key.' But before that he gave us chits for dinner, also paid for by the airline. 'There's an excellent restaurant here,' he said. 'You can go and have your dinner there.'

So four or five of us Indian kids went to the hotel restaurant for dinner. The others ordered French fries and toast, things we knew were vegetarian and thus safe. But I was trying to be adventurous. I thought of myself as a little more mature, maybe a little different compared to the others—more ready to experience the world and all it had to offer.

'What is your speciality?' I asked the waiter.

'Steak,' he answered.

I didn't know what 'steak' meant; it was a new word. None of us knew what it meant. 'I'll have that,' I said. 'I'll have the steak.'

'Good choice,' said the waiter. 'How do you want it?'

How did I want it? 'What do you mean?' I asked.

'How do you want it?' the waiter repeated.

'I don't know.'

'Do you want it well-done, medium or rare?'

I had no idea what he was talking about. But the word 'rare' sounded familiar, so I said, 'rare'.

Ten or fifteen minutes later, the waiter brought our food, including my steak. Rare. Full of blood. Oozing. I looked at it. Bhupen, who was a little more knowledgeable than me—he was a Brahmin from a family of lawyers—said, 'You idiot. Do you know what you're eating?'

'No.'

'This is cow meat. This is cow blood. You are Hindu. You cannot eat cow!'

'Well,' I said, 'you know, I ordered it. I should probably eat it.'

So I ate it. *I'm on an adventure,* I thought. *I might as well live it up.*

There was no storm in Montreal, but the ground was covered with a thick layer of crunchy snow. It was our first time seeing it. Bhupen and I went for a little walk, or at least we tried to. But it was slippery, and our shoes had leather soles. All this white stuff was beautiful, but scary. 'You can't even stand properly in it,' said Bhupen.

The next day the weather cleared and we flew from Montreal to New York. We had contacts there, friends of Bhupen's family who had invited us to stay with them for a day or two. But it turned out that his wife was heavily pregnant, due to have the baby very soon and obviously not up to paying much attention to us. Also, they had been living in New York for quite a few years, and I had the feeling they were a little ashamed of us, the two country bumpkins with few social graces and even less understanding of things here. We told them about some of the sights we wanted to see: the Empire State Building, the Statue of Liberty, Times Square. 'Okay,' they said, 'you just take the A-C-E, then you take the 1-3-9.'

'The *what?*' we asked, alarmed.

'The train. The A, the C or the E. The tube.'

We were completely lost. It was all so complicated. We were afraid, but at the same time we wanted to see everything. How do you take the train, and where do you take it till? When we asked people on the street, they were sympathetic. We did manage to see the Empire State Building, and we were caught up in the exciting hustle and bustle of New York. We also learned there was going to be a World's Fair in the summer, after our semester was over. We thought we absolutely had to come back for that.

Two days later we were on a Greyhound bus heading to Chicago. It was mid-December and bitterly cold outside. But inside the bus was hot and dry. You couldn't even open the window to get a breath of fresh air because it was cold outside. I was claustrophobic and suffocating; I felt like I was drying up. At every stop I would get down and drink three or four glasses of water. A lady passenger who noticed this, asked me, 'Young man, are you all right? Are you sick?'

We stopped in Pittsburg, Cleveland, Toledo, Fort Wayne, and other places along the way. And every place we stopped there were African-American people. Black people. We knew there were black people in America, but we had no idea there would be so many. The people in the bus stations were black. Many of our fellow passengers were black. The driver was black. We looked at them. They, no doubt, looked at Bhupen and me too. Brown people. Maybe they were wondering about us as much as we were wondering about them.

When we arrived at the Chicago bus station, the foreign student adviser, a Mr Heinrich, was there to pick us up. He welcomed us warmly, then drove us directly to the YMCA. (The first semester hadn't ended yet. The new semester, which was when we would begin our terms, was still ten or eleven days away.)

Our room was on the fifth floor. The problem here was the same as what I had faced on the bus. The room was hot, dry and suffocating. Neither Bhupen nor I were used to any kind of heated rooms. We couldn't figure out how to deal with it. You open the window, you freeze, but it feels good; close the window and it's warm, but you feel awful.

The next morning our education continued in the YMCA cafeteria. The free breakfast featured sausage, bacon and ham. We had seen ham before, but what were these other things? Clearly not something edible. And there were eggs. One fellow in front of me ordered his 'sunny side up', whatever that meant! Another chap wanted his eggs prepared 'easy over', or 'over easy'. We scratched our heads and ate toast.

In the cafeteria, though, we heard something shocking. Everybody was talking about it. And we had ours ears tuned in, listening to the conversations as best we could. The previous night someone had been murdered on the seventh floor, two floors above us. We didn't catch much more than that, so we didn't learn any details. But someone murdered in the same place we were staying in? Shocking! We had heard about Al Capone and the Mafia in Chicago. That was many years ago, but here we were now—and there was someone killed practically the moment we arrived. What kind of place had we landed in?

After breakfast we tried to find our way to the Illinois Institute of Technology—IIT—our school. We asked someone who told us there was a bus on State Street that would take us directly there. 'The fare's a quarter,' he said. We had money, including some change, but this 'quarter' denomination stumped us. What would that be? We knew twenty-five cents, but a *quarter*? We would have been equally confused had he said even 'nickel' or 'dime'. So we walked—in the snow and ice, slipping and sliding and holding on to each other the whole way, thinking Chicago was not a comfortable place to be in the wintertime.

At the foreign students' office, Mr Heinrich greeted us with a big smile and showed us some of the campus. IIT looked good, modern buildings, lots of students, lots of activity. When Mr Heinrich went back to his office, Bhupen and I continued looking around, and on one side of the campus we found ourselves on a bridge over a roadway. But this roadway was nothing like anything we had ever seen before. If we had ever heard of science fiction, we would have thought this was it. My God. What was this thing? Eight lanes going this way, eight lanes going that way. Cars packed together, speeding. Coming, going, like bullets shooting. Enough to make one dizzy. We just stood on the bridge and stared, mesmerized. My thoughts went momentarily back to Titilagarh, where as a child I would sit and watch an occasional cow wander slowly down the main street.

As we walked back towards the campus from the roadway I saw a student hurrying along who looked familiar. I stared at him. It was my classmate from Baroda, Bharat Thakkar. I shouted, 'Bharat!'

He looked up. 'Satu? You're here?'

'Yes. It's me.'

'What are you doing here?'

'I've come to study. What are *you* doing here?'

'I'm studying for my master's in mechanical engineering. Listen, I'm on my way to a final exam. See that building there? My apartment's in there. Take my key. I'll be back as soon as I'm finished.'

After the icy cold outside, Bharat's apartment was warm and cosy, homely. It had a couple of rooms, including a little kitchen. Obviously,

several people were living there. But nobody was at home when we
went.

With nothing to do but wait, Bhupen and I looked around, then
opened the refrigerator. 'My goodness,' said Bhupen, 'Look at all this
food here. Let's cook. We can cook a meal for them.'

I had never cooked before, but Bhupen knew what he was doing
in the kitchen.

So we cooked. And when Bharat came home from his exam along
with his Indian room-mates, we had a tasty meal ready for them.

'Wow!' they said, happy beyond words to come back from gruelling
exams to find such a welcome surprise. 'Listen, why don't you guys
move here? You can sleep on the floor instead of paying at the YMCA.'

'Okay,' we said. 'That would be great. You have exams now?
We'll feed you. Take care of things. Whatever you need. That'll be
our job.'

That afternoon we got our things out of the YMCA and settled
in to sleep on Bharat's floor. Every day the guys had a couple of
exams. They'd come back, and we'd have the apartment cleaned up
and straightened out. We'd have food ready. It was great. We had
companionship, we had something to do; we walked around, getting
used to the place. We stared at that incredible roadway again. We
were becoming 'adjusted'.

I had come to IIT to study for a PhD in physics. As far as I was
concerned, there were only two subjects truly worth pursuing: physics
and math. Everything else seemed secondary. But an academic adviser
said that depending on the nature of my research, a physics PhD might
take me six or seven years.

Six or seven years? I couldn't wait that long. I had thought that
with a master's already it might take me one or two. Anu was waiting
for me. I had to finish up and bring her over so we could get married
and begin our life together.

'Is there something I could do in a year?' I asked the professor.

He looked at my transcript from Baroda. 'Electrical engineering,'
he said. 'You could probably get a second master's degree in electrical
engineering in nine months.'

I wanted to study physics. Coming to Chicago was special to me
because I had been born in 1942, the year the atomic age began in
earnest at the converted squash courts at the University of Chicago, not

too far from IIT. This was where Fermi had set off the world's first self-sustaining nuclear reaction to deliver energy comparable to that of the sun. I was looking forward to visiting the site. To me, Chicago housed a temple of physics at the University of Chicago.

I had visions of Einstein and Newton and Rutherford floating around in my head. But if I could get a master's in electrical engineering in nine months, I could get a job, call Anu and get married. I had to send her a ticket. I had to be able to support us. I was hardly going to bring her over and say, 'Okay, now you go to work.' What kind of a man would do that? Anu would have to leave her entire family and come all the way to America, trusting in me. I wasn't going to tell her to go to work. No, I was going to take care of everything. That's what I was supposed to do and that's what I was going to do.

All these thoughts were racing through my head as I was sitting in front of the adviser. *Look*, I told myself, *if you have to let go of your physics, let go of your physics. So you won't become a physicist. It won't be the greatest tragedy in the world. The important thing is to get Anu here. We need to be married.*

'Okay,' I told the adviser. 'I'll do a master's in electrical engineering. That's what I want.'

In India I had studied some electronics as part of my physics coursework, but I had almost no idea of what went into a formal electrical-engineering curriculum. 'You need to take a course in control systems,' someone said. *Okay*, I thought, *what are control systems?* I didn't know. I had to figure these things out from scratch.

Meanwhile, Bhupen and I had to find a place to live on our own and move out of Bharat's apartment. We were both surviving on Bhupen's 233-dollars-a-month scholarship stipend. We couldn't afford the dorm; we needed something cheaper.

With the other Indian guys' help we found an apartment for 40 dollars a month. It was pretty awful, but we cleaned it up. We got a used bed from somewhere, a lamp somebody had thrown out in the garbage. We found an abandoned TV that we were able to fix up. Someone sent us to Catholic Salvage for more furniture, but their prices were too high. 'Where else can we go?' we asked. 'Joe's,' we were told. 'He's just around the corner.'

Joe's was a warehouse space packed with odds and ends of furniture. Joe himself was an African-American guy, very friendly, and his prices were right. We bought a few items, a sofa, a chair, a table. 'How do we get them home?' we asked.

'You haul,' he said.

'We what?'

'You haul. Hook a trailer up to your car. U-Haul.'

'But we don't have a car.'

'What do you mean, you don't have a car?' Joe looked at us. He realized we didn't look quite regular.

'Say, where are you guys from, anyway?'

'India,' we said. 'We're Indians.'

'Indians,' he said. 'Damn.'

He had an old globe in his office. We turned the globe and found India.

'Damn, that's far,' he said. 'Maybe I can give you a hand.'

So Joe brought his old van around and ferried us and our furniture to our apartment, even though it was in an Italian neighbourhood—not a place, according to him, he would ordinarily venture to.

With Joe around, I felt I had established a special bond with the African-American community around IIT. People on the IIT campus were very concerned about safety and security. Police cars were always roaming around, day and night. The difference in the poverty levels in and around the campus was striking. The south side of Chicago was more like a poor developing country compared to the richness of downtown Chicago. For us foreign students, this was striking. How could the most prosperous and wealthy nation in the world have this level of poverty and disparity?

Even with our 40-dollar-a-month apartment, we weren't going to be able to survive on Bhupen's money forever. I had arrived with 400 dollars in my pocket. I had paid the 360-dollar tuition fee for the semester, which meant I had 40 dollars left. I needed a job.

'I just met a Professor Trapp,' Bhupen said one day at the start of the semester. 'He's setting up an electromagnetic resonance lab. He's looking for a technician. Why don't you talk to him?'

So I did. 'Sir,' I said, 'I'm looking for a job. I have a master's in physics. And I'm doing a master's in electrical engineering.'

'That sounds good,' he said. 'How many hours can you work?'

'As many as you want, sir.'

'Are you sure? What will happen to your studies?'

'Not to worry, sir. I can handle them.'

I didn't know what I was saying. In fact, I didn't have any idea how difficult my studies were going to be.

'Can you start Monday?' he asked.

Yes, I could start Monday. I would have started that very moment if Professor Trapp had asked me to. I had a *job*! I had found a way to survive.

The work itself involved mainly taking measurements during experiments, which wasn't a challenge. But I made sure I did everything right. I was in the lab every day before Dr Trapp got in. I did whatever he asked as carefully as I could. If he had asked me to polish his shoes, I would have put the best shine on them he had ever seen. Not that he ever asked me to do something like that. Professor Trapp was a gentleman, friendly and relaxed. He made me feel comfortable. More importantly, he was happy with my work.

So I was all set at Dr Trapp's lab. It was my studies that were the problem. I just didn't get it. A lot of the concepts went right over my head. I couldn't understand why. In India I had been a good student. I had graduated with first-class honours. Why couldn't I understand this electrical engineering material?

I went to one of my professors for help. He said, 'Have you taken 416?'

'No.'

'Have you taken 415?'

'No.' *What* did the man mean?

He was talking about course numbers. I had signed up for '500 level' courses, without knowing anything about course numbers.

'Look,' he said, 'you better drop these 500 courses. You've got a master's already. You probably don't need the 300 courses. Sign up for 400-level courses.'

So there was a sequence to these things. Nobody had told me this. People just assumed you knew. Course sequences were common sense, something everyone knew—except me. In India, there were no courses in the same sense, let alone course numbers. There was a book you studied. You took your exam on the basis of what was in the book. That was it. Attending lectures might help you with the exam, but they weren't essential. In India, knowing the book was essential.

So I had to drop the higher-level courses. I was depressed. *Maybe this whole thing wasn't a good idea,* I thought. *Maybe I just can't do well here.*

Then I thought that the only way I could survive would be to take a lot of math courses. Math I knew I could do well in, no matter what level of the course I might take. So I started taking as many math courses as I could along with the electrical engineering courses. And I got As in math, so I was able to get the B average I needed to maintain.

There were a number of wonderful and unusual professors at IIT, different in some ways from my professors in Baroda. One was Dr Messenger, who taught a signal analysis course I took in my first semester. In one class he was trying to solve a particularly complex equation. The problem was on the board and Dr Messenger was trying various possible solutions, with no luck. 'Hmm,' he said, looking at us. 'This is a tough problem. I can't seem to solve it.' His bright eyes settled on one of the students. 'John!' he said. 'John's smart. Maybe John can solve it. Get up, John.'

So John got up and went to the board. Dr Messenger sat down in John's chair, looking at the board while John started working on the problem.

I was watching the board too, but I was also looking at Dr Messenger, wondering: What kind of professor says I can't do it, but my student can do it—and sits down in the student's chair to watch?

I'd just more or less arrived from India, where this scene would never have taken place. And, of course, John solved the problem.

'See!' Dr Messenger exclaimed. He was ecstatic. 'See! I told you he could solve this thing! I knew he could do it!'

What was going on here? What kind of teacher was this who would give credit to a young guy who could solve an equation he couldn't. My respect for Messenger rocketed straight up.

After class I went to him. 'Sir,' I said. 'Could I request you to be my adviser? I would be extremely pleased.' And Dr Messenger replied at once, 'Of course.'

~

At the beginning of the Fall 1965 semester, Bhupen and I moved to campus. By now we were really getting acclimatized. We were reading newspapers, watching the 5 o'clock news, understanding how Americans thought and felt. We were getting into the system. In Chicago, everyone, at least all our fellow students, seemed to be obsessed with football, which seemed a strange name for it since very few players ever actually kicked the ball. Our American friends went on and on about someone named Dick Butkus and somebody else named Gale Sayers. It was a mystery at first, a game with many large men, all apparently trying to kill each other. But eventually football permeated through our heads: touchdowns and field goals, downs and yards, first and ten. We began to understand it.

There was real violence on television too. Every night, we would watch the news about the Vietnam War and the rising resistance against it. All the young men seemed to be growing their hair long, so we grew ours out too. Vietnam was very much a part of campus conversations. Some of our graduating students had been drafted to fight the war. Defence companies had suddenly appeared on campus to hire engineers, and were paying them a lot more than other companies.

Our room was on the fourth floor of the graduate dorms, and all sorts of interesting people were around, budding scientists and engineers. There was one PhD student who used to shed his clothes the moment he got to the floor. All his clothes. He'd be completely, totally nude, and he'd just walk around that way. If someone called on the fourth-floor hall phone he'd get it and come in the buff to your door, announcing, 'Phone for you.' He'd even come and do homework with us—in his birthday suit!

I couldn't comprehend it. There were a number of Indian students on the floor in addition to Bhupen and me. We were all shocked. We couldn't stand it. It was such an astonishing violation of Indian modesty and norms. If I saw him I looked down at the floor. I couldn't talk, so intensely embarrassed was I.

Speaking of modesty, taking showers was also a big problem. The fourth floor had a common bathroom with an open-shower area. People took showers there, nude. Another shock. Indians do not do that in public. It just wasn't something we could wrap our heads around. We took to showering individually, at odd times, eleven or twelve at night, when nobody else was there.

After the first semester, once we had become used to things, Bhupen was elected head of the Indian students' group. One of his responsibilities, which I helped him with, was to greet the Indian businessmen who were showing up looking for ideas. To them, America was a gold mine, and they all wanted to figure out how to mine the gold. India was then a command economy, following the Soviet model. Her markets were closed, and foreign goods weren't coming in. But America was the land of plenty, overflowing with consumer goods. What the visiting businessmen wanted was to find a product that they could replicate cheaply in India. Since I was into electrical engineering, they'd come to me and say, 'Why don't you come up with a product for us that doesn't take too much money to manufacture. A simple product that we can sell at high volume?'

I would say, 'If I had an idea like that, why would I give it to you?' Of course, there were no ideas like that to give away anyway. Their sheer naivety was astonishing, but given our own experiences when we first arrived, we should probably have been at least a bit more sympathetic towards them.

At the end of the second semester I was one credit short of my master's, so I signed up for a summer course—in math—got an A, and graduated. Our math professor was a distinguished older lady who was an excellent teacher. While teaching, at times she would say, 'Al would have done this,' or, 'Al would have said that.' Finally, someone mustered up the courage to ask her, 'Madam, who is this Al?' She said, 'Why, Albert Einstein, of course.' Einstein was apparently a close family friend of the professor's. This was the closest I ever got to Einstein.

Right after graduating, Bhupen and I decided to go to New York to see the World's Fair, something we had promised ourselves we would do when we first landed in the city.

I had just graduated and so I had to give up my job at the lab. Bhupen was still working on his doctorate and living on the shoestring budget made available by his scholarship funds. But he somehow found an extra 125 dollars with which we bought a very used, old Plymouth car that we thought had a chance of getting us to New York and back. We had both learned to drive in an IIT parking lot and had even procured our driving licences. We thought we were ready for this.

One of our friends, a Chinese student named David Ho, said he'd like to come. We were happy to have him along. So off the three of us went in our 125-dollar Plymouth, and we made it to New York without a problem.

In New York we stayed with Bharat Thakkar, who had found a job there after graduating from IIT. The World's Fair was fascinating. General Motors had the biggest presentation, with a fancy Futurama ride that included an imagined trip to the moon. We saw new technological developments: lasers and fuel cells and radical designs for turbines. For technology buffs like us, it was a veritable feast.

After the fair we decided to drive to Niagara Falls. Bharat said he wanted to come along; then, another Indian, Om Gupta, said he'd also like to come. Then Om's wife, Rani, said that she was coming too. Then two more of Bharat's friends decided to come, which made eight of us, all packed like sardines in our 125-dollar car.

We didn't have room for eight people. Rani had to sit on people's laps, switching every fifteen minutes or so, since even though she was light, sitting on one lap became uncomfortable after a while. So off we drove to Niagara, three on the front-bench seat, four squeezed into the back, and poor Rani shifting from lap to lap.

Around midnight, David Ho was driving while the rest of us were dozing off. I was sitting next to David and at one point I woke up and saw that we were speeding. David had his foot on the pedal.

'David,' I said, 'ease up. This isn't a new car. Drive at forty-five or fifty. You're doing eighty.'

'Okay,' he said. But after a while he started speeding again. At 12.30 a.m., the car rolled to a dead stop. David had blown the transmission.

There were no cell phones then and it was the middle of the night on a dark road. But eventually a police car pulled up. Eight of us in one car might have been over the limit. But we were obviously students, and crazy-looking foreigners at that, so the officer let it pass.

'You need a tow truck,' he said, and made a call from his patrol car. A while later our rescue vehicle showed up. We all squeezed into the car, the truck hitched us up and towed us to a gas station.

It was now two in the morning. The gas station wasn't going to open until eight. It was cold. We couldn't just sit in the car and freeze, so the eight of us walked around the station area, shivering and hugging ourselves. There was an empty phone booth on the street, and when I looked inside, there was an intact phone-book. Leafing through it to see if I could find some Indian names I came across someone named Arun Patel.

I was delighted. My mind raced. 'Patel' was an Indian name, Gujarati, for certain. *We're in trouble. He's Indian. I'll call him,* I thought. *I'll wake him up.*

I made the call. A sleepy, annoyed voice answered.

'Hello?'

'Arun!'

'What? Who is this?'

'Arun, don't worry about that! Come here! I'm stuck. We've had a car accident.'

'Who is this?'

'Just come here. You'll find out when you get here.'

'Where are you from?'

'Baroda.'

'Okay, I'll come. Shall I bring something with me?'

'Yes, some pillows, blankets, those kinds of things.'

At three o'clock, Arun Patel actually showed up.

'What?!' he said. 'You?!'

'Arun, Arun. It's you?' It was Arun Patel, a classmate of mine from college.

'Arun, what are you doing here?'

'I'm now working in Buffalo,' he said. 'I'm living here. Everybody can squeeze into my car. Let's go to my house.'

So we all went to Arun's house and were able to get at least a little sleep.

It was an amazing coincidence with an equally amazing postscript. After this incident, Arun and I didn't see each other until ten years later when he called to say that he and his wife were in Chicago and suggested we meet up. By then Anu and I were married and living in an apartment in Chicago's Summit neighbourhood. When Arun and his wife rang the bell, I opened the door, and an instant later Anu screamed, 'Menashi!' This was followed by Arun's wife screaming, 'Anu!' And they fell into each other's arms. They had gone to school together but hadn't seen each other since those days.

But back in Buffalo, we still needed a new car. Our ancient Plymouth with its blown transmission wasn't anything worth fixing.

The next day we managed to find a used Chrysler for 200 dollars. It had a lot of miles on it, but it looked great, the black paint shone like new. It ran okay too and got us back to Chicago without any trouble.

Shortly after we got back, though, we found that underneath the shiny paint the car was rusted through. We realized this when one of our Indian friends, a heavy guy named Lal Dixit, was driving it one day and the floor on the driver's side collapsed under him. Chicago's snowy, slushy streets meant that pursuant to Lal's mishap, if you drove the car, snow and water would gush up through the non-existent floor like a fountain. You couldn't drive it from the driver's side; you had to sit in the middle, lean over and contort yourself to reach the pedals. It wasn't comfortable driving like that, but if we needed to go somewhere by car, we needed to go. People on the street would be staring, doing double takes, since there was no driver, but the guy sitting in the middle was leaning way over. You could hardly see his head. We finally sold that car to one of the IIT campus policemen for 20 dollars.

I graduated in January 1966 with a master's in electrical engineering.

Studying in America was an altogether different experience. In India, I was taught to remember facts. I was tested and graded only once a year on the basis of my memory. In the US, I had options to select courses and I was tested and graded every few weeks on a regular basis. I was taught to focus on problem-solving with critical thinking, collaboration, teamwork and a lot more. The campus experience was also important for us to learn about American culture and customs, things like Thanksgiving and football, Western manners, mindsets and interpersonal relationships. I made many new friends, Indians and non-Indians. We took part in conversations on Vietnam, the Arab–Israel conflict and space programmes. It felt like I had started my integration into the American melting pot. It was clear that America was all about individualism and innovations.

A short while later I found a job in Crystal Lake, Illinois, about 50 miles from Chicago. With some money coming in now, the time had come to write to Anu's father—her parents still didn't know what we were planning. It was a delicate letter.

Dear Uncle Chhaya,

Please allow me to explain our situation. Anu and I wish to be married. But be assured that we will not do anything that will upset you. If you are not happy to give us your blessing, we will wait until you are convinced that our decision is correct. We respect you and would never do anything that would distress our parents. I have spoken to my parents about our plans. They have given us their permission. We hope that you and Anu's mother will feel comfortable doing likewise.

I was utterly respectful. I sent the letter off with a clear heart and some trepidation, hoping for the best.

But when Anu's father received the letter all hell broke loose.

4

Love and Work

One phrase stood out in Anu's return letter to me. When her father read my letter, she wrote that the first words out of his mouth were: 'Over my dead body.'

Obviously, that was not what I had hoped for. But I was fairly certain that eventually he would come around. Hari Bhai Chhaya was an educated man, a sensible person. Every father would have some anger over a thing like this, with a beautiful, loving, special daughter like Anu. I was just going to have to wait it out. You get abused, okay, so you get abused for a while. It wasn't going to last a lifetime.

Unlike Anu's father, her mother accepted us almost immediately. She worked on the father to change his mind, and with Anu absolutely firm about what she wanted to do, the father began to see that he was going to have little choice in the matter, and before long, he acquiesced to our match. Soon after this, my family visited Anu's parents and formalized our engagement.

Since I was in America, my brothers, Manek and Pinu, represented my family at the engagement ceremony in Godhra. Then I began the process to bring Anu over. While this was going on, my dad wrote to me: 'Why not bring your younger brother over as well? America might be a better place for him.' So I had to wait a little longer to save up enough money for two tickets. They would be arriving in the late November of 1966. Anu and I would get married at the beginning of December, soon after they arrived.

As this was going on, I was working in Crystal Lake for Oak Electric, a company that made television tuners. Most of my friends who graduated with me had found jobs in the defence industry. It was 1966, and companies like Lockheed Martin and General Dynamics were sucking up graduate engineers like a vacuum cleaner. But I didn't want to work in defence since I felt strongly about Gandhi's philosophy of non-violence. I was hoping to stay in Chicago, but my job search had taken me out to this town an hour's drive away. My plan had been to live close to IIT and continue working towards a PhD part-time.

As I was looking for an apartment in Crystal Lake, a secretary at Oak Electric told me there was an elderly lady, a Mrs Wilson, who had a room to let out. Mrs Wilson, it turned out, lived by herself in a single, big family house. The room was nice, the location was convenient and she seemed very pleasant. So I took the room.

To Mrs Wilson and my work colleagues, I was 'Sam'—a name given to me by a secretary at Oak Electric. My actual name is Satyanarayan, meaning 'God of truth', a mouthful even for Indians. To my family I was always 'Satyan', to my friends I was 'Satu'. But my documents had my full name, which was too much for the Oak Electric person who processed payrolls. She decided that something simpler, something American that people in Crystal Lake could get their tongues around, would be better. So when my first paycheck came in, it was made out to Sam Pitroda. When I asked what was going on, the secretary said, 'Oh, I changed it. We had to open a bank account for you, so I thought that would be okay.'

How could someone decide to just change my name, I thought. But then I realized that if I were to have her change it back, my paycheck would be delayed for two more weeks. Plus, the name didn't really bother me. *If they want to call me Sam,* I thought, *okay, let them.* So I became Sam.

As Mrs Wilson and I got to know each other more, I found that I liked her very much. She was like a grandmother, warm and caring. When I came home from work we would sit around over a cup of tea and talk. She was lonely; she had no family nearby—her only son lived in Boston—so we kept each other company. If there was work to do around the house, I volunteered to do it. With most of my friends living back in Chicago, I had nothing else to do in Crystal Lake anyway. But even if I had, I would have helped out in any way I could. It was the natural thing to do.

I knew that she enjoyed my company as well. She appreciated having someone to talk to. I told her about my parents, my family, my girlfriend, about life in India. Over time she even began sending some things for my mother—small gift boxes with maybe a scarf or a nice sweater she had found while she was out shopping.

Meanwhile, Mrs Wilson was teaching me little things about American domestic life. 'When you wash dishes,' she said, 'you do it with warm water and soap, then you rinse them and dry them. You don't just leave them on the counter wet.' She took an interest in my life. There was a piano in the house, and she thought that maybe I would enjoy lessons, so she got me a piano teacher. She tried to fix me up on a date with the daughter of one of her friends.

'No, no, I can't do that,' I said, embarrassed.

'Why not? She's very cute.'

'I'm sure, but I can't date anyone.'

'You should really learn dancing.'

'No, no, I can't do that.'

'Why not?'

One day I said, 'Why don't we go out for pizza tonight?' I had a feeling she hadn't been out for dinner in years. 'Sam is taking me out for pizza,' she told the neighbours, and went to a beauty salon to get her hair done. Before long all of Crystal Lake knew about it. Mrs Olie Wilson had this young man who's living in her house with her—and taking her out to dinner.

The implications of these things went a thousand miles over my head. Being considerate and helping an older person out in any way you could was just an ordinary thing to do back in India. But word of all this got to her son in Boston, who was already beginning to get a little nervous, hearing his mother talk on the phone about Sam this and Sam that.

Finally, he panicked. It seemed to him as if this Sam person was exploiting her. Maybe he was after her money or the house. So he flew in to town.

'This is unheard of,' he told me. 'What are you interested in? What are you trying to do here?'

'I've never even thought of things like this,' I said. 'I'm doing this because this is what you're supposed to do for older people. I'd do this for my grandmother. I've just moved here for work. I have nothing else to do except be at home with her. What should I do when I come back home? There are two of us in the house, and she's treating me almost as she would her child. What else do you think I should do? She asks me to get the groceries, of course I get them. Wash the dishes? Of course I wash them.'

He wouldn't believe me. 'Look, what's your angle here?'

'I have no angle.'

'Do you have a social life?'

'No, not as you define.'

'Why is she sending things to your parents?'

'It's just a little gift of clothing or something. It's her business. Please.'

He thought I was interested in her property. When he left he still wasn't sure that I didn't have something up my sleeve.

Meanwhile, I was getting tired of my job working on TV tuners, which was neither challenging nor enjoyable. So I started looking for work in Chicago.

By now I had a small network of friends working as engineers in various firms, and someone told me about an opening at the Victoreen Instrument Company, which made test equipment for measuring radiation. 'You have degrees in electrical engineering and physics,' my friend said. 'They'll like that.'

So I applied and got the job, which meant a big jump in salary. I had been making 550 dollars a month, suddenly I was making 900. My job at Victoreen dealt with developing and maintaining nuclear instruments, which brought me back to Chicago, near IIT, to live. It also took me to national laboratories all over the country—Oak Ridge, Lawrence Livermore, Los Alamos, Brookhaven and others. I was travelling to interesting places and doing work I enjoyed.

~

By November I had saved up enough money for tickets for Anu and my younger brother, Pinu. Pinu only needed a one-way ticket since he was coming as a student. But Anu was travelling on a tourist visa, so she needed a round-trip ticket. Of course, she wasn't going to go back, so my plan was to get a refund for the return ticket, which would give me about 400 dollars, enough to finance our wedding celebrations.

One of my friends had just bought a beautiful new blue Buick. 'When your fiancée and your brother get here,' he said, 'we'll use my car to pick them up from the airport.' When the day came, I went to meet Anu and Pinu in my friend's Buick with Olie Wilson, Bhupen, and a few other IIT friends who were driving behind us in a second car. Mrs Wilson had brought along a warm coat with her for Anu, who, she was afraid would freeze solid in Chicago's cold and wind.

Seeing Anu after all this time was amazing. The only glitch was that when we got to my apartment, she couldn't find the return part of her ticket, the part I was planning to turn in for a refund. This meant that I now had no money for the wedding. It turned out later that she had lost it in the Buick. My friend had found it and put it in his glove compartment, intending to give it to me when we next saw each other, but then had forgotten about it. So, though I did get the ticket back later and applied for the refund (which I eventually received), it was too late for the wedding.

As usual, at the end of November it was cold, and even with Mrs Wilson's coat, Anu was shivering uncontrollably. She had left everything behind—her parents, her brothers and sisters, her whole way of life. And here she was, in this ice-cold city with a bunch of unknown guys in a miserable apartment—guys who no doubt were expecting her to cook for them since she was the only girl around, except that she had never prepared food in her life. Her family had always had cooks to do that for them. On top of that, she ended up twisting her ankle, not badly, but she was limping a little. I didn't want her to be hobbling around at our wedding, and neither did she. It was just one thing after another. Besides, with my next paycheck a couple of weeks away and no money in the bank, there simply wasn't anything to do but postpone the wedding.

My friends started wondering—the girl is here and they're not getting married. Something must be wrong. What was it?

One friend, Madhu Mehta, another engineering graduate from IIT, figured it out. 'Look,' he said, 'I know what's going on here. You don't have money. That's not good. Take my bank passbook. Withdraw as much as you need. Don't tell anybody, don't tell me, don't tell your fiancée, nobody. Just do it.'

So I took 150 dollars out of Madhu's account and rented a hall at the YWCA. By then it was close to Christmas. I thought, *Let's wait, we'll get married on 26 December. IIT's students will be gone then and the kitchen will be available; we'll be able to cook the wedding food there.*

With all the arrangements made, I typed out the invitation cards and sent them to my friends. I estimated that between them and their families, we should be prepared for about 100 guests. My idea was to have an informal celebration. Food, music, a good time. But Anu said, 'No, if we're going to get married, we need to have a priest.'

In 1966, in Chicago, there were no Hindu priests; at least none that I or any of my friends had heard of. This was going to be real trouble. I had borrowed the money, rented the hall, arranged with people to prepare the food. But how was I supposed to find a priest?

Finally, someone said, 'You should go to the University of Chicago. There's a professor of Sanskrit there, an Indian. Dr Joshi from Pune. It's possible he might officiate as a priest. Ask him.'

I found Dr Joshi's number and called him. 'Hello. Are you Dr Joshi? My name is Satyanarayan Pitroda, from Gujarat. May I ask if you are a priest? I need your help. I'm getting married. My wife is a Brahmin, and she wants a religious ceremony. Would you be able to do that for us?'

'Of course,' said Dr Joshi. 'It would be a pleasure.'

This was an exciting development that brought immense relief to me. I had found a priest where there were no priests. Anu was happy, which meant I was happy.

The next thing on the agenda was to get a marriage certificate from Cook County Court. We went there, and after waiting a bit the judge called our names.

'I have a few questions,' he said.

'Yes, Your Honour,' I said. Anu listened, trying to catch what was being said.

'Anjula Chhaya,' the judge said. 'Have you ever been married before?'

Anu caught that just fine, but she was infuriated.

'What?' she said, in Gujarati. 'How dare this person ask me such a thing! If I had been married before why would I be here? Who does he think he is asking such a thing!' She was fuming.

The judge was looking at Anu quizzically. Of course he didn't understand what she was saying, but clearly, something unusual was going on.

'Anu,' I said, desperately. 'Please. This is just a standard question. The judge has to ask it. He's not implying that you have been married before. Please, don't get upset.'

Anu was so outraged I thought she was just going to turn around and walk out. She was right on the edge.

'How dare he! I've come here to marry you! Why is this person insulting me like this?'

I looked at the judge. 'No, Your Honour. She's never been married before.'

'Mr Pitroda,' he said. 'She has to answer for herself.'

'Just say "no",' I whispered to her. 'Please.'

Anu hesitated a long moment, then said, 'No.'

Then I said, 'No.'

Then after we both said, 'I do,' the judge gave us the marriage certificate.

The YWCA hall was already filling up when we got there. Where were all these people coming from? There were well over a hundred already, and they were still streaming in. Indian weddings can be big, but we were in America now, and Americans only come over when invited. But these people were paying no attention to us. They were streaming into the hall from everywhere. Everybody who had heard about it was coming and they were all bringing two or three friends with them. 'I'm going to that guy's wedding.' 'You are? Good, I'll come with you.' 'Okay, let's go.'

Finally, the hall was packed with guests—Indians and a scattering of American friends. Mrs Olie Wilson was sitting in the front, like everyone's mother.

Then Dr Joshi, the priest, said to me, 'Where is your fire pot?'

The fire pot—I hadn't thought about the fire pot. In a Hindu marriage ceremony you need to have a fire. You have to hold your hands near the fire to signify your union. You need a fire, and you need a fire pot to put it in.

Thankfully, we found a pot in the YWCA kitchen.

The next question was: Where was the wood?

I had a penknife. Bhupen and my brother Pinu went out with the knife to cut branches from the trees on State Street. Somehow they managed to come back with a bunch of twigs and little branches. But it was 26 December, in Chicago, sub-zero, and the wood was frozen; the wood just wouldn't light.

So we had the pot, we had the wood. But we didn't have any fire.

Then my friend Mahen Tamakuwala said, 'Lighter fluid!' and he rounded up six or seven lighters from the smokers around and emptied the fluid on to the wood. And it lit up!

So now we had the fire too. Our close friends, Shyam Dixit and his wife, Chandra, stood in for Anu's parents. Other friends, Dilip Desai and his wife, Pratima, stood in for mine. We bound our hands together loosely and held them over the fire. We uttered the prayers. We walked hand in hand around the fire seven times and took the seven steps together, making our vows.

When we were just about to complete the vows someone rushed up to the front and said, 'Stop! Stop!'

'What is the matter?'

'Stop! NBC News is coming. They want to cover the wedding in the evening news.'

Everyone froze. NBC was coming! Dr Joshi was pleased. All the Indian girls wearing saris went to fix themselves up. Then they arranged themselves on the stage in a riot of rich reds, yellows, blues and greens.

A few minutes later John Palmer, the Channel Five anchorman, arrived with a camera crew. Anu was the obvious attraction, gorgeously dressed and resplendent in the gold jewellery her mom had given her. Dr Joshi had married us a few minutes before. Now he married us again, in front of the cameras.

With the ceremony complete, it was time for the feast—the array of Indian dishes our friends had prepared. But the guy who brought the dessert had left it in his car, in zero-degree temperature. It was frozen as hard as a rock.

'Hairdryers!' someone said. Some of the girls had hairdryers in their rooms. Soon, four or five hairdryers were blowing hot air over the surface of the frozen dessert. Mrs Olie Wilson was taking in this exotic Indian celebration with great interest.

Afterwards, someone asked me, 'Where are you going for your honeymoon?' I laughed. I had now spent Madhu's 150 dollars along with my entire recent paycheck. The wedding had soaked up all of it. I had exactly 1 dollar in my pocket—my total wealth until the next pay day.

A little later we were back at our apartment, together with my circle of close friends and their families. Pratima, Dilip's wife, told me to go out for milk, which I did. A gallon cost 67 cents, which reduced my dollar to 33 cents—the total corpus with which Anu and I began our life together.

~

Once we were settled in, Bhupen, who was still working on his PhD, moved in with us. So all of us lived together: Anu, Bhupen, my brother Pinu and I. Then Mahen Tamakuwala moved in, so we were five.

Our lives, Anu's and mine, were progressing smoothly. We picked up a black-and-white TV in decent working condition from the garbage, bought a used refrigerator for 10 dollars, a stove for 20 and a sofa for 40, and began our journey—with little money but lots of adventures. I remember once Anu started crying in the morning. In the evening, we were supposed to go to see an Indian movie at the IIT campus. This was the place to connect and socialize with all our friends. I was puzzled at her tears and asked her what happened. She said she was missing her mom and sisters back in India; if she was there, she would have gone with her sister to a tailor to get a new blouse stitched for this evening. Immediately, I took the yellow sari that she wanted to wear, cut the pattern for the blouse and stitched it, and she wore it to the movie that evening. I had never stitched a blouse before. For us, anything was possible and we were prepared to try new and innovative things. There was never a dull moment with all five of us together. It was one non-stop party—our romance with America. We were young. We were doing well. We were happy, and Anu and I were looking forward to having children.

Then my employer Victoreen decided to move to Cleveland. Anu and I moved with them, along with Pinu, but we felt that the normal course of things had been disrupted. In Chicago we had a group of close friends, most of them Indians living far from home, and we had become each others' families. But in Cleveland we knew no one. While we were looking for a place to live, we moved into a trailer. It was only temporary, but it didn't improve our feelings of isolation. I quit Victoreen Instruments and we headed back to Chicago. I was without a job. And in retrospect, that probably changed my life.

~

It wasn't long after we had returned to Chicago that my friend Madhu Mehta, who had loaned me the wedding money, told me about an opening at the Automatic Electric Company, a division of General Telephone and Electronics, GTE. GTE was a major provider of telephone services, a rival of Bell Telephone, which years later, after many mergers, became Verizon. Automatic Electric was a subsidiary that manufactured telephone equipment, including automatic switching machines that had made the old manually operated telephone switchboards obsolete.

As an electrical engineer I knew in general terms how telephone communication worked, but I hadn't had any experience with the systems that made phone connections possible. I also had no idea that telephone communication was entering a revolutionary era. But when I began working for Automatic Electric, I was assigned, completely by chance, to a small team that was at the extreme forefront of this imminent telecom revolution.

Bernie Rekeire and Mike Kelley, two senior engineers, headed the team, along with a Chinese-American scientist, Dr Chen. I was the junior person, together with Bob Lindsey who joined shortly after I did. The five of us were working to develop a new kind of digital automatic telephone exchange. Since I knew nothing at all about this technology, I had to learn on the job.

Luck smiled on me twice here—first, by placing me in a fundamentally important field just as it was about to explode and, second, by putting me on a team with talented engineers who were also friendly, nurturing people. The team bosses, Bernie and Mike, understood that Bob and I needed training and support, and they did everything they could to provide it.

Our team's job was to develop a way to connect telephone calls in which the transmission of the speakers' voices was done through the digital rather than the analogue mode. When people speak, their voices register ups and downs, moments of silence, variations in pitch and several other characteristics. All of these features are embodied in waves of sound. In analogue telephone transmission, these waves are carried through the wires that connect callers' telephones. But scientists at Bell Labs had developed a different, more effective way of transmitting vocal signals. They had worked out how to digitize sound waves.

What they did was sample the vocal sound-waves at different points, and convert those points into numbers. Those numbers could be transmitted and then reassembled back into sound waves at the other end of the transmission, so that the listener would then hear them as speech.

In order to accomplish this, the scientists at Bell had to overcome an immense challenge. Sound waves are continuous, and any single number that represents how a voice sounds at a given moment won't be exactly accurate. So how could one translate that voice into digits, and then translate it back on the other end of the line so that it sounds the same? The answer was to use brute force. The Bell Labs scientists sampled each sound wave 8000 times per second, assigning each sample a number. It was that array of numbers that they reassembled at the far end to achieve a clear transmission.

Digital transmission had great advantages over analogue transmission. It made for clearer sound; the digital signals didn't deteriorate over time and distance as analogue waves did. It was far faster, and it allowed for many more signals to be transmitted on one single piece of wire. Digital transmission significantly increased the capacity of the phone transmission lines. But it meant keeping track of and manipulating huge sets of numbers in microseconds.

Digitalization was a revolutionary development. But the process of actually transmitting digital signals and switching also needed to be revolutionized. That's what we were working on.

Connecting a telephone call between the calling and receiving parties goes through a series of steps. The first is when a caller takes the telephone off the hook, hears a dial tone and dials a number. That's the signalling part. Next comes the switching part, which routes the call. If the caller is in Boston and is calling a party in Chicago, what happens is that the numbers he or she has dialled first go to an exchange in Boston. In previous times that exchange was manned by an operator who fielded the signal and sent it on to a Chicago operator by plugging wires into the appropriate channels on her switchboard. But for many decades now, that exchange process has been handled by automatic switchboards.

The automatic switchboard—or just 'switch'—reads the numbers that have been dialled, say 312-567-1234. The numbers 312 mean Chicago, so the call is sent to the Chicago exchange, or switch. The Chicago switch reads 567 and sends the signal on to the switch that serves the 567 Chicago neighbourhood or subregion. The subregion switch reads 1234 and sends it to the subscriber whose number it is. That subscriber hears his phone ring, picks the receiver up, and the connection is made.

That's the switching process which by itself is fairly simple. What makes this simple process mind-bogglingly complex is that these switches are scanning hundreds of thousands of telephone lines at the same time. Of all those lines, they have to recognize the moment when any one receiver is picked up. When that happens the switch has to instantly access a database that tells it: This is John Jones's telephone; John Jones has paid his telephone bill; John Jones gets a dial tone so that he can make his call. Then the Boston switch has to connect John Jones's line with the Chicago switch, which is likewise monitoring many hundreds of thousands of lines and is simultaneously connecting an untold number of calls. If the receiver's line is busy, John Jones has to be sent a busy signal. If the circuit between Boston and Chicago is overloaded, say, because it's right after the Super Bowl, the Boston switch has to reroute the call through, for example, the Cincinnati switch instead of the Chicago switch. If the rerouting possibilities are overloaded, John Jones has to be sent a 'circuits busy' signal. And all this has to happen in a matter of milliseconds and microseconds.

These complexities are magnified by additional functions the switch is called on to perform, which have evolved over the years. If the subscribers have call waiting, the call-waiting signal has to be activated. If the caller has initiated a three-way or conference call, those additional lines have to be engaged. If the recipient wants to put his present caller on hold while he answers John Jones's call, the switch has to enable that. The switch has to monitor the call so that when the parties hang up, the lines are disconnected. If a party has neglected to hang up the receiver, that also has to be recognized and an 'off the hook' signal has to be sent. For billing purposes, the switch has to meter the length of the call.

Literally millions of these events are happening at the same time, which means that the telephone system has one of *the* most complex designs of any system in the world—far more complex than, say, for example, NASA's space station. And we, in our little team, were working out the problems involved in developing switches that would code, connect and decode binary bits of information—i.e., digitized voice signals. We wanted to build switches that GTE could use for its own networks of subscribers and that we could sell to other service providers.

Only two companies were working on digital switches in the US, Bell Labs and us. There was a bit of development going on in Europe at Siemens and Ericsson, and some in Japan. But the predominant activity was in the US. We were at the crest of the wave.

Designing the elements for digital switching was hugely challenging but also hugely exciting. We felt something akin to what I now imagine the creators of the Internet must have felt when they were developing the early protocols for computer networking systems. Indeed, our work on circuit switching for telephone networks was occurring at the same time as others were building packet-switched networks for computers. Later, as the two merged to form a global Internet, I was pleased to say that we participated in building digital networks which ultimately led to the Internet and opened a whole new dimension to communication.

As the least experienced of our engineers, I probably needed a little more support than the others, exacerbated by the fact that I was a foreigner. My English, for example, was fluent enough, but slightly eccentric. My English writing was, quite simply, bad.

After I gave my boss, Bernie, a report I had written about something I was working on, he took me aside.

'Sam, can I talk to you privately?' he asked.

'Of course.'

'Sam, look. You don't know how to write English well. But on this job you have to be able to write. It's a necessity.'

'Okay,' I said. 'I understand. Give me six months.'

In those six months I studied every book I could find on how to write. I read furiously. I did the exercises. I built up my vocabulary, spending my free time reading newspapers and magazines, noting words and phrases. And Bernie watched my progress. He encouraged me. 'Sam, you're really making an improvement.' 'Good Sam, that's good.' I knew he was overdoing it for the benefit of my morale, but I was grateful for his support. And in six months' time, a kind of miracle happened. I learned to write.

Before long the others were asking me to write up whatever we had that needed to be written. I took to it, and I began really feeling at home with the language. I wrote articles for trade magazines and professional publications, like the prestigious *IEEE Transactions and Telephony* magazine. I spoke on behalf of our team at conferences and industry events. I was also invited to be a guest editor for a special issue of *IEEE Transactions* on the topic of 'Telecommunications in Developing Countries', published in July 1976.

We felt that the best way to try out the new switching technologies we were developing was in the controlled environments of smaller systems like those of corporate offices, hospitals, banks and universities that might have 100 or 200 or 500 internal lines. These telephone switches, known as 'private automatic branch exchanges' then connected up to the public exchanges.

We built those smaller switches and started selling them. By then the whole telecommunications industry was picking up on these things. There was a general thirst to explore this field. Soon, I was being invited to all kinds of conferences in the US and abroad, giving seminars and lectures. People were lining up to hear about what we were doing. I started teaching a course at GTE on digital switching— What is it? Why do you need it? How do you convert voice signals to digital samples? How can you most efficiently transmit them? How do you generate digital tones? I started doing the same thing at industry trade shows as well, giving half-day or full-day courses in front of 500 or 600 people.

Over time, I realized that I was helping to socialize the idea of digital switching by creating a community of understanding for it. More than that, since we were working on the cutting edge of this technology, a great number of our developments were patentable. I had a certain knack for these innovations, and I began filing for and accumulating patents. Our GTE team was achieving significant recognition, and I was becoming quite recognized myself. I was the Indian guy who was developing interesting telecom techniques.

Every year, GTE held a dinner for its patent awardees. Hundreds of people attended, and the awardees were given a plaque and a 100-dollar cheque for each patent. The patents were in the names of the patent holders, but the GTE employment contracts specified that patents were to be assigned to the company. After four or five of these yearly dinners it was dawning on me that I wasn't ever going to be making a great deal of money *at* GTE, but that my patents were making a great deal of money *for* GTE.

~

In 1974, I was thirty-two years old and a senior engineer. In the back of my mind I had the idea that I wanted to be a millionaire before I turned forty. I used to tell my friends that ideally I'd like to have enough money at forty so that I could be free to do whatever I wanted to do—not that I knew what that might be, but the idea of having that freedom was growing on me. I wanted it. I didn't want to have a nine-to-five job after forty. If I had to, I would. *But ideally,* I thought, *by the time I'm that age I'd like to be done with money.* The problem was that I had no idea how to accomplish such a goal. Nor did I have any mentor to look to for answers.

~

That year my father and mother came to visit America for the first time. It was quite a thing for them to come to Chicago on a Boeing 747 all the way from Titilagarh. For Anu and me also it was a major event. By then we had purchased a house. We had cleaned it up, made it nicer. My brother Pinu was living with us, studying biomedical engineering at the University of Illinois. We wanted to impress upon my parents that their children were doing well. After nine years of marriage, Anu was pregnant with our first child, which was a great joy to all of us.

My parents had sent me to school and had watched my progress with pride, no doubt. But they didn't really know anything about what I studied or what it was I did for a living. One day while they were visiting, my father said, 'Tell me, what did you study in college?'

'Dad, I studied physics.'

'Really? Explain to me, what is physics?'

I explained it to him. Then he wanted to know about my work. So I took him to my office. By then I was well established at GTE. People respected me. I was a senior person; within the company I had a great deal of freedom. I wanted to show my father all this.

My father knew that GTE made things. To him that meant it must be some kind of a factory. And his idea of a factory was smoke, noise, tools and machinery. But in the office there were no machines, there was no noise. People weren't building things, they were just sitting at desks with papers and pencils. He thought it was a library. He could relate to a library.

'Do these people get paid to do this?' he asked. 'Sit around with paper and pencil? This is what you do?'

'Yes, Dad.'

It was a surprise to him. On the other hand, whatever I was actually doing, it was clear I was working hard. I left the house every morning before eight and I came home at six. He told me once, then several more times, 'Look, if you're working this hard, why are you working for somebody? Go work for yourself.'

'Dad, it's not that easy to start a digital switching company. It takes a lot of capital. You need a big support-staff, many people. You have to build an entire system with engineers and scientists and sales people. It's not something you can just go off and do on your own.'

'Whatever it is,' he said, 'I'm telling you, you shouldn't work this hard for others, you should work hard for yourself.'

He might be ignorant of these things, I thought, but ignorance can be a great asset too. It doesn't allow you to think of all the reasons you shouldn't do something—not that I was any closer to figuring out what I actually should do. But I realized that part of my success and happiness had to do with the fact that my dad never interfered or asked any questions about what I did and why I did it. He had full trust and confidence in his children. He worked hard, and provided us with security and love. I always felt that I would do the same for my own children.

But at work I was becoming increasingly unhappy doing what others were telling me to do. And one experience put me over the edge. I was assigned a project that I judged would take me three weeks to complete. My boss said, 'Give yourself more time. This has to be done exactly right, then it has to be thoroughly documented. Make it six months.' Then my boss's boss got to him with the same concern. 'No, no, no,' he said. 'You guys are trying to hurry this up. I need it done carefully. Timing isn't a problem. You really need a year to do it properly.'

By the time it got approved at the highest level, it had turned into an eighteen-month project. I was annoyed at the way it had been handled. It reinforced my thinking that I wanted to set my own agenda rather than working on other people's projects. In the end I did it in three weeks. I finished it, documented it and submitted my resignation along with it.

Everyone was shocked. Why was I doing this?

'I just want to do something else.'

'What? What else do you want to do?'

'I don't know. I'm just ready to leave.'

But the fact was that I had been approached by another Chicago-area company that was thinking about starting a digital switching operation. They had the investment money in hand and they were looking for someone with experience to run it. If I took the job, I would become a 10 per cent partner. This seemed to me about as close as I was going to come to doing a start-up on my own. It was something I was eager to pursue.

At GTE, I learned to use my education in physics and electronics while working on large digital switching systems. It required discipline, creativity and collaboration. In the process, I conceived products, filed patents, ordered parts, built prototypes, worked on documentation, and tested, evaluated and modified products. Eight years at GTE gave me the foundation I needed, teaching me about the domain of telecommunications, the domain expertise that I needed to build my future.

I firmly believe that without solid domain expertise in one particular field, it is difficult to build a long-lasting passion for work. Domain expertise teaches you to do something real, something that matters. To enjoy work requires commitment and passion. I have never differentiated between my job and joy.

5

Learning to Lead

The company was Wescom Inc. and was located in Downers Grove, Illinois, just outside of Chicago. It manufactured electronic equipment for the telephone industry. Wescom's then owner and president, Mr Clint Penny, had noted that digital switching was the future and had decided to get into the field while it was still in its nascent stages.

Clint Penny possessed an entrepreneurial soul. He had founded Wescom to compete against giant equipment companies like Western Electric, believing that even a smaller company could find ways to outperform large adversaries. He felt the same way about building digital switches. He was a fearless risk-taker.

Compared to GTE, Wescom was small, but the possibilities were vast. At GTE, we had been ahead of the curve and had started producing small switches. But the field was now wide open, and taking up this job would give me the chance to carve out a pioneering role for myself. It would be exciting, challenging, daunting and fascinating, all at once. And on top of that I'd enjoy an ownership position. I jumped at the opportunity.

Pursuant to discussions with Penny, his partner, Alan Brown, and Wescom Inc.'s chief engineer, Mike Birck, we decided to build a digital switch that would service 2000 lines. That would be attractive to big organizations—airlines, banks, insurance companies, hospitals—a market rich with sales potential. No one had developed a switch of this sort yet. We would be the first ones.

I was swimming with ideas on what to do and how to do it. The technology of the time was just about reaching a stage that allowed for true breakthroughs. Digital switches would give companies unprecedented abilities to maximize both intra-company communication as well as communication with the outside world.

I intended to build what the industry called 'non-blocking' switches. 'Non-blocking' meant that if a company had a 2000 line-switch, all 2000 lines could be used simultaneously. The previous generation of switches—which were standard everywhere—only allowed perhaps 200 out of 2000 lines to be used at once. They were elementally 'blocking' as opposed to 'non-blocking'.

Building an electromechanical, relay-based non-blocking 2000 line-switch would have required incorporating 2000 x 2000, i.e., 4 million relays, an impossibly intricate and expensive arrangement. Consequently, electromechanical exchanges were operated instead, on the basis of statistical probability. What were the chances that in a company with 2000 employees, there may be 100 or 200 or 300 employees using their telephones at any given time? The formula for determining such a probability was named after Siméon-Denis Poisson, the French mathematician who had developed the theory. If Poisson's distribution theory predicted that only 200 users would be on their telephones at any one given time, that was the number of relays a design would incorporate. If more than 200 users tried to make calls at once, the additional callers would not be able to get a dial tone. They would be blocked. Our digital switch was going to be able to unblock them. Digital switches didn't use electromechanical relays, resorting instead to low-cost, high-speed digital memories. As a result, it was possible to design non-blocking systems at a lower cost.

Another innovation I planned to use came from Intel, which was then just introducing their 8-bit processor, the soon-to-be-famous 8080. I had worked with Intel in one capacity or another at GTE, where we had used their earlier 4-bit microprocessor for various applications. I had met Lester Hogan, the semiconductor guru to Intel founders, Gordon Moore and Bob Noyce, and he and I had struck up something of a personal relationship. As a result, I was closely attuned to the development of the 8080, which I thought could provide the basis for a new kind of switch architecture.

Having the 8080 to work with put me directly on the cutting edge of a revolution that I had seen unfolding almost from the beginning, that I was really living through myself. William Shockley and his team at Bell Labs had invented the transistor in 1947, but for quite a few years the main application of this revolutionary technology was audio—tape recorders, hearing aids, transistor radios. When I was studying electronics in India—in the early 1960s—we were still working with vacuum tubes. In the telephone industry there had been some talk of creating an analogue switch using transistors, but that had never happened. So telephone switches continued to use electromechanical relays.

Then along came microprocessors—the packaging of many transistors together on a silicon chip. Intel's first microprocessor, which we had used to a certain extent at GTE, arrived on the market in 1971. It was a 4-bit microprocessor called 4040. The 8080 followed it, and it was powerful enough to give me the idea that I could build a switch architecture around 8-bit microprocessors themselves, which would free switches from their dependence on mainframe computers. In fact, at IIT, in one of our classes Dr Bruce Briely taught us about a 2-bit processor to understand basic computing operations such as addition, subtraction and 'shift'. However, at the time, in the early 1960s, we did not realize that he was teaching about a 2-bit processor. To someone like me, who had purchased a 2-input NAND gate integrated-circuit for 35 dollars, an 8-bit microprocessor on a chip was a miracle.

Before the invention of the microprocessor, mainframe computers the size of a building had been required to handle the various functions of switches, the connections, tones, timing, billing, and so on. But the new microprocessors had the capacity to control some of these functions by themselves. My idea was to use individual microprocessors to handle distinct functions. One microprocessor to scan lines, one to control routing, one to control tone generation—essentially, one for each of the major functions of the switch.

This would be a 'distributed' instead of a 'centralized' architecture. I designed my new switch to be non-blocking and distributor-controlled by using microprocessors, a network of small computers all communicating with each other, which together formed a new kind of switch. It incorporated other innovations as well, including duplicated controls and duplicated service circuits along with an advanced ability to detect and cure failures instantly, so the user would not notice any interruption. Its architecture enabled easy expansion of the system when more power was needed for additional functions, so in that sense it looked to the future. Because no mainframe was required, start-up costs were considerably less. Since the switch controlled the five major elements of telephone communication, we called it the 580—'5' for the five elements, and '80' because it was 1974 and '1980' implied the telecom future. The 580 was a five-function switch for the future—there was nothing like it on the market at the time. We went full steam ahead with the development and I took out the patents as we went along.

Building the 580 required large teams of hardware, software, mechanical, maintenance, reliability and systems engineers. The team also required technicians, testers, technical writers, sales, marketing and support staff. Some resources we took from Wescom Inc., some I hired from outside. To begin with, I had to prepare a development plan for the project for a period of two years, with a focus on finance and marketing. At the top levels there was Mike Birck, Wescom Inc.'s chief engineer, to whom I owed a great deal. Mike had interviewed me initially, so it was in part due to him that I was at Wescom in the first place. He was a brilliant engineer and also a wonderful teacher, a truly great support to me. Mike later founded Tellabs, which became a 10-billion dollar telecom company.

Our mechanical engineers designed racks, connectors, consoles— all the physical elements that went into the 580. We had logic designers, circuit designers, power supply designers, documentation people, software people working on call-processing systems, billing systems, maintenance systems as well as 'watchdog' timers, which would detect when some function was taking too long and would automatically divert it to a backup mode. We had over 100 designers, and 300 more in sales and manufacturing.

Most of our engineers had a narrow range of expertise; it was my job to work with all of them to bring this complex array of engineering functions together into a coherent, integrated whole. I learned from my engineers, and I developed my own ideas about how to do things. I had gained experience at GTE on self-healing controls, and had by now developed a fairly strong gut feeling and instinct about how complex systems should fit together.

The technical problems were daunting, especially in the software. There were no high-level languages then. There were no operating systems. Programs were written in machine language. We didn't even have a proper program to load floppy disks on to. We had to write our own.

I brought in Madhu Mehta, my IIT friend who had generously loaned me 150 dollars to get married. Madhu had a PhD in electrical engineering, but had gone back to India to help take care of his ageing parents. 'I've started this new company, Wescom Switching, with Wescom Inc., and I need your help in Chicago.' In India, Madhu was building early versions of computers for the local market. He joined us as a consultant, together with his Baroda-based group of young, talented Indian engineers, to help design part of our software in India. 'Outsourcing' was not a buzzword then, but we were doing it.

Despite the complexity of the engineering, I learned quickly that by far the biggest challenge wasn't engineering, it was people. And the key to get everyone talking and collaborating was that I needed to make sure they were happy with their work and functioning well together. At every stage I saw interesting human challenges. There were situations I had never dealt with before that sometimes surprised me, from personal conflicts to territorial issues, ego difficulties and even love problems. One of our young women engineers fell in love with one of Madhu's software engineers when he was visiting. They planned to marry, but back in India the engineer's mother had arranged his marriage with an Indian girl. Anu taught our lady engineer in the US how to wear a sari, and then I sent her to India to claim her fiancé.

I began meeting with all employees once a month. I told them where we were in terms of goals, what we had accomplished, how we were going to tackle our next phase. I wanted them to feel good about how we were doing, how *they* were doing. I wanted to instil in them a sense of accomplishment, an enthusiasm for the work we were doing. I would tell them about the mistakes I had made in my career, which they appreciated. I opened myself to criticism, which they weren't shy about providing. We were all making mistakes; that's how we learned. But in order to learn from mistakes you first had to acknowledge them. I tried to emulate that for the team.

The meetings were high-energy affairs. Everybody would get psyched up. But after a while, the morale level would dip down—A didn't do this, B didn't do that, C didn't give someone else the right documentation, there was so much to take in. And then at the beginning of the month I'd have another meeting, and they'd get excited again. From my mezzanine-level office in Oak Brook I could see the entire team downstairs, building the prototype. I had a clear view of the progress and problems. And that gave an extra charge to my own excitement about the work.

In 1974, there were hardly any Indian-American CEOs in the high-tech industry. Several African-Americans, including our janitor, took great pride in the fact that I was brown and the CEO. Every day he would wait for me, at the front lobby, while mopping floors, to say good morning. I would hug him every day, and that made both of us feel proud. I saw diversity as our great strength in the company. Once, a group of white senior managers complained that I seemed to favour Asian engineers. I needed to have a serious conversation with them on diversity as a fertile ground for innovation to make them feel comfortable once again.

I always thought of Gandhi and his life at Sabarmati Ashram in my dealings with people at work. My job was to make them all feel good, encouraged and empowered; I genuinely took an interest in their well-being. I strongly believed in an egalitarian and non-hierarchical organization strengthened with clean networking and openness to learn from each other and improve the overall productivity and efficiency.

At GTE I had learned about design, patents, documentation, testing and evaluation. I learnt about the immense importance of reading and writing. I had become comfortable with public speaking. At Wescom, in addition to engineering, I was looking at all the other aspects of the business as well—the financing, accounting, marketing, sales and customer service—in charge of the whole big picture of running a company. Management on this scale was of a magnitude beyond anything I had ever done. I knew nothing about running a company on this level, but I learnt on the job, and I had some great people teaching me.

One of my mentors was Tom Hughes, my marketing director. Tom was in his fifties then, very senior to me. (I was thirty-two when we started Wescom Switching.) Tom was, what I thought of as, a hard-core American, a deacon in his church, a football referee at his kid's school, a solid citizen in every way. We had almost nothing in common, but that didn't get in the way of our friendship, which developed quickly and deepened as we travelled all over the country together on sales trips—me making the technical presentations, Tom delivering the sales pitches.

Tom was a highly effective salesman, but he was far more than that. He took me to fine restaurants and taught me about food and wine. He instructed me on the importance of eating a good American breakfast. He would say to a cab driver, 'This is my father. I'm bringing him along'—his idea of humour. Tom was full of joy, and everyone around him couldn't help but feel it too.

When things started going well at Wescom, I bought a company car, thinking of giving it to Tom. But he said, 'I can't have a car if you don't have one. You're the CEO.'

'Tom,' I said, 'I live a mile away. You live 20 miles away. You drive the car.'

'If you won't take it,' he said, 'I won't take it.' For a week the car just sat there. Then one Friday I said, 'Why don't you just take the car over the weekends? On Monday we'll decide who keeps the car.'

Tom took the car out that Friday, when he and his wife went out to dinner. It was while they were driving home from the restaurant that a drunk driver smashed into them at high speed.

My phone woke me up at four in the morning. Tom's daughter was on the line. 'Sam,' she said, 'my dad's in the hospital. There's been a major accident.'

Anu and I ran to the hospital. Tom's wife, Joanna, and their daughter were there. Joanna was unhurt; the drunk driver had ploughed into the driver's—Tom's—side. But by the time we arrived Tom was already dead. I was completely heartbroken. He was not just my friend, he was my guide. I met with the family, his kids, his wife. At the funeral I was one of the pall-bearers. It was my first exposure to the death of someone I was close to, an ache that took a long while to subside.

I was acutely aware of how much Tom was teaching me as we went along. But, of course, in my previous jobs I had had my own bosses and had picked up a great deal from them through osmosis. My first boss was George at Victoreen Instruments, the nuclear measuring company. George's approach was simple. He hired people he thought had skills, gave them assignments, then gave them support. He was what I thought of as a comfortable—or comforting—boss. He made it clear that he believed in my ability, and he let me travel and learn by myself, which in turn enhanced not just my skills but my self-confidence too.

At GTE Bernie Rekeire and Mike Kelley were my bosses, and partners, in a sense. They were both ten or so years my seniors, and were friendly, caring individuals, who had what I would call 'nurturing' personalities. They believed in hands-on instruction, something that Bob Lindsey, the other junior member of our team, and I needed. But they did it patiently, in a non-confrontational way. 'Here's the way you do this kind of thing, like this. Do you understand? If you need more help, just let me know.'

I was lucky finding those sorts of bosses. They chose me because they thought I had the necessary talent. Then they supported me. But they didn't really manage me. And as I became a manager on a large scale, I did exactly the same thing. I loved my people. I left them alone. I made personal friends with them. I supported them in every way I could. I encouraged them to do good work. I never bothered them.

I did things that way because it fit my style and because I believed it was the right approach to management. I regarded myself as open, friendly and egalitarian, and those were the characteristics I brought to managing others. But I wasn't doing it to be popular. A good boss cannot and should not care about being popular. If my employees weren't at the right level, if they didn't deliver, I fired them.

Wescom was on an altogether different scale from our team at GTE. But I built on the lessons that had helped me in my own development as a scientist and engineer. A rigid, micromanaging boss who is constantly on top of his or her employees, questioning and harassing them, can turn off people's interest in their work. That management style can so easily become a barrier to the growth of skills and creativity a company so badly needs from its workers. In essence, I took what had been beneficial for me in my own work life and applied it to my own management methods. It was a style that reflected my own personality and my own idea of what can best help people realize their innate talents and improve their productivity. At the same time I read a wide selection of the popular, highly regarded business management literature around, most notably Peter Drucker. (I had developed the habit of reading regularly after Bernie Rekeire told me I needed to learn how to write.) The overall result was that I began utilizing management techniques that later became popular currency in Silicon Valley and elsewhere, which included principles like equality in management, a non-hierarchical management, flat organizations, open offices, flexible work hours, regular communication, and so on.

But my most important teacher and guide in all of this was Wescom's majority owner, Mr Clint Penny. Clint Penny was a character. An uneducated man hailing originally from Kansas, he was, by birth, a farmer who owned 18,000 acres of fertile land in Missouri. With his Midwestern accent, blue eyes and blunt ways, he fit my own mental definition of a hillbilly—though I would understand later that bluff, plain-spoken, jocular farmers weren't exactly the same thing as hillbillies.

Whatever his rural background, in the field of electronics Clint Penny was an entrepreneur of the highest order. He was a visionary who was able to scope out the future of telecom, even though he himself didn't know the first thing about electronics. He knew how to make money, and he knew how to enjoy the process—that was it. For some reason we had great personal chemistry together. He was thirty years older than me, and had very little connection to or even tolerance for things foreign— but he had found me, and both of us felt an almost-instant compatibility and sense of kinship, unexpected as that might have been. He believed I was capable, but he also knew I needed to learn.

~

In February 1975, our son Salil was born at Michael Reese Hospital in Chicago. He had so much hair that the nurses in the hospital would come and tell us, 'Your son needs a haircut.' Salil's arrival was great news for the Pitroda family. My brother Manek distributed sweets in Titilagarh, and I decided to buy my first (first-hand) car, a 1975 Buick.

~

Once we were well along in developing the Model 580 PBX (Private Branch Exchange), for large corporations to use for their communication needs, I went on a selling trip in 1975. My first stop was Japan, where I gave a talk on the 580 at the International Switching Symposium in front of a couple of thousand people. From there I flew to the Philippines. I met with the chief and top echelon of the National Constabulary Police in Manila and made my presentation. The 580 was a cutting-edge switch with microprocessors controlling the software, distributed control, and stored program control, which allowed for far greater efficiency through a special purpose on-board computer. I could tell I was dazzling the audience with all this new technology. When I was finished, the Philippino Constabulary bought a 400,000-dollar switch.

From the Philippines I went to Taiwan and made a presentation to their defence department, with all the generals listening intently. 'Mr Pitroda,' the top general said, 'you have convinced us. We will order this switch from you.'

As excited as I was about these orders, I was almost equally anxious. We had worked out the design for the 580, but we were only in the early stages of actually building it. When I got back to Chicago, I said, 'Clint, we've got almost a million in orders, but we don't have the product yet. What are we going to do?'

'Listen,' he said, 'never refuse an order. It doesn't matter if you don't have the product, just take the order.'

So I confirmed the orders.

Clint said, 'Now, I want you to find a guy to go back and forth between Taiwan and Manila, and give them the idea that there's lots of activity going on. Have him stay over there. Send him some cards, send him some hardware. He'll install what you send him, plug it in, unplug it, plug it in again. It'll be a show. Meanwhile, you guys here will be finishing the thing.'

I thought, *What a good idea.* But nobody wanted to do the back-and-forth travelling. No one in my existing team saw this as a productive way to spend the nine or ten months it was going to take before we had a finished switch.

Then one day I was at the supermarket and saw an Indian guy working one of the checkout counters, bagging groceries. I said hello and asked, 'Have you been to school? What do you do?'

'I'm an engineer,' he said. 'I'm looking for a job.'

'What kind of engineer?'

'Electrical engineer.'

'Why are you filling bags?'

'I haven't found a job yet.'

'Come see me tomorrow,' I said.

So he came to the office and I gave him the job. 'You're going to be trained and then you will need to go to the Philippines and Taiwan to install our systems. You will stay there for as long as you need to to get the systems working. Keep the light alive. Keep the lamp lit. You have to be constantly engaged with things. Go back and forth, tell them you have to go to the US. Be busy. Now and then I'll send some people you can take with you.'

And he did just that; he kept the clients satisfied that the right things were happening. And in nine months we had the switches ready and we delivered them.

Along the way, General Santos of the Philippino Constabulary announced that he needed to come and meet with me, which sent the whole place into a panic. 'General Santos is coming. What can Sam tell him?' The Philippines consulate called, informing us when the general would be arriving.

'We'll arrange to pick him up in a limousine.' I said. 'Please send me his schedule.' When they did, it turned out he was flying not to Chicago but to Indianapolis to visit a relative—200 miles away. So we sent the limousine to Indianapolis. And when he did arrive in Chicago, Anu and I treated him like royalty. The man had given us a 400,000-dollar order; we had to keep him as happy as possible.

This sounds like elementary business sense. But I was an engineer, not a businessman. I had spent my years immersed in designing systems, developing hardware and figuring out tone-generation problems, not business etiquette. I didn't know how these things worked. I had to learn them, and Clint Penny was my teacher.

The first 580 we actually installed wasn't in Manila or Taiwan, it was in Tulsa, Oklahoma, for American Airlines. The installation was, to put it bluntly, a disaster. After several years of back-breaking labour on development and production, the switch simply did not work. My distributor in Texas was Captain Jim Lovell, the chief astronaut of Apollo 13, who was now the CEO of the Fisk Telephone Company. He was the one who had sold the switch to American Airlines. I had become friends with Jim over the last two years. His astronaut colleague

Buzz Aldrin also got interested in our switch and he became a friend as well. It still amazes me, almost forty years later, that I got to know these two. I came to America after reading a story about taking man to the moon. Now I found myself to be, to my amazement, friends with these two legendary astronauts.

In any event, Lovell sold the switch to American Airlines, we installed it, and it didn't work. We tried fixes, and it still didn't work. Finally, Jim called. 'Sam,' he said, 'this is really bad. I can smell death here.'

'Don't worry, Jim,' I said. 'I'm personally coming to figure it out.'

So I flew to Tulsa, taking thirteen hardware and software engineers with me. Clint Penny also insisted on coming along. At American Airlines I tried and tried to figure out what was wrong, but the answer kept eluding me. I called Gordon Moore, one of the founders of Intel. 'Look,' I said. 'I've got a serious problem.'

'What you've got is a software problem,' he said.

'No,' I said, 'I think it's in the hardware. I think it's in the chip.' I called Gordon every other day; we tried to fix the thing together. It was a huge, nightmarish mess. I didn't sleep for fifty-four hours straight; I can't even imagine what I must have looked like. Finally, Clint put his foot down. 'Sam,' he said, 'you have to sleep.'

'I cannot sleep until this is done.'

'This isn't good,' he said. 'Something bad is going to happen to you. I insist that you go to your hotel room. I am going to stand guard and make sure you sleep.' He did, and I slept for a couple of hours.

In the end, we fixed it. It turned out that the Intel chip had a habit of randomly losing information. The 8080 and the Intel memory chips we were using were still in the early days of design and production, and weren't yet a 100 per cent reliable—something we had still not identified in all our testing.

But we figured it out—and everything worked! Jim Lovell was very nice about it. American Airlines was satisfied. Clint Penny was happy; his confidence in the project—and in me—was fully back on track.

~

At Wescom I started travelling a lot in the US, and to Europe and the Asia-Pacific. Wescom had offices in Chicago, Santa Clara, Hawaii, Tokyo and London. I was flying all over to market our products and attend seminars and conferences at various forums. In 1976, I was invited as a US expert by the Brazilian government, through the United Nations, to train people for a month and help them launch their digital switching initiative in Campinas, a Brazilian municipality in São Paulo. This was my lesson in globalization. I began to understand and appreciate the foods, cultures, customs, manners and markets of different parts of the world.

~

I began developing the 580 (private branch exchange) in 1974 using Intel's 8080 chip, which allowed for a new approach to switch architecture. Few people, if any at that time, recognized that the speed and power of chips was going to explode the way it did. Gordon Moore had predicted that the chip speed would double every two years and that the cost per chip would go down, but the truth of what came to be known as 'Moore's Law' took time to impress itself on the technology world. In the mid-1970s, we thought that if you could have a thousand transistors on a chip it was a miracle. Today, we build chips with a billion or more transistors.

Our growth at Wescom and the growth of chips and programming was a parallel story. We started with a more or less simple idea for private branch exchanges, or PBX. Several years later we evolved the PBX into an automatic call distributor. The automatic call distributor comprised a system that enabled calls coming into a company to be routed to specific terminals handled by operators or agents, for example, at airlines or service centres. A call coming in to an airline for a reservation could be routed to one of a group of agents, to a supervising agent and also to the supervisor of supervisors. The automatic call distributor could build a hierarchy of answering calls. It could handle high volumes of calls; it was non-blocking. It was an essential tool for businesses that depended on high telephone traffic, where incoming calls were constant and smooth internal connections were necessary. We were the first to build digital call distributors. We developed them for Continental Airlines, Frontier Airlines and United. The future for these and similar technologies we were developing seemed limitless.

In the middle of a busy working schedule at Wescom, I was again back at the Michael Reese Hospital at the end of January 1978, waiting in a maternity area for our second child. The doctor came out and said 'Mr Pitroda, you have a beautiful little daughter. Both she and Mom are doing very well. Please come with me.' I was thrilled to hold my little princess, Rajal. Now, our family was complete. I remember sitting outside our small little house in Brandywine with both of my kids on my lap, dreaming about their future. It was time now to move to a bigger home.

~

Clint and Alan together owned 90 per cent of Wescom Switching—everything other than my 10 per cent interest. Faced with the need for more cash to fund their personal priorities, they decided to sell the company in 1979. To facilitate the sale they hired the Wall Street investment bank Salomon Brothers, which made a deal with major manufacturing corporation Rockwell International for 27 million dollars.

Clint and Alan did not share their plans to sell the company with me. I was a minor partner with no say in the company's future, so they probably didn't feel the need to. In retrospect, they probably also didn't want to spook me into doing something disruptive. So I knew nothing about any of it until the deal was struck. When I found out, I was told that Don Yakley, president of the Rockwell telecom division that was buying us out, was coming to see me.

On the given day a limousine pulled up at our office and Don Yakley stepped out with two of his senior people. 'We've bought the company,' Yakley told me. 'We need to discuss arrangements with you.'

'Wait a minute,' I said. 'I'm not selling you my share.'

There was a long silence. Yakley looked perplexed.

'What do you mean? We bought the company.'

'You bought it from Clint and Alan. You didn't ask me. You didn't buy my share. They were my partners. Now you're my partner.'

Yakley gave me a long look. 'Rockwell can't have you as a partner. It doesn't work that way. We want to buy you out.'

'I'm sorry,' I said. 'I'm not selling.'

There was really nothing else to say. They left to regroup and rethink, not happily.

Paul Miller was my attorney, a wonderful man and a good friend, Harvard- and Yale-educated. He was, by heritage, a Boston Brahmin—as sophisticated as they came. 'Paul,' I said, 'this is a once-in-a-lifetime opportunity to make some money. I'm not going to just let it go.' We talked it over, and I decided on a course of action.

Back at the company I went to see Clint. 'You know,' I said, 'you really should have told me.'

'Sam, you're just a small owner, we didn't want to bother you.'

'Well, I'm not selling.'

'What *are* you going to do then?'

'I'll do whatever I have to do, I have nothing against you or Alan, quite the opposite. But this is for my family.'

That afternoon I called Ed Spencer, the CEO of Honeywell, hoping that he would be interested in buying the company.

'Ed, this is Sam Pitroda.'

As soon as I explained the situation to him—Clint and Alan's decision to sell, the Rockwell deal, my talk with Rockwell—Ed said, 'Don't do anything. I'm coming up to Chicago with my team.'

Ed flew in with his team on his corporate jet the next day. He looked at things and we talked. He liked what he saw. When he had had a chance to put the numbers together he offered us just under 40 million, far better than the Rockwell deal. I was also talking to a couple of other likely buyers—Emerson Electric and Loral, but it looked as though Honeywell's offer was going to be the highest.

At this point I had not yet discussed what I was doing with Clint or Alan. I was confident that if I could make a bigger deal they'd pull out of the Rockwell understanding and come along with me.

Then one day when I was sitting at a bar at O'Hare Airport in Chicago, waiting for my flight to be announced, the man sitting next to me said, 'Excuse me, are you Sam Pitroda?'

'Yes?'

He introduced himself and informed me that he worked for a Saudi Arabian prince. He said, 'We've heard that you're selling Wescom. I was planning to get in touch with you. We're interested in buying it.'

After some discussion, it seemed to me that the guy was actually legitimate. It made sense to at least meet with his principal and talk seriously. Then I thought, a Saudi prince? This is getting a little out of my league. I was comfortable enough talking to Americans, but if I was going to meet with a Saudi prince I needed to have Clint come along with me.

So the Saudis came to Chicago and Clint and I sat down with them. One of them was the cousin of Adnan Khashoggi, a global arms dealer and one of the world's richest men. We talked and came to an understanding, and the numbers we spoke about looked positive, better than Honeywell's offer. Then Clint and I flew to London to finalize the deal with them. Everything was ready to go. The final price was 40 million dollars. The terms were better than the two deals we had in hand. Closing was set for Chicago in thirty days' time.

Thirty days went by and we were set to close when word arrived that no money had come in. The prince had changed his mind. He wasn't going forward with the deal.

Clint was completely pissed off. We had been jerked around. 'Clint,' I said, 'that's why I wanted you to get involved. I don't know how to work with guys like this.'

With the Saudis out of the picture I went back to Ed Spencer at Honeywell. He was eager to go ahead. 'It's 40 million,' he said. 'We have a deal.'

We made no announcements, but a couple of days later the *Wall Street Journal* published a story with the headline: 'Honeywell Offers to Buy Wescom'.

That day I got a surprise call from Don Beall, CEO of Rockwell.

'Sam,' he said, 'what are you trying to do?'

'Don, what I'm trying to do is get the best deal we can.'

'Look, I don't want you to shop around. What do you want?'

I had never seriously thought about what price I actually wanted, and instead had just been looking for the highest bidder.

He said, 'Just tell me right now. What do you want for Wescom?'

I wasn't going to take the time to work out any numbers. I knew what the other deals were. 'Around 50 million,' I said.

'Done!' said Don Beall. 'We'll need to close before Christmas.'

After that it was just a matter of working out the details and, finally, just before Christmas, Don flew in lawyers from all over. Rockwell jets landed at O'Hare from three different places. Paul Miller met with all of them, and after a prolonged back and forth everyone agreed and they closed. When I was called back into the room, Paul said, 'Sam, it's done. This is yours.' He handed me a cheque for 2 million dollars. 'They'll pay the remainder in stages,' said Paul.

I looked at the piece of paper. I had never seen so many zeroes on a cheque before. In addition, Paul had negotiated a three-year contract for me with Rockwell at a salary of a half-million dollars a year. I was going to come on board as vice president for technology and engineering. At that time the US government Certificates of Deposits (CDs) were paying an interest rate of about 12 per cent. I thought, *My God, if I put 2 million in CDs at 12 per cent, I'll never have to worry about money again. Almost a quarter million a year for the rest of my life? I'm done!*

While driving back from Paul Miller's office, I looked in the rear-view mirror. My face stared back, but what I saw there was my entire life. I was a multimillionaire. I was a thirty-seven-year-old kid with a 2-million-dollar cheque in his breast pocket. How in the world did that happen? I thought of my parents, my school, my teachers, the people who had been important to me. What a crazy journey. I had had no particular plans to do any of the things I had done. No vision, no road map. Nothing. Nobody had pointed out a path. I just had some vague idea about making some money before I turned forty. And somehow, miraculously, it had happened. I was an entrepreneur, and I had learnt to lead with a focus on both Gandhian values and American work culture.

But I also realized that I was living multiple lives. As engineer, entrepreneur, inventor and businessman, I was dealing with the competitive American business landscape. And on the other hand I was part of a traditional Indian joint family with three generations living together under one roof. I had to balance out my roles on both sides. By now my parents had come to live with us. Anu's brother Yashesh and their father had also joined us. Because of our joint family, raising our children was a lot easier for me personally. There were several family members looking after Salil and Rajal, so I could focus my attention on work.

I came home from signing the deal.

'Anu,' I said, 'we sold the company. This is the cheque.'

Anu looked at it. It hardly meant anything to her, as money wasn't high on her agenda. We had a simple dinner. Rice with some dal and yogurt. The usual. The next morning I went to the bank and deposited the cheque. And that was it.

6

Dreaming Big

My bank, Northern Trust, had experience in handling large accounts, but I don't think they were used to ordinary people just walking in from the street with a 2-million-dollar cheque. At the teller counter they asked me to wait, very politely. A few moments later a private banker and investment counsellor were asking me to sit down so they could tell me about the various investment instruments that were available for me. The next thing I knew I was being bombarded with information about fixed and variable rates of return, short- and long-term strategies for wealth growth, tax consequences, shelters and endless arcane possibilities, all of which were more than a little overwhelming for me. Before this windfall, Anu and I had never even had a savings account. We had always got by with one checking account, which rarely had more than 500 dollars in it.

America was still very much the land of golden opportunities, a way of getting out of poverty and launching yourself into a better life. And one by one, our family members were coming over to America to build their new lives. Four of my sisters and their husbands; my

younger brother, Pinu; Anu's brother, Yash; his wife; my parents and
Anu's father; then my older brother, Manek, and his family; and even
more came in as people got married and had children—the list went on
and on. At its peak we had more than ten people staying in the house.
We'd save enough money for one ticket, then the next person would be
ready to come. We'd pay one tuition, then the next would be due. Anu
was taking care of everyone's day-to-day needs. Earlier, she had also
taken on a job as a data-punch operator to help finance bringing over
and supporting our family. Our plan was to help them further their
education in the US, and then turn them loose to pursue their dreams.
It was great living together and having our family with us. But one
consequence was that we hadn't had to bother about how to handle the
extra money—there just wasn't any.

We had bought a new house a year before Wescom's sale, in the
suburb of Downers Grove, a genteel white community of large homes
and small nuclear families. If Anu and I had situated ourselves in the
inner city of Chicago, our neighbours might not have given us more
than a second glance. But in Downers Grove we stood out. There were
so many of us, and we looked different from the neighbourhood's other
residents, to say the least. Then there was my friend Bhavesh Das. He
was looking to buy a house and I told him, 'Bhavesh, the house next
to mine is up for sale. Why don't you buy it? I'm travelling a lot. It
would be so helpful to have you close by.' So Bhavesh bought the house
and moved in with his wife and children; of course, there was a lot of
friendly noise and back and forth between the two houses, all of which
had the neighbours on edge.

The new house had a large finished basement, perfect for parties
and also for meetings of what we called, for lack of a better name, the
India Forum.

The India Forum had its origins back in 1966 when some of us
were students at IIT: Bhupen, Madhu, Bharat, Mahen, Dilip, Prakash,
and a few others. Our studies kept us busy, and America itself was a
constant fascination; we were all getting more and more comfortable
here. But at the same time we missed home terribly. We had left
everything behind us, miles away. Underneath, we were lonely; we
longed for India.

Someone came up with the idea of getting together once a week to
chat and have a little party for ourselves, to help assuage our loneliness.

We did that, and we continued the tradition after we all graduated and went out to work. Gradually, these get-togethers became a little more formalized. We met every Sunday from ten to one. From ten to eleven we had a speaker. Afterwards, we had coffee and tea and question-and-answer time. Eventually, our initial group grew to fifteen or twenty regulars. We did this for nineteen years, fifty weeks a year, year after year.

Early on, one of us would be the speaker, telling the rest about whatever they were doing in their professional lives, or maybe about some other interest they had developed or knew about in enough depth. Later, we began inviting speakers for all kinds of issues, from the Arab-Israeli conflict to the Vietnam War to homosexuality to economics, anthropology, philosophy, sociology, US foreign policy, and more.

We were all eager learners, so anything went. Prakash, the psychiatrist, gave four lectures on normality—what makes a normal person, or what makes a person normal? How do you define a normal human being? This was a fascinating question to us. So many of these topics we had never thought about, or even knew existed. One speaker had written a book on caste and politics, another on India's Naxalite Maoists. At one point, Dennis Brutus, the South African anti-apartheid poet, had a visiting professorship at Northwestern University. He fell ill the Sunday he was supposed to come, but his nineteen-year-old daughter came instead and gave a great talk on his behalf—and so we learnt first-hand about apartheid.

We began our India Forum meetings in our one-bedroom apartment in Chicago's Summit neighbourhood, but then the Chicago Latin School gave us a conference room. When Anu and I bought the house in Downers Grove we moved the meetings to our big basement. At some point we began to think of the India Forum as a kind of informal institute of learning. I certainly did. Someone like me, whose whole training and professional world was engineering, could never have learnt anything about psychology, economics, philosophy or any of these other subjects. But the India Forum changed this for me.

As time went by we started publishing a magazine. We wrote the articles ourselves, designed it and had it printed by a neighbourhood press. We cut, stapled and distributed it, not just among ourselves but to Chicago's university campuses: Northwestern, the University of Illinois, the University of Chicago. Eventually, our meetings became so well known that speakers of repute coming to Chicago would ask if they could get some time at the India Forum. We were sought after.

The India Forum stayed together for nineteen years, the first part of which coincided with the Vietnam War and the anti-war movement. Most of us who came to the sessions were Indians. There was one white person who started showing up consistently at meetings, week after week. He sat there and took notes. At first we wondered who he could be, and then someone figured out that he must be with the FBI or CIA. The war was going on, war protestors were becoming more and more militant, violence was in the air. The 1968 Democratic Convention in Chicago had exploded into riots, police beatings and massive arrests. And we were, we realized, an organized group of potential foreign radicals talking about anything and everything—maybe even planning something. So we were given our own FBI monitor. And since he was there for every meeting, and since he seemed like a nice guy, we'd invite him along if we went somewhere afterwards for more talk or a bite to eat. He told us his name was Herbert. We doubted it was, but we didn't mind.

Inevitably, a lot of our talks were about India and its problems: poverty, health, issues facing women. I gave a talk on telecommunications in India, how rudimentary it was and how important it could be. All my friends started asking questions. What made me think telecom was so important? Why not food or clean water instead? Telecom was something for the urban elite. It was exotic, fancy, sexy. Telecom wasn't going to solve any of India's great problems.

'Sure,' somebody said, 'modernizing India's telephones would be a great idea. But you can't worry about urban India. You have to worry about rural India—that's where the poverty is.' Someone else said, 'What's the point of developing telecom if you don't have the human resources for it, the engineers and technicians?' Another said, 'India doesn't produce anything you'd need to build a modern telephone system. Unless you wanted to be obligated to foreigners, you'd have to create a whole industry. How do you think you could ever do that?'

Most of the discussion that followed my talk bordered on the sceptical, but it was intelligent. It created all these ideas running through my head. I knew how telecom developed. Modern systems in the Western world were urban; they featured big exchanges and high telephone densities. In the US every household had a phone or two.

The obvious approach to modernizing India's systems would be to import the Western model. But what would that actually do for India, where there were 600,000 villages—many of which had no phones at all?

There was a need for a different way of doing it there. Indian telecom would have to be rural telecom. To do it effectively you would have to develop a customized, uniform system of exchanges that would make sense for that population, in that climate. That would mean, as someone pointed out, indigenous production. You'd have to build the human resources for this, engineering talent and local manufacturers. The goal shouldn't be density, like in the West, it should be access.

In the West, if you were rich you were supposed to have lots of phones. With almost a billion people in India, one would think you could never get every person a telephone, but maybe we could find a way to give almost everyone access to a telephone. If you defined your goals carefully and figured out a comprehensive plan, you could make a huge difference. It might take twenty years, but it would make an impact.

These kinds of grandiose thoughts were fermenting in the back of my mind, but meanwhile I was working for Rockwell International, one of the world's major manufacturing conglomerates. Rockwell made printing presses and industrial equipment and truck parts, but they were especially well known for their high-tech electronics and aerospace components that played a significant role in America's space programmes.

At Rockwell I was vice president for technology and engineering and head of strategic business development for digital switching in Illinois, Iowa and Texas. Again, I found myself in learning mode. Wescom had taught me a great deal about running a business, but Wescom was a small, entrepreneurial company. Rockwell was a giant, with a culture and processes that had been developed over decades.

After Rockwell acquired Wescom, I had a couple of management meetings with senior Rockwell executives. One meeting brought together twenty top Rockwell managers, including Sy Rubinstein, the head of the aerospace division. Rockwell was the prime contractor for NASA's space shuttle, and Rubinstein had been chief engineer for the programme. Other division heads were there as well, the cream of Rockwell's people.

After the general meeting we broke up into small groups. As soon as we did that somebody said—'Okay, you take notes, you're the chairman, you get the pizza, you make the coffee.' And people just did it. Somebody at random divided up the tasks and everybody did what they were supposed to.

That had happened at all the big meetings. I was so impressed. These men were chief corporate executives, but nobody ever complained saying, 'I made coffee three times,' or, 'I ordered the food last time.' There was no hierarchy. I thought, *Could this ever happen in India?* Maybe it didn't happen at other big American companies either, I didn't know. But in India, with all its rigid deference and hierarchy? Never.

Since part of my responsibilities were in Dallas, I kept an apartment there and travelled back and forth frequently in one of our corporate jets. Don Beall, Rockwell's president, used to hold meetings every month in Dallas with seven or eight of us from operations in the Midwest. We'd make presentations to the team, have lunch together and discuss key issues. This was routine practice at Rockwell.

I learned from that. I also learned from Rockwell's approach to planning. Each of Rockwell's businesses put together a strategic three-year plan. Then they each had an annual operating plan that was revised and re-articulated as the year progressed and conditions changed. These were big businesses, but their planning was agile and responsive. They used management resource planning techniques that integrated the purchasing, production and inventory-control functions. I saw how the chiefs of the various divisions worked: printing technology, space technology, semiconductors. Rockwell was loaded with managerial and technological talent and had developed ways to effectively integrate and utilize their skills—it was a superbly managed giant enterprise, and was a great developmental experience for me. As Rockwell was a prime contractor, I even got to visit Florida to witness several space shuttle launches.

But I knew that after three years, when my contract was up, I would leave. I was still in charge of the Wescom technology. But I was backing away, letting others do a lot more. It was understood that I was going to move on from there in some fashion. If I stayed at Rockwell I would become one of the mainstream corporate executives, with a career path that might lead me towards becoming a major division chief one day. Or I could decide it's time to move on, time to do something else.

Rockwell would have been okay with either. I had a lot of friends there, not just in management but in technology, and they were working on world-leading projects too. But more and more, India was on my mind.

~

Shortly after we sold Wescom in 1980 I had taken a trip to India. I realized that I had gone through substantial change in my life in the last decade. From being a foreign student from India, I had become an American citizen by 1977, with a wealth of experience in technology and management. I had learned new ways of doing things, acquired new tools and behaviours and, in the process, my mindset and manners had changed completely.

I decided to go to Delhi, the capital. I'd never been there, except for two days. During my first year of college, at the age of fifteen, I led a tour of India for about thirty students from our university. In Delhi, we had an opportunity to meet Prime Minister Nehru and see the Red Fort and other Mughal-era monuments. My idea now was to invite my parents to Delhi and take them to see these World Heritage Sites. They had been living with us in Chicago for a while, but had recently gone back to Titilagarh. I didn't know anything about Delhi hotels, but someone had told me that the best hotel was the Taj Mahal, so that's where I got a suite.

As soon as I was settled in, I tried to call Anu to tell her I had arrived safely. But the call wouldn't go through; there seemed to be something wrong with the line. I tried a couple of times. No luck. When I called the desk to complain, they sent somebody up. But the call still wouldn't go through. So I went to sleep.

This reminded me of the fact that I had never made a telephone call before leaving for America in 1964. We had no phone at home. Neither did any of my relatives. If someone had a phone he was generally deemed too rich to be my friend. Our family didn't need a phone. Similarly, we had never owned a television. However, I knew how to design one on paper.

The next morning I looked out of my window and saw a large funeral procession passing on the street below. But it looked a little odd—a funeral, but not an ordinary funeral. I went downstairs to see, and it turned out that this was a funeral for dead telephones. People were carrying a funeral litter, but instead of a body, the litter was piled with dead, old, non-functioning telephones.

That was intriguing. A dead telephone demonstration. Telephones, my speciality, being paraded through the streets. When I asked the doorman what was going on, he said, 'Oh, it's just the phone problem. It takes ten years to get one, and then they never work. People get upset.' The next day in the newspaper I saw a big article on the dead-phone demonstration.

My parents arrived the following day, my mom carrying boxes of food with her. She thought that her boy was staying somewhere by himself and would need to be fed. When they got up to my room, she began to unpack. 'Your sister cooked this for you. All the things you like.'

'Mom,' I said, 'this is the best hotel in Delhi. Let's go downstairs, we'll eat at the restaurant.'

It was quite wonderful taking my parents to see the famous sights, but the whole time I was thinking about those dead phones. I couldn't get it out of my head—the idea that this phone situation needed to be fixed. And with a lot of arrogance and even more ignorance I thought, *Who better to fix it than me?* This is something I need to do. I am going to fix it!

I was, of course, working for Rockwell, but over time this idea became a fixation. When I told Don Beall, he said, 'That's fine. Whatever you want to do, we'll support you. You want to go back and forth to India, don't worry about it. Take time off. I'd like you to stay with us when your contract's over, though. Maybe we can do something with Rockwell in India.'

I was moved by Beall's generosity. Rockwell had treated me well right from the beginning. But his interest was in developing a business in India, which wasn't what I had had in mind. 'Don,' I said, 'I'm grateful. But I think I need to do my own thing over there.'

At home I told Anu about what I had decided. 'We've got more than enough money now,' I said. 'I don't really need to work any more. I'm going to spend the next ten years fixing India's telephones.' I don't think it came as a surprise to her. She had been hearing about India's phones ever since I came back from that first trip to Delhi.

Then I told the India Forum members. They thought that if I was serious about it I ought to first talk with the Centre for the Study of Developing Societies in Delhi, a leading Indian think tank. Some of our friends were key people there—Rajni Kothari, Ashis Nandy, Dhirubhai Sheth, Bashir Ahmad—distinguished sociologists and political scientists, deeply engaged in thinking about ways to modernize Indian society.

On my next trip to India I met up with them. 'I have this idea,' I said. 'I'd like to see if it is possible to fix India's telephones.'

These were people who understood Indian society in depth. And they were interested; they questioned me in detail about what I had in mind. They told me how difficult such a thing would be, the level of bureaucratic resistance I would have to face, the bottlenecks that would hinder any effort at changing the system that was already in place.

I listened carefully. But I was finding it a little hard to concentrate. We were meeting in Rajni Kothari's office, and he was sitting in a chair that had wheels and which gave off a disconcerting squeak every time he moved or made a gesture. Strangely, I was the only one in the room who seemed affected.

Finally I said, 'Wait, I'm having a hard time focusing.'

'What's the problem?' said Kothari.

'It's your chair, the squeaking. Do you mind if I fix it?'

I asked an attendant to get some oil and I promptly greased the chair.

'Now we can talk,' I said. 'I don't understand, didn't it bother you?'

'No,' Kothari said, 'I never noticed.'

'How long has it been like this?'

'I don't know. Probably for years.'

One of the others there, a Harvard-trained social scientist, said, 'For years? Let me tell you a story. In my house, the latch to the bathroom door is broken. When you go in there to use the toilet, you can't lock the door. So what happens is that since you can't lock it, people who go there make a noise, *hmm hmm hmm*, like clearing your throat—so that nobody will come in. When you're in the bathroom you have to keep making the noise. Everybody in the family does it.'

'How long has this been going on?' I asked

'Twenty years, maybe.'

'Wait a minute. For twenty years you've been making that *hmmm hmmm* noise in the bathroom? Why in the world?'

'Because that's the way it is. It's not that bad. We're used to it.'

That struck me at once—the attitude of 'It's okay, it doesn't matter.' The chair squeaks, you don't notice. The latch is broken, it doesn't bother you. You live with it.

To me, this attitude was a big problem. I'd been living in the US for the last twenty years. I had got conditioned. Living in America had changed me completely. If something's broken, you don't just leave it alone. You fix it. Even if it's not so important, you still fix it. And here I was in a country where people's minds just didn't work that way. In India, life is more about *'Sab chalta hai'*, or 'anything goes', in a sense—letting things be as they are.

I had now started going to India at intervals of every few weeks, exploring the possibilities for my telecom idea and reading everything I could on the Indian telephone system. And every time I was there, I felt this compulsion to fix things. If I was in a cab, I'd find myself trying to fix the doorknob that was falling apart. Every time I landed in Delhi I would realize I had entered a different world. Everywhere I looked I'd think, *This has to be changed. That has to be changed. This needs to be cleaned. That thing is too crooked. This other thing is put together all wrong.* It went on and on in my mind. I was supposed to worry only about telecom, but I was seeing this vast array of non-functioning or poorly functioning things that I just wanted to repair. It was making me obsessive. For instance, I'd be talking to someone—an intelligent, interesting person—but would notice that his socks were down around his ankles and that his shirt needed cleaning; in other words, he needed to be fixed.

Later on, when I was starting to become a public figure in India, a critic wrote something along the lines of: 'Who does this Sam Pitroda person think he is? He's constantly finding things in India that he says are wrong. He thinks he needs to fix everything.' The critic wasn't saying this as a compliment, but I can't say it was that far from the truth.

Still, I loved spending time in India, travelling, meeting people, soaking up the country. I'd think endlessly about the contrasts. America—with its individualism, its opportunities, its direct talk, the way people didn't dance around problems but confronted them, and the American sense of equality that meant so much to me. But at the same time I understood more about India. I began to feel the essence of India, what India stood for. Diversity. Complexity. Chaos. Confusion. Contradiction. Love. Affection. Tolerance. Joy with family and friends. All of those things I had absorbed back there in my youth, but had never understood properly. It all started to make sense to me. Rediscovering India after living abroad is a time-honoured tradition. Gandhi and Nehru both did so, along with many others. And I followed in their footsteps.

But while I loved re-finding the India I had left behind in 1964, I wasn't getting very far with my telephone endeavour. My idea had been to first get an in-depth understanding of the system and its problems and, second, to figure out how I might be able to bring about a fundamental transformation. After a year's worth of meetings with engineers, industrialists, politicians, academics, and others, I had accomplished my first goal. I had a clear grasp of how the telephone system worked and the different levels of its problems. I had also developed a plan for transforming it. I thought I knew what had to be done and how to do it. But I had made almost no progress in finding a way forward. The Indian political and technological landscape was a Gordian knot I couldn't untie and had no way to cut through. I was a single individual, an outsider with no particular weight behind me.

I had, in fact, made some interesting contacts. Early on I had even spoken with a committee, set up by then Prime Minister Indira Gandhi to explore the restructuring of telecommunications, which was headed by H.C. Sarin, an officer in the administrative service. A friend, Damodar Bhartia, had sent a newspaper clipping to me in Chicago about the committee, so I wrote to Mr Sarin requesting a chat with him. I didn't realize, though, that I had signed the letter as 'Sam'—not 'Satyanarayan'—Pitroda. Sarin, as I learned later, thought I was Italian. He thought there was some Italian executive based in the US who was trying to sell him something.

He wrote back, saying: 'Sorry, we aren't entertaining foreign companies.' When I sent a second letter explaining that I was Satyanarayan Pitroda from Orissa and Gujarat, he said, 'Come.'

My meeting with Sarin's committee went well. I was bubbling with enthusiasm, I spoke forcefully. Sarin and the others were receptive. Sarin said, 'You have some good ideas. I'll support you.

I like what you're saying.' I felt as though I had won an important victory. But there had been no follow-up from the Sarin committee.

For over a year now I had been travelling to India and back every two weeks or so. Since there were no direct flights from Chicago, I'd take the Air India out of New York. Always Air India. On the flight I could listen to music, look at people, hear the languages of India. Air India allowed me to start easing into an Indian frame of mind. But as time went by I'd find myself standing in the boarding line at JFK wondering if it was worth it. I was leaving Anu behind with our two little children, Salil, six, and Rajal, who was three. And where was this getting me? Anu tried not to be reproachful, but she'd tell me, 'You know, the last time you came back the children hardly recognized you.' I often thought to myself while standing in line there: *Don't you think it's time to shut this down and start living like a normal person?*

On the other hand, how could I shut it down? Everywhere I went people would tell me, 'Yes, telephones. That's the most important thing. The telephones just don't work. They're miserable. It drives you crazy. You can't even get one installed.' One friend, who had a PhD from Oxford, told me, 'When I was younger, my parents decided I should get married. So they showed me all these girls. But after a while they all began to look the same. So I decided that I was going to marry a girl with a telephone, because then I won't have to wait ten years.'

Then at one of my meetings in India someone said, 'The only possible way for you to get your plan going would be to meet with Mrs Gandhi.'

Okay, I thought. *Right. But how am I supposed to meet Mrs Gandhi, the prime minister of the country?*

Back in Chicago I discussed this with Anu's father. He was a high-ranking official, then a judge. Maybe he would have an idea.

'Well,' he said, 'I know a member of Parliament, a very decent guy. Why don't you meet him next time you go?' And he gave me this person's number.

Anu's father's parliamentary friend turned out to be the hereditary Maharaja of Baria, the tiny remnant of a princely state in Gujarat. I called him—his phone worked. I introduced myself. 'Hari Bhai Chhaya is my father-in-law, sir. He told me I should come see you.'

'Come, come, come,' said the Maharaja. 'Come right away. We'll have gin and tonic.'

So I went to Baria and presented myself at the Maharaja's home in Delhi. In the reception hall he was sitting on a big chair, surrounded by twenty or thirty dogs. He was the Maharaja, and his hobby was dogs. He had lots of them.

We had hardly said hello when he called out, 'Gin and tonic!'

A moment later two servants appeared with gin and tonics.

The Maharaja beamed at me. 'You'll come every day. Yes? We'll have gin and tonic. But tell me, why did my friend Hari Bhai Chhaya send you here? What do you want to do?'

I explained what my plans were and how I had been advised to meet Mrs Gandhi to further said plans.

'That's not a problem,' he said. 'I'll arrange it.'

I sat with him for most of the afternoon, then met with him several more times. As visitors came to see him, he introduced me: 'This is Hari Bhai Chhaya's son-in-law. He wants to fix India's telephones.'

'Aaaah,' they said, 'that's not possible. That is so extremely difficult.'

Everyone I saw had a negative attitude. Everyone talked about why it couldn't be done. Bureaucracy. Corruption. Incomprehensible delays. It was as if they took great pride in talking about why things couldn't get done in India. Back in America, I don't think I had ever, even once, in my entire working life heard, *It can't be done.* Sometimes people would say, *I don't know how to do it*, but never *It can't be done.* Here, it was exactly the opposite.

But the more I heard this negativity, the more I was convinced that it had to be done. *If all these people say it can't be done,* I thought, *that means it* has *to be.* And if the Maharaja was unable to introduce me to Mrs Gandhi, then maybe I could find a way to do it myself.

The Maharaja of Baria was the very soul of generosity. His warm smile said everything. This young man in front of him has come all the way from America? He wants to do something good for India? We should help him do it. And while we're at it, we should have a gin and tonic.

The Maharaja had connections with the right people. Many dignitaries and members of Parliament would visit him regularly. He let them know of my plans and, within days, I received a call from the prime minister's office. Mrs Gandhi had agreed to see me. A ten-minute time slot had been reserved for my appointment.

At first I was overjoyed. I had an appointment with Mrs Gandhi! That was a triumph in itself. How many private citizens with an idea in their head could ever hope to see the prime minister in the flesh? But then I realized that ten minutes was just not going to be enough. Ten minutes wouldn't give me time for anything other than my introductions. I needed to lay out my plan in a comprehensive way that would convince her of its urgency and feasibility. I needed at least an hour.

So I told her office, 'Look, I don't want to meet for ten minutes. If Mrs Gandhi is really interested, I need to see her for an hour.'

That line threw them off. I could hear the astonishment in their voices. Who is this crazy person? The PM gives him ten minutes and he says no? *You* don't say no to the PM for a meeting, the PM says no to *you*!

I said, 'Whenever she's ready to meet for an hour, I'll come.'

When I visited the Maharaja of Baria next I told him what had happened. He thought for a moment and said, 'You could try to get to her through her son, Rajiv. I know someone close to him. Try there.'

I contacted this person close to Mrs Gandhi's son and was asked to come to his residence. But when I did, Rajiv wasn't available. 'Sahib's in a meeting,' I was told. 'He can't see you now.' I came again the next day. 'No, Sahib's taking a shower. This is not a good time.' It was a little humiliating, but I didn't care. Sahib could be taking a shower every day, but I wanted him to know that I was not going to go away. If Rajiv Gandhi was the path to his mother, and this person was the path to Rajiv Gandhi, then I was just going to keep at it until he agreed to see me.

While this was going on, by some serendipitous chance the *Chicago Tribune* came out with a big story about me and some of the things I had done as a telecom innovator and businessman. And, somehow, somebody in Mrs Gandhi's office had got hold of the story. I was, it seemed, a known person in the United States, at least in the telecom industry. I didn't know they had read the article, but the consequence was that I got a call one day from the prime minister's office. 'Mrs Gandhi will give you an hour.' She wouldn't be able to see me immediately, but she would give me an hour of her time.

We set up the meeting for a date several weeks later. Back in Chicago I worked on my presentation and gathered my physical slides—there was no PowerPoint then. I procured an extra bulb in case the projector bulb burned out. After almost two years of back and forth, this was my one opportunity. I couldn't risk anything going wrong.

When I went through customs at the Delhi airport, the customs officer scrutinized the projector. 'This is a camera,' he said.

'No,' I said. 'It's a projector.'

'It says Kodak. It's a camera.'

'It's not. Really. It's a projector.'

The inspector turned to another inspector. 'This guy says it's a projector. What's a projector?'

'I'm not sure. Look in your book.'

He looked in his book. 'It's a camera,' he said. 'You have to pay duty.'

'Look,' I said, 'this isn't for me. It's for Mrs Gandhi. I'm making a presentation to her the day after tomorrow.'

'Oh,' he said. 'I'm so sorry. Please proceed.'

My meeting with Mrs Gandhi was scheduled for 6 p.m. at her home office. I arrived an hour early to make sure everything was in order. I had to find the best spot to set up the projector. I checked the plugs in the walls to make sure they were working. In India, the electricity had a habit of going out. I told the staff that once the meeting began I didn't want anyone coming in with tea or coffee or food. In my mind I could visualize attendants coming into the room to serve refreshments and someone spilling something or stepping on a cord. Things like that happened. I had seen it before.

By six I had everything set up and ready to go. I had checked the slides to make sure they were in the right sequence. I had checked the projector to make sure it was working. I was checking it again when a member of the staff came in and said that Mrs Gandhi would be half an hour late. Her previous meeting had spilled over into my time.

In the meantime all the other people were arriving. Mrs Gandhi had invited her entire circle of advisers. The whole Cabinet. The finance minister, the minister of technology, all the other ministers, the who's who of Indian politics, and also her son, Rajiv, whom I had been trying to get a meeting with.

Rajiv Gandhi and I were about the same age. I introduced myself to him and got the immediate impression that this was someone I could talk to. There was something welcoming in his manner. Something clicked.

With half an hour to go before his mother arrived, Rajiv and I fell into a discussion. I explained to him that I had this idea—to bring telecom development to India in an Indian way. I told him I was convinced that telecom would change the face of India. A good telecom system would connect people in a way they had never been connected before. It would help tie the separate regions and states together. It would spur economic development, especially in the rural sector. It would create educational opportunities. It would help strengthen Indian democracy.

'But we have to do it differently than they do elsewhere—in developed countries. We have to start with rural exchanges. Smaller exchanges that we design ourselves, for our own conditions. We have to look at it in terms of access instead of density. We have to train our own people so they'll become experts in software. We need to establish a manufacturing base for it. If we do this, it won't just generate indigenous development, it will create exports.'

I squeezed in all the material I could, but he picked up on it instantly. Rajiv Gandhi was a quick study. He just got it.

When Indira Gandhi came in, Rajiv sat next to her. I could half hear him saying, 'Mom, listen to this. This guy has ideas.'

I went through the presentation, one slide after another. I had organized it as clearly and comprehensively as I could. The developed world had 800 million people and 400 million telephones, one for every two people. India had almost 800 million people and 2.5 million telephones, one for every 280 people, many of which did not work. We were even further behind other developing nations like Mexico and Brazil. Our system operated on a patchwork of outmoded exchanges provided by different companies originating from different foreign countries. Our technical resources to maintain this crazy quilt of a system were vastly inadequate. We had virtually no ability to expand service in a way that would meet continually growing demand.

I laid out the particulars of what we needed to do to transform this system—build it out with the best modern digital technology and make it accessible not just in the cities but also in the villages, where 70-plus per cent of India's population lived. My strategy for India's telecom development was based on indigenous development, accessibility, local production, ancillary industries, the digitization of networks, rural telecom and young local talent. I explained that the existing telecommunications agencies could not be expected to accomplish this. We needed instead to create a core research and development group that would design uniform equipment meeting uniform standards, especially exchanges, focusing on the countryside first and then the cities. This core group would require government support, but it needed to be independent of the existing bureaucracy. Building indigenous equipment would require us to establish local manufacturing. In the process we would modernize our phone systems, provide access for the bulk of our population, and develop our own technology, entrepreneurs, human resources and industrial base.

To make this happen I essentially wanted to create a bypass— something to circumvent the existing system. I was concerned that the existing organizations and vested interests would kill any new initiative. By now I had learned that the Indian systems worked on perks, privilege, patronage and personalities—not on performance and productivity.

I don't think Mrs Gandhi or the others in the room understood everything I was saying in the presentation, especially regarding the specifics of the technology. But what Mrs Gandhi did understand very well was the core of my vision. When I finished, she looked at me and said, 'Good.' And then she smiled.

For me, *connecting* India was a big dream. I strongly believed that a diverse and complex nation like ours could expedite the process of modernization by linking people and places. Connecting India would substantially enhance access, openness, networking, collaboration, cooperation, conflict resolution, decentralization and democratization—and as a result would enable social, political and economic transformation. I was convinced that the movement would begin new conversations and help change the mindset, leading to improved education, skills, trade, commerce, governance, growth and overall prosperity. This could indeed be a once-in-a-lifetime opportunity for me to help modernize India. This was important to me because of the striking poverty within India, and the disparity between India and the US. This had the potential to become India's 'New Deal'.

Part II

Dreams, Democracy, Development

7

Indigenous Development: C-DOT

After Mrs Gandhi left the room it was as though the floodgates had opened. All the ministers wanted to talk to me. They had heard her 'Good' and caught her smile. She had given me an hour—that in itself was a message. She had basically said: *This idea has merit. Go ahead with it.* This led to a whole new journey full of unknown territories in an equally unknown country I had left about twenty years ago. It was the beginning of a battle with Indian traditionalism, bureaucracy, old mindsets, negativity, and many other barriers. I had no idea that this would ultimately lead to a bigger battle to help modernize India.

I had, during my presentation, described the foreign exchange ramifications of indigenous production versus imports—which made the finance minister want to have a talk with me. I had also laid out the consequences for science and technology—which made the science and technology ministers ask to see me. Everyone was lining up to make appointments.

As I talked with the group, I realized that Rajiv Gandhi was going to be my ally in whatever was going to follow. However brief our discussion had been, I felt I had a friend in him. He understood the message of modernization through telecom and technology. He had a similar vision, and his political support was crucial for the implementation of the plans. From my understanding of India's prior successful strides in development in atomic energy, space, agriculture and milk production, I had realized that to succeed it is important to have domain expertise and political will together with the right chemistry between national leadership and professional experts.

My meetings with the ministers started the next day. The finance minister said, 'Tell me how much money you'll need. What level of foreign exchange will we save?'

The fact was that I did not know. I did not have answers to everything. I had presented the bones of a plan at Mrs Gandhi's house, but I had not done the careful cost analyses yet, that would come later. At this stage I had ideas, not numbers.

But I had made up my mind that whatever questions the ministers asked, I needed to answer them. The exact answers, of course, could wait until I had done the research. But if I simply said, *I don't know. I'll have to review it. I'll get back to you*, that would have been the end of the discussion. Even with Mrs Gandhi's nod of approval, I was still an outsider with no particular standing coming into a labyrinth of powerful conflicting interests. I needed to embody confidence. I needed them to be persuaded that I knew what I was doing and that I'd be able to deliver. I told the finance minister with great certainty and confidence that the project would cost 36 million dollars.

After a spate of discussions with the then electronics minister, Dr Sanjeeva Rao, and several parliamentary and technological committees, the administration decided that the time had come to assure itself of my antecedents and credentials. A four-man team was sent to Chicago to check me up, a sign of real seriousness, I thought, especially when I saw who all would be doing the checking—G.B. Meemamsi, head of the Telecommunications Research Institute; Professor M.V. Pitke from the Tata Institute of Fundamental Research; Dr Gupta, secretary of the Department of Electronics; and Mukesh Mathur, joint secretary in the telecommunications ministry. These were among the leading people in Indian telecom. Meemamsi and Pitke had themselves done significant work in electronic switching. The government couldn't have sent a more distinguished group. If these four decided to get behind me, my credibility would be beyond question. I'd have the standing I'd need in order to move through the maze of approvals that lay ahead.

The team was in Chicago for eleven days. I took them to GTE, Rockwell and Bell Labs. They spent time with engineers and scientists who knew me and my work. They saw my facilities at Wescom and the switches I had designed. They examined my patents. They met Anu and the children. I'm not sure how much doubt they may or may not have had before they arrived, but by the time they were done talking and looking and questioning, I was sure they finally thought of me as a credible individual.

At my house we discussed the details of what I wanted to do. What exactly was the full plan? How would it work? What were the stages? How did I see it all unfolding? Together, we began to prepare a note for the Cabinet's approval.

This kind of note typically takes over a year to prepare. Multiple ministries get involved, and multiple consultations are essential to develop a sense of consensus with the various ministries. I needed to gather all the relevant data: How many people in how many fields? How much funding? What were the management procedures? What were our specific objectives and timelines? Once I had fully fleshed out all the details, the plan had to be presented to each of the ministries that had jurisdiction over any of its parts. Each ministry needed to comment, then the ministries had to consolidate their comments— which seemed to me an interminable amount of inter-ministerial wrangling. Only when the consolidated report became ready did the project go to the Cabinet for approval.

The core of my plan dealt with establishing an independent organization outside the government, which would be funded and owned by the government but would enjoy autonomy, flexibility and freedom of action. I knew that without autonomy this would never work. Being subject to the byzantine procedures of the electronics or telecommunications ministries would strangle the project in the cradle. To make it viable we had to find a way around the bureaucracy.

As the note concretized and moved forward, I met Rajiv Gandhi a number of times. He had, by now, begun to enter the political world, though he wasn't yet formally a part of the government.

'What name do you want to give to this thing?' he asked me at one point.

'It can't be a "department",' I said. 'That would imply we're part of the system. It has to be a "centre", so it's deemed independent. It can't be telecommunications. If we say it's telecom then everybody will think we're invading their turf and undermining their authority. So not telecommunication. Maybe "telematics"? Telematics is generic. Nobody has a telematics department. How about the "Centre for the Development of Telematics"? C-DOT.'

C-DOT sounded about right. It was a centre. Autonomous, but ultimately under government authority—that meant a governing body of Cabinet secretaries and a three-person operational board. Dr Meemamsi, Dr Pitke and Mukesh Mathur agreed to serve. Later, Mr Mathur was replaced by Mr Mahajan.

C-DOT would develop a product or products which would be manufactured in India by public and private sector companies under licence, and be used and supported by the telecommunications department.

The biggest problem, I felt, would be the user. The telecommunications department would have to agree to use it. It was a grave possibility that C-DOT would come up with the best, most relevant and effective telecom equipment, only to find in the end that it would simply not be used.

This wasn't an idle fear. India's non-functional telecommunications systems had generated avid interest from international equipment-makers such as Siemens, Ericsson and Alcatel, who saw the country as a vast market ripe for exploitation. In fact, a government committee had been established to evaluate proposals from these multinationals, and while our C-DOT plan was still taking shape, a major deal had been worked out with France's Alcatel. Both Indian and French political and telecom players, including the French government, were heavily invested in this agreement, so the general opposition regarding creating an indigenous industry was intense. Alcatel and its advocates argued that the French switching equipment was ready to go, having been developed at huge expense. Alcatel was poised to export ready-made switches and even to set up a plant in India to make big digital exchanges. Given India's needs and lack of resources, the argument for importing equipment generated considerable political support.

But my approach had its own advantages. C-DOT was going to produce small switches first, fitted to rural needs, transitioning later to the larger switches required by urban centres. I was focused on opening up telephone access to India's villages, where over 70 per cent of the population lived. We were going to design these small switches—128 and 256 lines—to withstand India's specific climatic conditions: the heat, humidity, salt and dust. I had been conceiving the switches as virtually maintenance-free—an essential characteristic, considering that the scarcity of trained technicians meant that broken equipment in India usually stayed broken. This is why India needed indigenous development. Once these switches went into the field I didn't want anybody to have to touch them to maintain them. Then, of course, C-DOT was going to generate a pool of highly trained, native software and hardware engineers as well as a new manufacturing base for the switches themselves and the necessary ancillary products. Instead of sending Indian money overseas for imports, C-DOT would build up our own technological and industrial capacity to export as well.

I worked hard to publicize the advantages of indigenous production. India was a giant country full of talented people and manufacturing potential. There was no reason we should be at the mercy of foreign technology and foreign industry if we could in fact create and produce high-tech products ourselves. Making things at home instead of importing them—the concept of swadeshi—was the backbone of the Indian independence movement, it is a philosophy deeply ingrained in our history, and it was a philosophy I was determined to bring to telecommunications and technology.

～

On 26 April 1984, the Cabinet approved the creation of C-DOT and set aside a whopping 36 million dollars to be used over a three-year period. I had made the presentation to Mrs Gandhi in 1981. For three years I had been hammering away tirelessly at my own expense, with passion, perseverance and patience.

For me, this was the beginning of a whole new journey. I'd be in a new environment, with new people, new tools, a new culture—facing an array of unknowns. If this wasn't a challenge worth taking on, what would be? It was all quite romantic, actually—at least to me. I had a chance to make a huge impact on a large number of people. I was going to connect the unconnected. I was going to help make India the country of a connected billion.

It probably would have been a good moment to sit back and celebrate. But all I really felt was a surge of energy. I was ready for this. I had laid out all these plans. Now, I had to bring them to life. And we only had three years. I needed to get moving.

Ten years ago I had built Wescom Switching from the ground up. I knew what was necessary to design and manufacture switches. But I was on a different playing field here, one that was littered with explosive mines. At Wescom, all I had to worry about was creating and marketing a product. The challenge there had been the engineering. C-DOT, on the other hand, was a national enterprise, so much bigger in purpose. And because it was a national enterprise it would be living in the uncertain world of politics and public opinion.

I didn't know this territory, but I did know it was full of danger. I needed to be extremely careful, especially about how I handled myself. C-DOT was an Indian enterprise, not a Sam Pitroda enterprise, and as Indian as I might have been, I was still an outsider here. I didn't advertise it, but I wasn't even an Indian citizen—I had become an American citizen long ago. I could so easily be pegged as a self-aggrandizing interloper, an outsider with his own hidden agenda. The more the spotlight was on me, the bigger the target I would become and, correspondingly, the more fragile C-DOT's existence would be.

The Cabinet's approval was news—the government was undertaking to transform the telephone system after so many years of misery and dysfunction! A press conference was called. 'I don't want to be there,' I told the electronics minister. 'This has to be an Indian initiative; I'm only the catalyst. Let the department take the lead here.' When the press conference happened, I was back home in Chicago.

The newspapers were not kind. They were sceptical about whether this could work. Why did the government approve such a scheme, brought to them by a person who's been away from the country for twenty years? The *Economic Times* was appalled at the administration's decision to create its own telephone exchange dreamed up in a foreign land.

India Today published an article by T.N. Ninan that said: 'On the strength of one non-resident Indian's promise of delivering the goods, the Government is willing to invest 36 crore in one ambitious do-or-die research venture.'

That was the general reaction—that the administration was making an ill-advised bet on the word of a non-resident Indian, to the tune of 36 million dollars. I had convinced the government to put this money up for a difficult project in a vital area, a project that should have been addressed in a far more serious and accountable fashion. The whole tone was to delegitimize the C-DOT initiative; they wanted to dismiss this one-person affair, conjured up by an outsider.

Soon after the press conference I flew to Delhi. I thanked the people who had been instrumental in getting C-DOT approved and launched. Now I had to operationalize it.

Just as I began taking the first steps I got a call from the electronics minister Dr Sanjeeva Rao. When we sat down together, he said, 'Now that this is approved, we need to understand what you want out of it.'

'Sir, I don't want anything.'

'Please, I need you to be candid,' he said. 'What do you want?'

Everyone—both those in favour of and opposed to C-DOT—assumed that, at bottom, I was going to ask for something substantial. What did I really have in mind? I was, after all, an American-style businessman. I had built and sold a company for millions and drawn large paychecks. I could not be doing this without my own interests in mind.

'Are you thinking of selling your proprietary technology to C-DOT?'

'No. Not at all.'

'Are you planning to license the technology that comes out of C-DOT?'

'No, I'm not licensing anything. I'm not taking anything. I'm going to have teams of young engineers in here. I'll help them develop it; I'll guide them. But they'll do it.'

'Look,' said Dr Rao, 'Rajiv Gandhi has asked me to check on this. He's personally asked about what you might want.'

'All I want is the opportunity to serve and do it right. That's it. Nothing else.'

'All right, I understand that. But what about your salary and benefits?'

I had read about US President Franklin Roosevelt's dollar-a-year men—industrialists who came to Washington to join the Roosevelt administration by offering their experience for a greater cause. I had also seen Gandhiji and others giving everything they had and sacrificing their life for India.

'I'll charge one rupee a year.'

I found it difficult to explain this to him properly. The only thing I really wanted was to put my energies to work for this great Indian cause. I had been working for money for the past twenty years. That was fine. I was glad I had done it; it had turned out well. But I felt the need for something beyond that, some deeper kind of fulfilment. And what could be more fulfilling or better suited for me than this? Gandhi called this 'public work' instead of the pursuit of money. There were many like Gokhale, Annie Besant, and others, who did what they were doing for the public, foregoing riches to make India better.

I also felt it was essential to demonstrate that I was not in this for my own benefit. If I was seen in any way as a greedy manipulator I'd never be able to generate the confidence and loyalty I was going to need to see this through. I had to be completely above suspicion. I was clear from the beginning that either I could build a big business of my own and make lots of money in telecom in India, or help build a nation and not make a dime. I couldn't do both, though. I had to take my pick.

Dr Rao didn't press further. He understood. 'Okay,' he said, 'I'll convey this. What about your title, then? Director? Chairman?'

'No. I do not need any title.'

'Look, you should be the head of C-DOT. That's the only thing that makes sense.'

'No, I don't want that. I can be an adviser. I don't need a fancy designation to get the work done.'

'Who do you think should be the head, then?'

'Dr Meemamsi. He's the most senior person. He's a good man and a good scientist.'

'You don't want to be on the board?'

'No. But I'll be available to all the board members. I assure you I'll get it done.'

'Okay. What's next on your agenda?'

'We need funding, offices and people.'

'You'll have to talk to Rajiv Gandhi about that,' he said.

Rajiv Gandhi was in charge of the Asian Games that had taken place in Delhi in 1982. He had built the infrastructure and had overseen the management. 'Why don't you take the space at Asiad Village, where we have office space and hundreds of apartments?' he said.

I thought, *What a great idea*, and went to see it. It was a wonderful space with only one drawback—it wasn't air-conditioned. We were going to have young software engineers working at all hours, with computers all over the place. Air conditioning was a necessity.

When I looked into it, I found that air-conditioning equipment of the type we needed had to be imported. Retrofitting the buildings for it would take nine months. I only had three years. In thirty-six months I would have to deliver. I wasn't going to take nine months to set up an office. I needed an office now.

I started looking at hotels. During the Asian Games a lot of hotels had been built that were now standing empty. I found one called the Akbar Hotel in Chanakyapuri, owned by the government and essentially vacant—with air conditioning.

When I told Rajiv about it, he said, 'Sounds like a good idea.'

So we took over floors eight and nine of the hotel. But furnishing hotel rooms for offices was also going to take some time. We had to design furniture for the space: cubicles, partitions, work areas. I couldn't just take desks and stick them in the hotel. The place had to be wired differently. We had to install good lighting too.

I planned it all out, the layout, the furniture. I hired contractors and furniture makers. I heard, 'This will take four to five months to get done.'

Fine, I thought. *I'm going to hire the engineers. They'll all be young, most of them more or less just out of college. They're used to dorm rooms. They can work on the beds until we get the furniture put in.*

The next question concerned hiring. What was the best way to do this? Dr Meemamsi had about ten key engineers who had been working with him for many years at the Telecom Research Institute. Dr Pitke had a similar group at Tata. Dr Pitke's team were hardware guys. Dr Meemamsi's group did systems and software. Dr Pitke's group was based in Bangalore, while Dr Meemamsi's was in Delhi. It was an easy decision to make. I'd start our hardware operations in Bangalore, and our systems and software in Delhi.

I was in a hurry; I made most decisions on the fly based on my experiences and gut feeling. The thirty-six-month time frame was already crowding in on me, and I was just off the starting line. I flew to

Bangalore and found office space in a new four-storey building in the middle of town. We signed a lease.

Now we had to hire people, about 200 engineers. We put out a newspaper ad: *Graduate engineers wanted. Software. Hardware. Systems analysts.* We received 1400 applicants. I had Meemamsi's and Pitke's key people screen them, then I saw the survivors myself. I didn't want to look at their credentials, the courses they had taken, their GPAs, their references. They were all recent graduates from good schools. The screeners had already checked those things. I wanted to see if they seemed comfortable with themselves, if they could communicate well, if they were enthusiastic and whether they would get behind the vision of what we were building.

With the initial hiring complete, everyone moved in and began working—the Bangalore hardware group in their new space, the Delhi software group at the Akbar Hotel. I went back and forth, but my own office was in Delhi at the hotel, in one of the bedrooms.

The Akbar was a scene. I could just imagine what my colleagues back at Rockwell would have made of it. Our software engineers, a hundred or so of them, set up shop in the bedrooms, where they had a chair, a bed, a night table and a little desk—not exactly an optimal environment for programming. But the kids loved it. (They all seemed like kids to me; I was forty-two at the time and most of them were little more than half my age.) They especially loved the place because it was air-conditioned. With Delhi's abominable heat, they could just come inside and it would be blessedly cool. They thought they were in heaven.

To bring about generational change to the telecom industry in India, in a 'greenfield' project, it was essential to think of not just technology and management but also about privatization, deregulation, ancillary industry, local manufacturing, human capacity, affordability, scalability, sustainability, and a lot more. In 1984, the Licence Raj was flourishing and there was very little entrepreneurial effort to privatize local industries. The telecom industry was a monopoly owned by the government.

The most critical challenge for us in the beginning was to create a new work environment—with a new work culture, habits, standards and ethics—to empower our people with the passion to get things done in the shortest possible time-frame, while still focusing on quality and performance. For this to happen, it was essential to shield young talented engineers from the day-to-day hassles related to antiquated procedures, bureaucratic bottlenecks, financial controls and hierarchical feudal management

The first step was training. I needed to explain the project, the technology and the overall architecture I had conceived for our switches. What exactly where we going to build, how would we build it, and what would the software look like—the hardware, the packaging, the documentation?

To do this, I assembled everyone together in Delhi. Each day I gave hours and hours of presentations on how we would construct the switch, the new things we would incorporate, the microprocessor we would use. (By now Motorola had produced the groundbreaking 68000 16-bit chip.) Unix was becoming a reality by then as well. We were going to use the Unix operating system and the C programming language— such a far cry from the start-up of Wescom, only ten years earlier, when there was only Unix and machine language for microprocessors. As an additional teaching tool, I distributed a sixty-two-page collection of articles I had written for various professional journals on digital-switching technology.

Training our engineers was anything but a simple process. They were smart—you could just see the intelligence sparkling in their eyes. They had all been to top schools. Their enthusiasm was off the charts. But they were so young. Most of them had thought extremely little, if at all, about telephone switching—more or less like me when I started with GTE. On the other hand, of course, the fact was that they weren't conditioned by the take-no-chances file-shuffling attitude ingrained in so many Indian enterprises. Their minds were clear of that. They were ready to think differently, and they were eager to learn. Which was why I was only hiring young people in the first place.

But the young team required a lot of orientation, support and love. They were going to find themselves under the tremendous pressure of keeping to schedules, meeting deadlines, working full-out week after week and month after month. Indians going to work for the government or most Indian companies would never experience such things; they'd usually be in sluggish workplaces where there were minimal expectations, and an extremely small—if any—sense of urgency, but permanent job security. Our young team had to be prepared for the stress of a work culture they'd never heard of before. They were looking for exciting work, new learning opportunities, but not job security.

They also needed a lot of technical training. 'I'm sending you to Chicago,' I told them. 'We're going to send you in teams. I have a friend from Bell Labs who is going to teach you Unix and C++. You'll get to see how they do things at Intel and Motorola.' Sending my young people to the US would open their minds and would give them the basic instruction they needed and, equally important, I'd make sure they got some exposure to how American engineering companies worked, so they would be able to understand American work habits and ways of thinking.

When they arrived in Chicago, Anu and her brother, Yash, took care of them. They picked them up at the airport, carrying coats along so they wouldn't freeze. They told them what to eat. And often, Anu fed them herself. It was a family effort. The entire initiative depended on getting our engineers up to the mark quickly. And to give them credit, at their end, our engineers were more than willing—willing to completely give up their professional lives for this. They were every bit as fired up as I was.

I learned one thing immediately: To motivate our young people we needed to make public commitments, and for this we needed the support of the media. So I went to the press and said: 'C-DOT is going to build a modern digital telephone switch in thirty-six months for 36 million dollars. We have rented offices. We have hired 200 engineers. This is our commitment to the Indian people.'

That was a story: Thirty-six months, 36 million dollars, a veritable revolution in the telephone world. It caught people's attention. Now everybody in the media was interested in hearing what this thing was. How many people had ever heard of a telephone switch? What was it, and why was it so important? What exactly was it going to do to the existing dysfunctional telephone system?

So the media showed some excitement. The coverage turned positive, very different from the scepticism and sarcasm that had greeted C-DOT's launch. Not that the critics disappeared entirely. 'What is this?' I'd read occasionally. 'They are luxuriating in air-conditioned offices? How much is that costing the taxpayers? These people have said things publicly that they know they will never be able to deliver on.'

We couldn't avoid whatever criticism or disbelief that persisted around us. I learned to disregard the critics myself, but they became motivators for our young engineers. 'Sam made a commitment? They think we can't do it? Now watch us *do* it!'

In my own work life I had been part of well-run companies where good engineers, scientists and the staff worked hard in essentially happy environments. But I had never seen anything approaching C-DOT. The kids at the Akbar had total freedom. They were basically fresh college kids, barely a year or two out of university, still possessing that youthful spirit. They came and went when they wanted. If they worked past 5 p.m., room service sent up dinner—at C-DOT's expense. The result was that they more or less lived there. They had beds. They'd fall asleep in their rooms when they were exhausted and get up to work, without brushing their teeth.

If I was working late, I stayed at the hotel myself; I kept my clothes and toiletries there. One night at around ten I went to the lobby for something and there was an older couple waiting by the elevator.

'Excuse me,' I said, 'can I help you?'

'Yes, maybe,' the husband answered. 'Our son works here, and he keeps saying that he works until ten or eleven. He tells us he works for the government. But that can't be. Nobody in the government works past five. We need to check on him.' So I took them upstairs. There were four or five youngsters working in one room, spread out on the bed and on the floor cushioned by pillows. They were eating something and programming at the same time. The parents were puzzled. 'It's this late and they're working?'

Similar efforts and excitement abounded in Bangalore also. Since they were building hardware, their day-to-day progress was visible on the floor with the equipment and wires running all over.

Trying to understand these kids, I found myself thinking about the psychology lectures and discussions we had had at the India Forum. What made these young people tick? What could I do that would make them better-adjusted, more effective workers? I realized that a lot of parents might have the same concerns. So I told everybody, 'If your parents so desire, bring them to work. I'll tell them what you're doing.'

We had problems, of course. Almost immediately I realized that the Bangalore guys and the Delhi guys didn't get along well. The first time they all came together for a meeting in Delhi, the Delhi guys took a tea break. They were tea drinkers. In Bangalore they liked coffee instead. A petty difference, but indicative of the cultural differences. They were from different tribes—North Indians and South Indians, software and hardware. They didn't see the world quite the same way, whether they were in Delhi or Bangalore.

Another issue we faced was regarding gender in the workplace. It dawned on me, fairly early on, that there were no women in the organization. I was still travelling back and forth to Chicago then. I told Dr Meemamsi, 'I'll be back in Delhi in six weeks. When I come back, I want thirty women here.'

'Why do you want that?'

'I just do. Put an ad in the paper, say only women should apply.'

'That will be a problem. There'll be an uproar if we do something like that. It will seem like discrimination.'

'Don't worry about it,' I told him. 'I'll take up the responsibility. But I want women in the organization. I can't have an organization with only men. If you can't find women engineers, hire women administrators, hire secretaries. All the team leaders should have one.'

Dr Meemamsi put the ad in the paper, and six weeks later when I came back from Chicago I saw thirty women, mostly working in administrative functions. Now there was one woman as a part of each team. I couldn't have been more pleased. My secretary, Renu Baweja, was extremely smart; she was an excellent organizer, she had a quick mind, she took notes in shorthand fast. From the first moment she started working for me, she made my life easier.

But after some time I discovered that not everything was going as smoothly. One day I came out of the elevator to find four or five women talking near my office door.

'What's happening here?' I asked.

'Sir, we'd like to talk to you at some point.'

'Come. We can talk now.'

'No, no, sir. It doesn't have to be now. We don't want to disturb you.'

'No, come now. Let's talk.'

I brought them into the office. 'Tell me,' I said, 'what's the problem?'

They told me. 'We've been here for a month,' they said. 'Our bosses don't talk to us, not at all. They ignore us completely. We come here every day, but we have no work to do.'

That was my fault, my American conditioning got in the way of my need to think Indian. In the US what could be more normal than women in the workplace—still mostly secretaries in those years. But our Indian team leaders were confused by it all. They were young men; they weren't used to talking to young women in this setting. They were shy. It wasn't part of their culture. Women hardly figured in the Indian workplace. Almost all secretaries in those days were men.

The men didn't know what to do, and the women didn't know how to deal with their silence. I thought, *I have to get this out in the open.*

So I told the women, 'Don't worry. While your bosses aren't talking to you, I'll give you some lectures on telecom.'

I had them come for the talks. I explained how telephones work. I told them why Indian phones had such problems and what we were going to do to fix them. I described digital switching. I talked about indigenous development.

The women loved it. They began to relate to what we were doing, which they really had no idea about before. They started to see themselves as part of the team.

I lectured the men too. 'We all have aunties at home,' I said. 'We all have our mothers and sisters. Think of your co-workers here as your family members. Don't look at them as outsiders. My secretary, Renu, handles all my work. She takes care of my chequebook, she keeps my schedule, she organizes my meetings. She talks to my wife if I'm too busy and have to send her a message. So, beginning tomorrow, when you come to the office, let your secretaries handle your schedule. Start with that. I want you to be focusing all your attention to your projects. Let them support you in doing this.'

Wescom was where I had first recognized that, in a business, managing people was, if anything, more basic than the work itself. If a company wasn't running smoothly, it wasn't going to reach its goals. By 'running smoothly', I mean seeing to it that the organization was well structured enough so that its parts were integrated and that people were working effectively with each other. To achieve this, a manager had to wear a psychologist's hat along with his or her other hats. But dealing with American psyches was one thing—Indian psyches were a whole different universe.

If the underlying American orientation towards others was egalitarian, Indians naturally saw the world as hierarchical, and they acted accordingly. They couldn't help it. It was in their blood. This ingrained deference of theirs was a hindrance to efficiency and creative work. But this wasn't the culture that I wanted to build at C-DOT.

To give an idea of the true state of India's phones, it's enough to say that C-DOT, established to revolutionize the telephone system, only had two phones itself. If I got a phone call, I had to go into a nearby workroom where one of them was located. Typically, I'd go in and there might be four or five people working on a problem together. The moment I walked in they would all jump to their feet and would remain standing there stiffly until I finished my conversation.

I said, 'Guys, listen. If I come in for a phone call, don't stand up. Do your work. Don't waste your time. I get calls all the time.'

But they were simply incapable of doing that. The next time I went in, everybody jumped up again. After three or four days of this, I had completely had it. I had to come up with some strategy to short-circuit—what was to me—this maddening mindset that afflicted not just this little group but the whole organization. I understood whatever I did was going to have to be long-term, a consistent effort at deconditioning. But I thought I'd start with something dramatic.

The next time I went into the workroom, one of the women was there along with the men. As usual, everyone jumped to attention. I went to the woman, the most vulnerable of the group. I wanted to make a scene, so I put my face close to hers. 'Don't you get up!' I said. 'I don't like you getting up! How many times have I told people that?'

The poor woman was trembling. She sat down. The men were shocked. They sat down. I made my phone call and walked back to my office. After that the word got out. 'He really gets mad if you stand up.' Next time I went, nobody stood up. They were wary, but they kept their heads in their work.

This hierarchical dysfunction showed up everywhere. One day I had to send my secretary, Renu, to Bangalore. But one of our financial officers said she wasn't allowed to fly. 'She's in the category of employees who aren't allowed air tickets, sir. We cannot pay for them. She has to take the train.'

'No, she's going to fly.'

'No, sir. Truly, it's a government regulation. She has to take the train.'

'The train takes a day and a half. She has important business there. She needs to fly. If someone has an issue with it, tell them I authorized it. Please now, get her the ticket.'

That diktat sent a shiver through the organization. On the one hand I knew that our people, most of them anyway, held me in affection. On the other hand, could it possibly be that I was becoming mentally disturbed? A secretary taking a plane? Impossible. Absolutely unheard of.

But the word did spread. Everybody here was going to be treated equally. The boss was non-hierarchical. I talked to my driver. If he did some favour for me I gave him a little hug. People noticed this. Hugging a driver—unbelievable! In the lobby I waited in line for the elevator. In India, at that time, the elevator used to be booked, for someone in my position, so it'd be ready for you the moment you arrive. But I would wait for it along with everybody else. If somebody saluted—the doormen had a habit of saluting—I really couldn't stand it, so I would go over and give him a hug.

I wanted to create an egalitarian culture, so all these little (and sometimes big) demonstrations were helpful; they complemented various egalitarian organizational structures I put in place. I included all of our support staff in our monthly progress review meetings. I encouraged a sense of equality among the engineers by not giving out job ranks—senior, junior, etc.—for anyone other than the leaders. I protected the engineers from the administrators and the load of paperwork that in other organizations was typically so onerous.

But sometimes my American ways created problems. At meetings I might say to someone, 'Look, the way you're going about this problem isn't correct. That's the wrong approach to it.' I'd say something critical like that and notice that the recipient would sulk. The young engineers tended to take criticism not just personally, but very personally.

That wasn't good. We were getting into the thick of the design phase already, and I needed to hold everything together: Delhi, Bangalore, men, women, the government, the media, finance. I needed the engineering to move ahead with all due speed and with no unnecessary bumps. But this was a problem. If people made mistakes, they needed to have them pointed out to them. They needed to learn from them, not fall into a funk every time I said something was wrong with the way they were doing something.

One of the things I started doing was bringing over some of my friends from America to give seminars and training in specific areas. We paid for their travel expenses, but they were happy to donate their time. They'd usually come in for two weeks. I'd take them to see the sights at Agra; we'd have a good time together, and they would teach. Bharat Thakkar came to teach about reliability, Alan Stewart taught transformers, Ranga Swami taught mechanical design. At the time I became aware that the unfortunate personal reaction to criticism was a widespread problem, I invited Dr Prakash Desai to come by. Prakash was one of my oldest friends, a charter member of the India Forum and a distinguished psychiatrist at the University of Illinois.

Prakash spent two weeks at C-DOT talking with people. At the end he gave me a report.

'Your young men,' he said, 'have three issues. Generally speaking, they suffer from fragile self-esteem. Everyone is ready to be hurt. That's one of the elements that define Indian character. This low self-esteem has a lot to do with Indian child-rearing practices. So you must constantly pump up their self-regard. They don't get an adequate dose of it from their parents. They don't get it from their teachers or their supervisors. They're expecting it from you, and you're not doing enough of it. You're doing well as far as the group goes. But not individually. There you're not doing well. When you psych everybody up as a group, they're all energized. But they do not get it from you as individuals. So you have to attend to that.

'Second. As a result of their fragile self-esteem they aren't good team-players. They are hierarchical and feudal. In order to be a good team-player you have to be ready to either lead or follow, depending on where the knowledge lies, not depending on age or seniority. You need to respect yourself and respect others, not be vulnerable to perceived disrespect. Working well with a team requires a strong sense of security, which, generally speaking, they don't have. So you not only need to give them more self-esteem, you have to teach them about teamwork. You're lucky they're young; you can mould them to an extent. Older people would be imprisoned by their conditioning.

'Third. They don't distinguish between criticizing *them* and criticizing *their work*. You think these are two separate things, they think it's the same. So when you criticize somebody's design in front of ten people, he will think you don't like him. Because of your American experience, you know it has nothing to do with him personally, it has to do with a particular piece of work. But that's not how he sees it.'

How interesting. I digested the information. Then I called a general meeting. I said, 'Dr Desai has analysed a problem I've noticed—that when I criticize someone's work, it tends to affect them personally, which I think is getting in the way of progress. He has told me to be more careful. I will learn. I want to apologize to anyone I may have inadvertently hurt. I don't want you to think that my pointing out some mistake of yours means that I'm insulting you. I am not. I'm simply calling attention to an error. That's the way I am trained. So please understand that if I criticize your idea, I am not criticizing you. You're my colleagues, you're my heroes. But you can't have good ideas every day. None of us can—including me. So you can also tell me when I don't.'

I was grateful to Prakash for his astute analysis. I think it had some effect. What was really going on was that I was learning my own culture, as Indian as I am. I looked like them, but I was not like them. My mind was shaped and conditioned elsewhere, and this phase at C-DOT clarified that.

After a couple of months I felt that we had our legs well under us. We were moving forward on the design front. We were more or less organized. We were becoming an object of attention. Newspapers and magazines were writing stories about us; there was a buzz. Men and women were working together at C-DOT. The management was non-hierarchical. These were all novel concepts, and people were interested in reading about them. My leadership style at C-DOT was based on clearly communicating our purpose to all our team members to ensure that we were all aligned, all the time. In addition, I had to break my vision into manageable pieces of work for the various teams to operationalize, manage and monitor. I also had to provide and display the appropriate discipline, hard work, sincerity, honesty, character, ethics and morals. My energy and enthusiasm had to be contagious to gather momentum and mobilize forces.

~

I was in Chicago watching a news programme when a news alert came on. Indira Gandhi had been assassinated. Two of her Sikh bodyguards had fatally shot her in her garden, apparently as retribution for the Indian army's assault on the Golden Temple in Amritsar several months earlier. Her elder son, Rajiv Gandhi, had been appointed prime minister prior to a special election.

Immediately, riots broke out all over Delhi, coupled with widespread killing and arson. Sikhs being murdered, Sikhs being hauled in by the police. It wasn't clear if the violence would spread and what might happen next. I stayed in Chicago for a couple of days, then flew to Delhi, a traumatized city.

By then the situation was calming down. Stability was starting to return. But what all this might mean now for C-DOT I had no idea. Mrs Gandhi had been the linchpin of our efforts; she had given us what we needed to go forward. What would happen next when some new person and party came in to power? After spending all this time and energy getting C-DOT through the Cabinet and then setting it up—would that all be gone? I might have to start the whole journey all over again.

For a while I had pangs of worry about it. But as the special election grew closer, it seemed pretty clear that Rajiv Gandhi was going to win. The media was projecting him as a young, energetic tech-savvy modernizer. If he did win, I was sure it would give C-DOT a tremendous boost.

8

Path to Development

At the end of December 1984 Rajiv Gandhi was elected prime minister. His party, the Congress, swept to power on a wave of sympathy. On 5 January 1985 I went to see him.

I had thought a good deal about this meeting. The election had given Rajiv a massive mandate. He was young and charismatic, untainted by any hint of corruption. He was in a position to bring about great generational changes to life in India. I knew he had to be in the process of defining the goals for his administration and ways to achieve them. He was dreaming big. I had a big dream for India as well, one that I wanted to share with him. *India could be poised for revolutionary development and growth,* I thought, *and technology could be a key driver to expedite this process.*

We spent an hour together at his house. I described for him what I was thinking of, my plans, and how telecom and IT could change the face of India. I felt we ought to emphasize information and communication technology to expedite developments in vital areas like agriculture, health, education and governance, and to create jobs as well as rev up foreign exchange. I could help and was ready to do whatever was needed.

Rajiv was just about my age, only two years younger. He himself was a techie of sorts. He had studied engineering at Cambridge University. He had been a commercial airline pilot and a radio ham (operator). He liked to tinker with radios and televisions, and had a feeling for tools. He had a grasp on how things could be made to work, which was similar to the way I saw myself.

He was also used to the egalitarian system. He wasn't impressed by the sycophancy that's so ingrained in India. This meant that we could talk and exchange thoughts in a straightforward manner. It meant we could relate. He was also the only prime minister who had ever held a 'regular' job—unlike a politician—while he was a commercial pilot, so he knew what work life and culture meant, with schedules, commitments, responsibilities and teamwork, something else that made it easy for us to understand each other.

Moreover, as we talked it became clear that his own vision for India included the kinds of things I was talking about and wanted. Technology, we both believed, was the prerequisite for development. Technology, especially telecom, could strengthen India's democracy; it could level differences and enhance feelings of community among the country's disparate regions and peoples.

Rajiv Gandhi had grown up amidst the Congress Party's liberal, non-sectarian ideology, the main force behind the Independence movement. He had gone to school in England and had married Sonia, an Italian woman he met there. Meanwhile, I came from America, with the different orientation I had imbibed in that country. On several fronts we had a basis for understanding each other, and for friendship.

As our discussions deepened, I realized that if I truly wanted to be a part of the kind of changes that were on the agenda, I would have to make up my mind about where I needed to be based. Did I really want to jump in fully and help, or did I want to remain a part-time player juggling between Chicago and India? I hadn't felt the realization that clearly before, but I did now, seeing it was the same as making the decision. 'I have decided I'm moving to India with my family,' I said. 'Lock, stock and barrel.'

'Good,' Rajiv said simply. We didn't discuss the matter further. There was no job title, no job description, just a shared vision for

India. It was understood that I would come and work, not just on C-DOT, but on telecom, information and other technology-related initiatives.

I knew I could go off somewhere instead, build a company and probably make millions and live a very comfortable life. But the opportunity to help build a nation—my India—was unique, challenging and romantic. However, it required a great deal of personal investment and family sacrifices. It was clear from our meeting that this was indeed an extremely rare opportunity, and that if I didn't grab it, history would never forgive me. The risk was huge, but the potential rewards were huger. I also felt inside that if I did not rise to the occasion, nothing would get done. Connecting India was my calling.

Now that Rajiv was prime minister, I thought it would make sense to give him a brief on C-DOT's progress. He had been a huge help in getting the project off the ground; I knew he was genuinely invested in it. But I wanted to show him exactly what we were doing. No laypersons understood what a digital switch was or what a 128-line or a 256-line rural exchange might be. RAXs (rural automatic exchanges) and PBXs—it was all Greek to them. What did the thing look like? How big was it? What did it actually do?

'I can have a demonstration for you outside your office,' I said.

'Excellent,' said Rajiv. 'Set it up.'

The excitement at C-DOT could hardly be described in words. 'The PM wants to see our design?' 'The PM is interested in what we're doing?' The kids were absolutely over the moon.

On the given day a small team of our youngsters set up the exchange near Rajiv's office. I went in to meet with him first. When we walked out, six or seven of the C-DOT engineers were standing there with the equipment. From the outside the switches looked like nondescript metal cabinets. But the insides were a complex array of printed circuit cards with microprocessors, software, electronic components, ports, links, buffers, backup power sources and other elements that made these devices among the world's most intricate machines.

Rajiv shook hands with all of the C-DOT youngsters. One of them said to me afterwards, 'I'm not washing my hand for a month now.'

The switch prototypes we demonstrated for Rajiv Gandhi were the skeleton of the 128-line and 256-line exchanges designed for rural use. We had promised the government a family of switches from 128 lines for rural use to 40,000 lines for urban areas. My plan was to design every component of the small exchanges so that we could incorporate them as modules into the larger exchanges. We'd be using the same cards, processors and software. Everything was modular, flexible, expandable, scalable—and affordable.

But we wanted to start with the smallest exchanges, which we intended to install in rural villages. I wanted people in these small, remote places to be able to easily call their relatives and friends living in other places; I wanted to give small business owners the ability to connect with their customers and suppliers elsewhere, so that they could expand and build their businesses—none of which was possible with the current generation of scarce and unworkable phones. Villagers, the vast majority of the population, were isolated in stagnant social and economic enclaves. I intended to break them free from their barriers and connect them with each other and the rest of the world.

All over the globe, higher growth has been correlated with increased telephone density. The general wisdom was that if you were rich, you had a lot of telephones, and the corollary was that if you had lots of telephones, you were bound to be rich. In the industry of telecommunications, the prevailing wisdom was to start with the dense rich areas and work your way outwards.

I had a different view. My approach, which I talked about in every forum possible, was to not worry about telephone *density* in developing countries like India, but to focus on *access* instead. Telephone density in the cities is not going to touch life in the villages, which is where India's challenge lies. We needed to worry instead about improving access to telephones for everybody.

That, in essence, meant public phones. I wanted to make phones available to rural people, the village dwellers. Don't give a phone to the rich man for his and his family's personal use. Instead, put it in a shop or a pharmacy or a school or a bus station. Put it on the street, somewhere where ordinary people can use it.

But whenever I talked about public access, people thought immediately of the Western-style coin-operated public phones. I constantly heard things like, *You can't have a coin-operated phone;*

the people won't have coins; they'll be vandalized; you won't be able to maintain them.

But I wasn't thinking of coin-operated phones. 'Coin-operated phones are the Western model,' I would say. 'They're expensive to make, they're expensive to install, they're expensive to maintain. That's not what I want. What I want are public phones operated by a phone manager or phone entrepreneur. Give phones to an unemployed person or a disabled person. Set up a table in a tea shop. People will come to make calls. The telephone will generate a receipt for each call. The users will pay the phone person. The phone person will pay a fee to the phone company and keep the rest.' Ultimately, these public telephones came to be known as Subscriber Trunk Dialling/Public Call Offices—or STD/PCOs—set up with yellow signs all over the country for people to make calls anywhere without having to own a telephone. The public telephones created roughly 2 million new jobs in the country and provided livelihood to many families, especially the underprivileged and the handicapped. They also connected every corner in India to each other and to the rest of the world.

Because of these public telephones and their clear utility for common people, it became easier to privatize the telecom industry in India in 1994. But we weren't thinking of industrial progress at that time. We were thinking about connecting India from the bottom-up.

Our engineers understood this concept and were committed to delivering a phone system that would satisfy local Indian needs and assure access. Together, we designed small 128-line exchanges that incorporated the most sophisticated technology, but we ruggedized them for local conditions. They were humidity-, dust- and monsoon-proof. They did not require air conditioning, which necessitated a design breakthrough since switches built for high-temperature and high-humidity environments invariably needed air conditioning. Beyond that, the Indian electrical grid was notoriously undependable; we couldn't have the switches overheating every time the power failed.

Our answer to the heat problem was, first, to use low-powered microprocessors. That meant the switches were a little slower than the standard commercial switches, but in our circumstances that was irrelevant. Then we gave more space to the various components and configured them differently from what was standard in order to increase the so-called 'vertical chimney' effect, which would efficiently dissipate the heat from the microprocessors. Our switches weren't sleek, they were bulkier than they might have been. But I wasn't concerned about aesthetics. I just wanted them to work in a hostile Indian environment with dust, humidity and heat, and without air conditioning.

From the beginning I had several objectives for C-DOT. The first, of course, was to design and build switches. For C-DOT itself I had selected recently graduated engineers—our average age was twenty-three. I did this in order to get people who hadn't been conditioned yet by the system, into the system. But I had a second goal in mind too. Indian schools were producing wonderful engineers—as good as any in the world. But, typically, these young people looked overseas for employment. Engineering jobs in the US and Europe were far more attractive and lucrative than jobs in India. The West was where the action and the opportunities were. It was an example of the brain drain. My second objective for C-DOT was that it would keep many of these smart, young people *in* India. C-DOT and its inevitable spillovers would nurture our native hardware and software talent and provide a home for them. From the beginning I had thought of C-DOT as a catalyst, or at least a model, for high-tech growth in India generally.

Another objective was regarding the manufacturing front. I talked a great deal about indigenous production, how India could build its own telecom system instead of spending cash reserves on imports from multinationals. As we made progress on switch designs in Delhi and Bangalore I began organizing the manufacturing effort.

The first step was to enlist people and companies to build the equipment. To do this I called a conference in Delhi where we presented our manufacturing plans and announced that manufacturing licences would be available for a fee of 4 lakh rupees. There was more than a little opposition to this approach; it seemed to some a random and overly casual way to build a manufacturing base. 'Sir,' I heard, 'this is not possible. How can you let just everybody get a licence?' My idea was to build multiple manufacturing capabilities for telecom equipment and train a large number of people at various locations in the private sector.

My answer to that was, 'Why not? They're paying 4 lakh rupees, let *them* worry about it.' That might have sounded a little flippant. But the fact was that no one in India had ever manufactured telecom equipment privately. So it wasn't as if we had a group of experienced manufacturers to choose from. No one in India had ever produced telecom transformers. (Eventually, I had to send someone from the US to teach them.) No one had ever made connectors before, no one had fabricated serving boards or electronic racks. We were going to have to build an entire industry of manufacturers and vendors from nothing.

When I invited potential producers in to buy licences, I knew that the licensees would be novices in telecom manufacturing. But I had lined up ancillary industries that would provide materials and components. I would direct the manufacturers to these sources. I would teach them how to fabricate and how to assemble to the required specifications. I would teach them how to test. My plan was to create a new native Indian industry from the ground up.

So, in a sense, the process was random, but I was certain the incentives would generate the necessary interest and, eventually, the necessary manufacturing expertise. Which is what happened, sometimes, in unexpected ways. One day at the Hyderabad airport a young man came up to me. 'Mr Pitroda, I've read about you, you're doing wonderful things. I'm a mechanical engineer. Do you think I could do something?' I happened to have a connector in my pocket, a telephone jack—a dime a dozen in America, but hard to come by in India. 'Here,' I said, 'make this in India. Go to the US, figure it out.' Six months later he was making connectors.

At the Delhi licensing meeting, forty-eight people came forward to buy manufacturing licences. Forty-eight was too many, I knew that. More than a few of them were bound to not have the resources or ability. Inevitably, some were going to fail.

But this kind of entrepreneurial risk-taking was not part of the culture, particularly in government-sponsored industries. People in the administration said, 'How can you talk openly about people failing? It's absolutely not acceptable.'

My answer was that we had to accept it. 'The fact is that some of them are going to fail. There's nothing to do about it. Failure is a part of life, and a precondition for success. It is okay for failures to happen.'

That caused some consternation. Ever since Jawaharlal Nehru, India had embraced a command-driven, socialistically oriented economy. Privatization of this sort was a new idea, a different kind of culture. The expectation of failure sounded harsh, even unsavoury. It smacked of cruel, crass American capitalism. 'It's okay to fail,' I said. That might have seemed blunt and unsympathetic, but it was the truth.

I had envisioned that we would be creating a sizeable industrial base, but I think the scope of it wasn't immediately evident to almost anyone. Even Rajiv Gandhi himself wasn't aware of the extent of what all was happening. But he had implicit trust that I would be able to manage, and I didn't want to burden him with anything that wasn't absolutely necessary. 'The best thing I can do is give you the gift of time,' I told him. I didn't want to come to him with a set of problems for him to solve. I wanted to solve them for him. As prime minister he was bombarded by the problems of the world. I didn't want to add to that. *Why am I your friend if I'm going to add to your burdens? I'm not going to give you problems. I'm going to relieve you of problems. That's my job.* That's what I thought.

That was my attitude. Rajiv liked that. I made no demands. I never asked for any favours. And there weren't many people around him who didn't want something. My intention was that whatever time we spent together should be time saved for interesting and innovative ideas. I wanted him to feel good with me, not look at me as someone who needed to be managed.

He and I both experienced that most people in India take thirty minutes to deliver a thirty-second message. The real message normally comes at the end of the meeting, and people invariably have a hidden agenda.

Once the manufacturing licences were awarded our engineers got even more excited. It wasn't abstract designs, systems and algorithms any more. They could sense that things were beginning to come to fruition. Some of the teams moved into a new phase, creating plans and teaching tools for the manufacturers to use. We prepared forty-eight sets of drawings. We set up a training room. We made videotapes demonstrating assembly methods. We trained the engineers to use the testing equipment.

All this had to be done on the fast track. Everyone understood what was at stake and that we needed to work as hard and in as disciplined a manner as we were capable of. People had been working hard before, but now it seemed as if the place had gone into overdrive. The young engineers were putting in twelve-hour days, some far more. They took pride in it; they felt totally committed. If someone needed to fly from Bangalore to Delhi to solve some problem, they just did it. I told them, 'Don't wait for permission. Do it. When I see it, I'll sign it. I'll backdate it. If you have work to do, don't wait for permission—do it. Do you have to go to the US to figure out how to fix something? Go. Don't worry about junk, about irrelevancies. Just get the work done.'

~

The 128-line rural automatic exchange was C-DOT's first product. To unveil it to the public we booked the big function room at the Taj West End Hotel in Bangalore. We invited the relevant group of Cabinet ministers. I organized the presentation and laid it out. The kids in Bangalore were working on it non-stop.

I flew in to Bangalore the night before, to hear that everything was on track. We were ready to go. 'Good,' I said, 'let's go straight to the hotel. I want to have a look at the room.'

The first thing that caught my eye when I walked in through the door was a line of sofas and armchairs in the front row.

'Why are these here?' I asked the hotel manager.

'For the VIPs, sir,' he said.

This was the last thing I wanted. C-DOT was supposed to be as egalitarian as possible—an ongoing struggle. I was not going to tell our engineers and staff that they were less important than anybody else—why folding chairs for them, and sofas for the higher-ups?

'No,' I said. 'I want the VIPs to sit on the same chairs as everyone else.'

The hotel manager and his assistants were horrified at the thought that the hotel might be seen as being disrespectful towards the ministers. They insisted that protocol had to be followed; the VIPs had to be seated properly.

'Look,' I said, 'this is not *your* function, it's *our* function. Please get rid of these things for me. I'm not sending this kind of signal, that VIPs have a sofa and everyone else has to sit on a chair.'

I also decided that I wasn't going to say anything myself at the event. I strongly felt the same way I had when we announced the creation of C-DOT. I was the driving force at C-DOT, no question. But there were countless extremely talented people involved, and this was a national project. The telecommunications minister was the one who ought to be making the speeches, not me.

The launch went beautifully. The ministers gave speeches. I stayed in the back, where I could easily watch the proceedings. I was filled with pride for what our young team had accomplished, and filled with confidence that we could accomplish everything else we had promised. Now we had to get these switches up and running—in thousands of interior villages.

This was not a job for the faint of heart. I was big on giving pep talks to C-DOT's people. Some might have even thought I was a little overenthusiastic. But we all needed to be psyched—myself as well as the young engineers. Getting to this point was one thing, keeping up our energies for the long haul in front of us was something else altogether. The RAX was a triumph, but it was only the beginning.

As part of the launch, we announced that we would install one RAX a day. Our slogan was: 'An RAX a Day'. For India's 6 lakh villages we would need somewhere between 30,000 and 60,000 rural exchanges. If we installed one a day, that would mean only 365 a year. To install ten a day, which I actually thought was feasible, would still mean a ten-to-fifteen-year project.

But the installations didn't happen overnight; everything had to be geared up. So after a month, when 'An RAX a Day' didn't swing into action, a newspaper headlined the event, calling it: 'A Hoax a Day'.

All the engineers were mighty upset. 'Sir, look what they're saying. "A hoax a day". This is not fair! How dare they say that!'

'Don't worry,' I told them. 'Let them write whatever they want. We'll get there. We have to concentrate on putting out one RAX a day. Then we'll go up to three, four, five a day, ten a day. We are going to fill up the country with them.'

Insulted as they were, the engineers put themselves on a war footing. After a month we were producing two RAXs a day. Ultimately, we did go up to ten a day. All the fabricators had to speed up and coordinate. More transformers, more connectors, more racks—it all had to be lined up. And all of it was, of course, indigenous production.

Along with the rural switches we needed to provide public telephones. For that, we designed public telephone installations we called STD/PCOs, which meant a telephone, a big, yellow STD/PCO sign, or sometimes a yellow stand-alone phone booth. The yellow was designed to stand out in the same way the red British telephone booths stood out. If you saw yellow, you knew a public phone was around. The phone had a little meter that came with it to monitor the length of the call and bill it accordingly. The phone was manned, but the customer did the dialling. At the end of the call, the manager collected the fee—20 per cent for him, 80 per cent for the phone company.

Public telephones were the property of the managers. The phones provided them with their livelihood. They maintained them and took a lot of care to ensure they weren't vandalized. They often took the units home at night and plugged them in in the morning at their tables in the booths.

The idea was not just to make phones accessible but also to employ a large number of people. We instituted a policy that gave job preference to people with disabilities. Later, many women became phone managers as well. These public telephones poured out of our manufacturers as our switches were installed in village after village. Eventually, we placed more than 2 million of them throughout rural India. Everywhere you went there was a yellow public-phone. In villages behind mountains, across deserts—the yellow phones dotted the landscape. Now almost everyone could make or receive a phone call. Village kids found they could earn a few pennies by running off to find people if a call came for them. If Sanjay wanted to reach his sister, Radha, who lived in another province, he called the phone in her neighbourhood, where an enterprising kid would run off to find her. 'A call for Radha from Sanjay!'

In a short while, the phones became the centre of social activities. Something like an adda (the sociocultural tradition of people gathering together to talk and eat on a regular basis), much like the French salon. People socialized and spent time with each other where the phones were, while waiting to make or receive calls, make business arrangements, or just chat with friends. So the booth managers started selling things like tobacco, cigarettes, candies, a few sundries. It was a simple idea, but a fertile one. People loved the phones. They created jobs, and they did what I had envisaged they would do from the beginning. They gave people access to the world beyond the confines of their distant and isolated homes. The phones brought them a step closer to modernity. The telephone was no longer a luxury, but a necessity. A farmer could make a call to sell his produce, a mother could speak to her son working in another state, a local shopkeeper could order his supplies. People started using public phones in a variety of ways.

As we installed an increasing number of rural exchanges, we also designed and manufactured our next switch, the 512-line exchange. The smaller switches we placed in villages, the larger ones, capable of routing calls from ten or twelve villages, we installed in market towns. Rural exchanges and public telephones flourished simultaneously.

~

In all of this I was hands-on, designing, managing and cheerleading throughout the way. But as we went along I was also absorbing lessons and drawing conclusions. Telecom for India was in its infancy, but I was convinced that the exchange of information enabled by telecom and IT would eventually have the same kind of effects in India as it had had in the US. Connectivity would be the basis for openness, accessibility, networking, economic development decentralization and democratization and, as a result, fundamental social transformation.

I was convinced that the lack of information exchanges was directly connected with poverty. In India, as in many other parts of the world, poverty has a lot to do with the poverty of information and knowledge. However, knowledge is power, and not many people like to share their power. If people can get information and knowledge, in whatever form they need—be it agriculture, business, soil, water or health—it adds to their prosperity, directly and indirectly. I had seen, first-hand, the effect that telecom and IT was having on economic life in America. I was sure that India could move in the same direction too. All it needed was political will.

Telecom would be an economic and social driver. You could already notice the beginnings of that in the villages as the public phones made their appearance and became a part of village life. I could see that they would empower people politically as well. If you can pick up the phone and call your elected officials yourself, it gives you a certain perceived power. You can reach out to them. You can question them. You can ask them for information and explanations. You can make your presence felt. With phones you can organize things quickly across great distances.

India, I thought, was ripe for what I conceived of as generational change. Telecom was a big idea. Looking to the future, it had the potential to catalyse a pervasive, society-wide transformation.

As I immersed myself more and more deeply in the Indian environment I continued to think about the fact that there were two ways to go about creating this social transformation. The first was to create a big private business in telecom. The country needed digital switching coupled with local production. You could build a large company to do these things; you could 'entrepreneurize' it. This was a path to great wealth.

Assuming you wanted telecom to have a nation-building impact, the prerequisite was political will. Without political will and visible ongoing support from the government leadership, it is difficult to execute big ideas. I would have been nowhere without Mrs Gandhi's approval and Rajiv Gandhi's political will, support and enthusiasm.

And along with political will, you need domain expertise to get things done. In India, with its bureaucratic habits and stultifying procedures, you absolutely need young, fresh talent. But managing young talent is an art in itself. It requires an unconventional approach, with a focus on collaboration. It translates to egalitarian management methods and selfless commitment on the part of the leadership.

Young people need clear and simple goals. Not 'simple' in terms of how the goals might be achieved—there are few human enterprises more complex and challenging than building digital telecom systems— but simple in terms of being well defined, single-minded, explicit and clearly articulated. Youngsters need to be guided every step of the way. They need new work culture, work norms, work ethics, work habits.

At times, all this felt like an immensely frustrating uphill battle. So it was important to me to have my own guide—just as I was a guide to the young engineers. I needed to have an internal compass to find and preserve my moral and psychological balance. In my case I looked to Mahatma Gandhi for help.

Gandhi was embedded in my brain—his moral power, the way he never turned away from what he had set out to do, but also the fact that he arrived in South Africa as a lawyer, looking to make some kind of a career for himself. Yet, he found something completely different, a social mission. He became a new person, a person who devoted his life to what he called 'public work'.

I did everything I could to keep our young people excited. We had parties, cultural programmes, performances and camps. With all the cheerleading and motivational talks, the drama training from my university days came in very handy. These were morale-building activities. But I also needed our people to feel like they were a part of something larger, that their work was essential to the growth and health of their country. I wanted them to feel proud. They weren't just holding a job, they were vital cogs in an endeavour that contributed to India's well-being.

Finally, I understood early on that even though our young engineers were so engrossed in creating C-DOT, it could not possibly be the farthest point on their horizons in terms of career and life goals. They were going to seek their own mobility, their own paths upwards—aspiration and ambition were part of their youthful natures too. I wanted them to see C-DOT as a rich environment that would help them progress in their lives. Doing their best at C-DOT would help them open avenues to their futures. At C-DOT they would build their skill sets and their résumés; doing their best with us would contribute to wherever they would be going over the next twenty or thirty years.

I tried hard to get that message across. It was part and parcel of envisioning C-DOT, not just as a telecommunications project, but as a springboard for Indian engineering talent. And after a year or so of operations a chance came along for me to make my point. Two of our managers came to me and said, 'Sir, we have a problem—bad news. We have seven people who want to go to the US for further studies. We're angry, sir. We want to fire them immediately.'

'Fire them?' I said. 'Let's throw a party for them.'

'What do you mean? They're taking advantage of us. They're ungrateful. We trained them and now they want to leave us.'

'I'm happy they're doing that,' I said. 'What a great thing. Our engineers are going abroad. They'll take with them all the things they've learned here. They'll be our ambassadors. Of course, they should go.'

So I had a big party for them. I gave a speech. 'I'm so proud of these seven young people. They're leaving us. But they'll take with them great memories of C-DOT, memories of love and affection. Now, if you guys have any problems, you can call them in the US, and they'll give you answers. Look at them as your extension over there.'

The speech was a hit. I meant every word I said. And, in fact, it has played out very much like I thought and hoped it would. Today, there are several hundred C-DOT engineers in Silicon Valley. In 2011, I had lunch with forty or fifty of them. 'Sir, I was there in 1987.' 'Sir, I was there in 1991.' It was like an alumni reunion. C-DOTians are everywhere in key leadership positions in companies in the US, Australia, Europe, the Middle East and the Asia-Pacific. They are well-accomplished, well-connected, well-informed people who take pride in themselves.

~

But C-DOT itself was only a mere part of the larger picture, where we needed a comprehensive strategy. You could not say, *I'll design the product, but I don't know how to manufacture. Or I don't know how to set up ancillary industries. Or I don't know how to create standards.* All these needed to be part of an overall plan.

We also needed to be media-savvy. The press was going to carry our message. In India's political environment, the tenor of that message would be important, perhaps critical. I knew there would be hiccups along the way, but I felt that if C-DOT was running well and doing its job right, the reporting would be positive.

A big part of doing the job right was to have a clear cost–benefit advantage in mind. Whatever we did, it had to be not only better but less expensive and affordable as well. We couldn't build all this fancy technology and then find out at the end that it could be bought for a cheaper price abroad. So it had to be affordable, scalable and sustainable. But if it wasn't affordable, the rest would be irrelevant. We were clear on the point that what works in developed countries would not necessarily work in India. We needed an Indian model of development to meet Indian requirements.

I didn't fully understand all—or maybe even most—of these things when we started out. I distilled their essence as we went along. But I did know one thing clearly that stayed with me daily at C-DOT. That in order to accomplish what I wanted, C-DOT needed to be a part of the government, yet separate from it. In the first two-plus years of C-DOT's existence I felt I had succeeded in establishing this healthy, functional bypass. C-DOT was organized and productive. Our costs were one-fifth of what it would have cost to import the equivalent equipment. We were scaling up, moving towards our ultimate goal—the 40,000-line urban switch.

But on that switch we were running behind schedule. I had promised a thirty-six-month time frame, and the large urban switch was going to take forty or forty-six months to deliver. But, in fact, a delay of this kind didn't mean anything. C-DOT's work was vast—the design, the manufacturers, the ancillary industries, the 6 lakh villages. In the big picture, a six- or twelve-month delay for the large switch was immaterial. But that was my engineering self speaking. I didn't foresee how an essentially irrelevant thing like this had the potential to come back and bite me with a vengeance. This delay was used later by a few to harass me.

~

Now that C-DOT was on track, my presence was becoming far less crucial. From here on, the main work would be fine-tuning, which wasn't an area I wanted to focus my attention on. With Rajiv Gandhi in office, I had a window of opportunity to do other things. If I spent a lot of my time refining C-DOT, the chance would slip away. In 1987 I began thinking seriously about what those other things might be.

Rajiv and I had spent a good deal of time talking about how technology could help address poverty, inequality, inclusion, basic human needs and some more of the country's most acute problems. These were serious conversations, in the sense that the possibilities excited both of us. But to that point they were no more than discussions between friends. However, the more I spoke to Rajiv, the more I got sucked into dreaming big to modernize India.

But as we talked, and as I scaled down my participation in C-DOT, I began to think about these things more consciously. To enable some coherence on the subject—for myself as much as for anything else—I put together a fifty-page paper outlining the areas where I thought technology could play a critical role: literacy, water, agriculture, transport, energy, health. I entitled the paper: 'India in 2011'. What kind of an India did we want to build in the 21st century? When I shared that presentation with Rajiv, he asked me to have a conversation with some of his staff in the prime minister's office. Gopi Arora, his secretary, liked the plan and we collectively agreed with the prime minister to launch this vision document on national television on 14 August for public discussion. However, the government got busy with the Punjab Accord and our plan to start a national conversation on India in the 21st century got derailed. Similarly, I had also done a detailed document on the building of the Congress Party, right after Rajiv Gandhi's speech at the centennial celebration of the Congress in Mumbai. The plan was to operationalize his vision of the party for the future, a plan we had to also let go of due to our day-to-day firefighting activities.

9

Technology Missions

In the August of 1987, the initial three-year period for C-DOT was up. To mark the anniversary, we decided to present a report to the nation at Delhi's big Vigyan Bhawan and give a live demonstration of our telephone exchange to the prime minister and others. We invited 1200 people from all over the country—businessmen, manufacturers, scientists, academics, government ministers, students and all the major media, in addition to Rajiv himself. The C-DOT teams from Delhi and Bangalore provided a live demo and displayed the exchange components and associated hardware we had developed.

I gave a little introduction at the podium. It was outlined in the 'Report to the Nation', as follows:

Mr Prime Minister, distinguished guests, and friends from C-COT, it is a pleasure to present a report to the nation on C-DOT's accomplishments in the last three years. Perhaps someone might be curious to know why, when C-DOT has been an open book right through. The answer is that this great nation of ours had reposed in us 'super trust' of developing a sophisticated digital telephone switching technology and products on our own from scratch for Rs 36 crores in thirty-six months. Now the question is, how far have we been able to come up to her expectations. Did we size up to it? The questions posed are as difficult as the answers themselves. But our endeavour would be to answer these queries frankly and honestly for you to judge. According to us, the task was not, and has not been, a simple one, by any yardstick. In fact, for quite some time it was considered to be a great gamble by many. However, we believe it has proven to be a great initiative on the part of the Indian system to challenge the genius and the drive of our young people.

The Centre for Development of Telematics was established on August 25, 1984 by the government with the following objectives:

- To develop sophisticated telematics technology and products indigenously
- To digitize India's telephone network to improve overall service
- To be prepared for the integrated service digital network of the future

C-DOT is a scientific society funded jointly by the Department of Electronics and the Department of Telecom. The main goal of C-DOT has been to develop accessibility and rural communication with a focus on self-reliance, labour-intensive and capital-sensitive programmes. At present, C-DOT has 425 people with an average age of 25 years. In Delhi, there are 215 working on software, systems and administration. In Bangalore, there are 210 people working on hardware and production. C-DOT has now developed small, medium and large rural exchanges, private automatic exchanges, and other exchanges for the digital networks.

In spite of all our accomplishments, we still have miles to go. We are conscious of the fact that designing a family of digital switching systems will not solve the telecom problems of India. We need to manufacture, install, maintain and service these systems for a long time to come. We recognize that qualified and dedicated people coupled with management skills to mobilize and motivate their capabilities are the ultimate limitations of development and not capital or technology. Finally, we would like to thank our families for allowing each one of us to spend long hours at work, the media for fair coverage of our ongoing activities, and all those individuals, organizations and government agencies who have supported us.

Mr Prime Minister, please allow us to say publicly that without your personal involvement from 1981, our dream to build self-reliance in this vital technology of tomorrow as part of the ultimate goal outlined by our founding fathers of an independent India would have remained only a cherished reverie never to be achieved—but only to be deferred, delayed, distracted and dead. Through your concern, commitment and continuing encouragement, it has been possible to deliver this development to the nation. Mr Prime Minister, thank you for your vision, support and presence.

Then one of the young engineers stood up and made a direct call to a colleague in Bangalore, the two describing and explaining the designs, the products, what they were and how they worked, all in clear layman's terms, for the benefit of everyone in the hall. Then Rajiv spoke for fifteen minutes. He was impressed. Judging from the media accounts the next day, the entire country was impressed. I was proud of my team and very happy.

That was my concluding report on C-DOT, my way of saying: *C-DOT is working well and it is on autopilot. This is the product and the process. Everything is on track and being implemented. Our engineers and administrators have the work in hand.* Now it was time for me to move on.

~

It is an understatement to say that I was acutely aware of what my relationship with Rajiv Gandhi meant, not just in terms of the opportunities it gave me but also personally. I treasured that bond. His thoughtfulness towards me and, equally, towards Anu, was something that touched both of us deeply.

I started commuting to India in 1981, but decided to move my family there in 1985. Of course, doing that meant uprooting them, which gave me a deep feeling of anxiety. Salil was ten, Rajal seven. They had been born in Chicago, they were enjoying their schools, their family and friends. Chicago was their home. A big move was going to create a major disruption in their lives. Anu herself hadn't lived in India for about twenty years. How would she feel about moving? I thought that at the very least I had to introduce her to Rajiv, so she could see for herself why I wanted to do this, and could begin getting comfortable with the idea of this transition.

My chance came when Rajiv went to Washington to see President Reagan in June 1985. I didn't have an appointment with him, but I called the Indian ambassador. 'Please tell the PM that I'm going to be in Washington with my wife. We would very much like to meet him.'

The ambassador said, 'There is no way you could do that. His schedule is solidly booked.'

'I understand,' I said. 'But if you would please ask him. Just say that Sam Pitroda would like to see him.'

'Certainly,' said the ambassador. 'I'll tell him.'

Anu and I went to Washington, not having any idea if Rajiv would be able to make the time. Three friends came along with us, Dr Prakash Desai, Rajiv Desai and Dr Divyesh Mehta. We were being tourists and seeing some of the sights, when I heard from the ambassador that Rajiv was free for half an hour—between Caspar Weinberger, the then defence secretary, and George P. Schultz, the then secretary of state. All of us were free to come.

The meeting was at the Indian Embassy. It took us a while to get through the heavy security, and as we walked in I saw Weinberger leaving. When we got to the meeting room, I said, 'Mr Prime Minister, this is Anu.'

'Anu,' he said. 'Welcome. Come, sit here next to me.'

I knew Anu's heart must be racing. This was the prime minister talking to her, charming, good-looking, in such a warm and welcoming manner.

'Anu, I know Sam wants to come to India. I want you to make sure the children's admission to school is taken care of. It's very important, and Sam may not understand these things in Delhi. Let me know. It's essential to get them into the right school.'

He was speaking to Anu in exactly the sort of language she wanted to hear. I couldn't help thinking what a truly exceptional person he was—what an effort he made and how relatable he could be.

Now, as I was finishing up with C-DOT, my relationship with Rajiv had only deepened. He would call me at night sometimes, at ten or ten-thirty. 'Sam, come.' So I would go with Anu to his home and we would talk, just the three of us.

But my personal feelings aside, I knew that my relationship with the prime minister had more or less given me carte blanche to take on whatever role I thought would make most sense post-C-DOT. I was thinking hard about how to bring technology to bear on India's most pressing problems and what I might do to further that. We had talked about it. I was now beginning to get some clarity on what I wanted to do.

Additionally, I was part of the Scientific Advisory Council to the Prime Minister, chaired by Professor C.N.R. Rao, a world-renowned scientist in the field of super conductivity and materials science. Other members of the council were Dr Ganguly, Dr Tandon, Dr Mashelkar, Dr Narsimha, Dr Raha and Dr Lavakare—India's most distinguished scientific minds. These were the people who had spent their lives in research. As a scientist, I wasn't anywhere near as accomplished as them, but I interacted with them regularly, so I was able to learn valuable lessons in agriculture, health, biotechnology, vaccines and other areas from them.

This group was always pushing for more research funds. But they also understood the need to use science and technology for the improvement of society. That was one of the main items on their agenda. What do you do with all this knowledge if not help the common man?

Being part of these discussions had helped me refine my ideas on the best ways to use technology to address specific problems. I was just about ready to make a proposal to Rajiv, when one evening I got a call from his principal secretary, Mrs Sarla Grewal. 'Mr Pitroda,' she said, 'can you come over right away? We have an emergency on our hands.'

I was alarmed. 'What's happened?'

'Please,' she said, 'just come.'

When I got to her office, she told me. 'The PM is so angry, he just fired the secretaries of water and agriculture. He exploded at them.'

'What do you mean "exploded" at them? Why? What exactly happened?'

'They were reporting to the PM on what they were doing about water and agriculture. He was so furious at their presentation that he fired them both on the spot. This hasn't *ever* happened that the PM would fire two senior people like this. It will cause huge problems, big disruptions in those departments. I'm sure you can convince him otherwise. Please help.'

That same night I talked with the two department secretaries, effectively, the COOs of their ministries. But they didn't have much to add to what Rajiv's secretary told me. 'We were making the presentation. The PM thought it was really bad quality. He just fired us.'

I called Rajiv's office and told them we'd like forty-eight hours. Would his office please ask him to put the decision on hold for that time? Then I told the secretaries I wanted to meet with them the next day to better understand exactly what the problem was.

We decided to tackle the issue of water. 'We've been asked to ensure adequate water supply for rural India,' the secretary said.

'All right. How much water is needed?'

'Enough. Many places don't have adequate water resources.'

'What kind of water are you talking about?'

'Water.'

'Let me ask you some questions. Do you know how much water a dog drinks?'

'What? What do you mean?'

'I want to know. How much water does a dog drink, a buffalo, a camel, a cow, a cat, a donkey, a goat? How much do people need for bathing, how much for cooking, washing, drinking? Please get this information—then we'll talk.'

The water secretary had simply not looked at the problem this way. He hadn't broken the issue down into its component parts, which one would imagine would have been the first thing on his agenda. But he and the agriculture secretary were bureaucrats, not specialists. They didn't get into the details. They were responsible for planning, but they didn't feel that a technical understanding was essential for the planning function, or at least for their function. In their presentation to Rajiv they had shown a kind of feel-good, advertisement-type video on India's water and food production—pretty generalities with little substance. Rajiv was a nuts-and-bolts kind of guy. I understood how those presentations must have infuriated him. No wonder he had stopped them midway and fired them.

I said, 'Look, if you don't break the problem down, how can you understand how much you need, and for what purposes? You'd require 20 litres per day, 50 litres, how much? And for whom? There are almost exactly the same number of animals per village as people. You need to know how much water they use, how much the people use. You can't plan without knowing these things. You certainly can't report to the PM without specifics.'

Before long they came back with studies showing hard numbers on water requirement and use in the villages. They needed 30 litres per day per person, 40 litres for cattle.

'Okay,' I said. 'What are the problems? What do you need?'

They ticked off the challenges: Excess iron in the water supplies, excess fluoride, and occurrence of guinea worms coupled with high bacteria counts. They needed water-testing labs, geohydrological surveys, satellite imagery and education programmes.

It wasn't that I knew much, if anything, about any of these issues. I was simply asking questions they hadn't asked themselves before they put together their presentations. A whole new horizon had appeared in front of the officials. There was a lot of technology in water and, of course, in agriculture as well. So we restructured the presentations together. Forty-eight hours later we sat down with the prime minister. They gave their presentations again, and this time he was happier with them. He took back their dismissals.

Thinking about all this, I concluded that now was really the time to look at not just telecom, but at some of the other areas I had identified in the paper I had done earlier, specifically in terms of where and how technology could most effectively impact development. Which of India's problems were most amenable to generational change, and what kind of organization would it take to accomplish the transformations that might be achieved?

In fact, I was not the first to think along these lines. Several years earlier the national five-year plan had identified more than a dozen areas where science and technology could and should be fruitfully applied to national development. Moreover, the plan had discussed the efficacy of the 'mission' approach to addressing problems, i.e., utilizing special task-driven teams or organizations to accomplish specific goals. The mission approach would bring management, coordination and motivation to the efforts, which, by their nature, crossed over bureaucratic boundaries. Providing clean, adequate water, for example, involved the health, agriculture and education departments and others at the national, state and local levels. It required bringing scientists and technologists to focus their attention on specific problems.

The fact that there was no guiding, unifying force behind attempts to address these kinds of large problems meant that they typically got bogged down in a haze of territorial confusion and a multiplicity of priorities. This resulted in a psychology of impotence and somnolence, with little or nothing actually getting accomplished. The mission approach was a potential cure for this malaise.

Even though the five-year plan had established a number of projects to cut through the bureaucratic tangle, they had gone nowhere. Nobody understood them. Nobody was invested in them or wanted to take responsibility for them. They were, as one commentator said, 'black boxes'. No one knew exactly what was inside them or how they were supposed to work.

But the five-year plan had suggested what the needs were and how they should be addressed. With this as a base, together with Rajiv, I decided that the missions should concentrate on five sectors: Rural drinking water, literacy, immunization, edible oils and telecommunications. Later, we added a sixth: Dairy production.

The National Technology Missions were launched to give new focus to development, where we shift from directing people to empowering them. These were launched in 1986–87, at the initiative of the then Prime Minister Rajiv Gandhi. The mission approach was required to create a sense of urgency, missionary zeal and infrastructure for technological self-reliance and improved delivery systems. It was also required to provide management focus, improved communication, improved centre–state coordination and organized information to substantially increase people's participation. The delivery of these basic needs required a unique integrated approach to make use of modern technology and tools to understand grass-root realities and the talent of our young intellectuals, professionals and technocrats. It also required cooperation between the various agencies, the active participation of women as well as strong political commitment at the state and district level. To succeed in these missions we needed to rejuvenate our existing institutions, simplify antiquated procedures, decentralize planning, mobilize available national resources, eliminate the duplication of efforts, provide modern management for motivation, mobilization and monitoring, and focus on quality and continuity; there was also a need to bring social auditing by people outside the system, and bring traditional community participation back into our mainstream.

I would come on as adviser to the prime minister for the Technology Missions with a ministerial rank. My overall objective would be to mobilize technology to benefit the people, especially the rural population and those in the sectors we had identified. In addressing these six areas, I would attempt to integrate technological interventions with government efforts, private industry and volunteer resources. My job would be to coordinate the ministries and galvanize the work already being done. I would keep everyone involved and focused on goals and timelines. I'd operate independently and bring in new methods of management. All these functions were right up my alley. I wasn't a specialist in any of the mission areas other than telecom, but I could be the catalyst for all of them.

The first requirement was the staff, i.e., a secretary, someone I could rely on as a kind of 'chief of staff'. This was going to be a vast job. I had more or less created it for myself and I was ready to tackle it, but I knew I'd need someone with exceptional talents alongside me.

I found that person in Jairam Ramesh, a brilliant young man educated in India and then in the United States at Carnegie Mellon and MIT, specializing in engineering, economics, management and technology policy. Ramesh had been working as an adviser to Abid Husain at the Planning Commission, which had devised the five-year plan. Husain and I were close friends. He was a colourful man with an open mind, a generous heart and a deep understanding of government institutions. He was a strong supporter of the Technology Missions concept, and generously offered me his advisership. Ramesh personified exactly what I needed—he wasn't just broadly knowledgeable, but full of ideas, energy, enthusiasm and drive.

Next, I hand-picked the mission directors. The team comprised Gauri Ghosh, Dr Misra, Dr Shenoy, Dr Rao, Dr Randhawa, Mr Narayan, Dr Kurien, secretary of health, Jairam, Dr N. Ravi and myself.

We now had in hand an interesting organizational structure. Each of the mission directors reported to their respective ministers: the immunization director to the health minister, the literacy director to the education minister, the edible oils director to the agriculture minister, and so on. At the same time, however, their objectives were defined by the Technology Missions, and they were accountable to me as adviser. In this structure one of my jobs was to resolve conflicts. I met regularly with the various national Cabinet ministers and also with the ministers and chief ministers of each state. My approach was to make sure the ministries got appropriate credit for our accomplishments, which had a beneficial effect all around.

In each of our mission sectors, my sermon was always that technology is an entry point to bring about generational change. Bringing the right technologies to the forefront would allow for radical new approaches to fundamentally transform existing conditions.

In the realm of water, for example, perhaps our most formidable problem was that there were over 100,000 villages without adequate sources of drinking water. Water had traditionally been located in these places mainly by dowsers and water diviners using age-old methods. Instead, we called in space research experts to provide us with geohydrological mapping so we knew exactly where to drill wells. Our success at finding water sources went up exponentially. At the same time, we had to use technology and build plants to remove excess iron and fluoride from the water. We also had to build many desalination plants to get drinking water from salty seawater.

A large percentage of Indian villages had water sources, but not clean water. We identified 100,000 of these villages and set up testing laboratories in each district. We instituted standards and established treatment facilities. We had over 30,000 villages with guinea worm affecting people's health, and education, training and safe wells were needed to avoid contracting infection through feet in water.

A major challenge was posed by the Mark 4 model water-pump that was used all over India. When these pumps broke down, they often stayed broken because the villages didn't have people with the skills to fix them. Our response to this issue was to print and distribute many thousands of easy-to-understand repair manuals. We knew that when these got into the right hands, a huge number of these Mark 4s would stay operational, significantly increasing village water supplies across rural India.

We printed the manuals in each of India's fifteen languages, Gujarati, Bengali, Oriya, Malayali, and the rest. But we had a major problem with distribution. When we shipped the leaflets, we feared the state minister's office might keep 200 of the copies, the secretary might keep 100 and somebody else would keep fifty. By the time manuals finally reached the right local officials, their number was vastly diminished—only a couple of hundred out of a thousand, not nearly enough. And then we'd face logistical errors such as the Kerala officials being saddled with the Gujarati-language manuals, and the Bengali officials getting the Malayali manuals. It was all simply a mess.

The first challenge for the Mission on Immunization wasn't technological per se, it was infrastructure-, supplies- and decision-making-related. India's record of childhood immunization was abominable. A large percentage of the children had never been immunized against measles/mumps/rubella. But polio was then a much graver problem. In 1987 India had the largest number of polio patients in the world. Polio vaccines had been around for over thirty years, and we had still not been able to accomplish anything close to universal immunization. It was a national disgrace.

There was one simple bottleneck with regard to the polio issue—an ongoing conflict between those who wanted to use the Sabin oral vaccine and those who favoured the Salk injected vaccine. The two camps of physicians and medical scientists were fighting it out in public. The citizens, of course, had no idea what to think. Everyone was confused, and meanwhile parents lived in fear over their children's health.

When we understood what was going on I called a meeting of seventy of India's top immunization people. Jairam and I met with the assembled experts in Delhi. I told them, 'We have three days. We won't be leaving this place until we can tell the nation what our stand on the polio vaccine is. Are we going to go with oral vaccines, or the injected variety? But we need one voice. I'm not qualified, you are qualified. Now you have to decide.'

Dr Jacob Jones was an expert on vaccines, and he provided the necessary leadership during these difficult discussions. Everyone decided, finally, that oral immunization was preferable. The problem here was that the oral vaccine is a lower-virulence live-virus vaccine, which means it needs to be kept cold during transportation and storage. It requires what is called 'cold chain' handling, which mandates the use of cold-chain equipment. But how do you get refrigeration into every part of India? So I called a meeting of industrialists at CII (Confederation of Indian Industries). The whole logistics of the cold chain had to be worked out.

And they did work it out. It took time to get everything in place and start immunizing, but the process worked its way through until almost every Indian child had been immunized. And in 2013, twenty-five years after our intervention, India was finally declared polio-free.

The immunization intervention had other consequences as well. In 1987, when the Technology Missions were launched, India had zero polio-vaccination production capability. I wondered then: *How is it that India has the world's largest number of polio patients and perhaps the world's largest population of children with polio, and we don't produce a polio vaccine?*

No one had an answer to that, so we did the research and I went to the prime minister. I told him it would cost us up to 300 million dollars to establish proper polio-vaccine production. When he approved the initiative, we sent teams to France and the USSR to study their methods. After that we drew up plans and the government made the investment. In a few years the company that had been established under the science and technology ministry was blending and producing all of India's polio vaccine indigenously.

In fact, some of the problems addressed by the Technology Missions were as much societal as they were specifically technological—immunization, for example, and literacy. These areas often required a driving hand with strong political backing to break logjams and create new procedures. In a broad sense, creating new processes to solve problems was itself a kind of technology, at least according to my definition. In my view, 'technology' encompassed the design of new production systems as well as breakthroughs or advances in hardware. Technology is not merely a device or a gadget. It is, at its heart, a way to solve a problem, whether it involves software or hardware.

The Mission on Literacy illustrated that. New devices were helpful here. We developed and put into production a solar-powered lantern, so that people in areas without electricity would be able to read and perform all their other functions at night with ease. We designed and produced plastic blackboards that performed much better than the traditional models and didn't use up wood resources. But improving literacy was not primarily technological in that sense. Instead, it had to do with motivating people and providing training and materials—but most especially, it was about motivating people.

Vastly improved literacy (and numeracy) was crucial to India's socio-economic development. But it was also a prodigious challenge. When the Technology Missions got under way the country's literacy rate was at just about 50 per cent. Several hundred million adults were illiterate, the majority of them women.

The question was—What is the best way to attack this? Children were being taught to read in schools, but adult education depended on, first, motivating people to learn and, second, providing teachers and study materials. With such vast numbers, it was clear to me that some kind of mass mobilization was necessary, which was not something the education department was set up to do. The plan of action now included launching literacy campaigns throughout the countryside. We set up organizing committees and created a massive volunteer effort. We sent street theatre, acting, circus and music troupes into villages, endeavouring to teach whole populations about the importance of literacy in an entertaining, appealing manner. We wanted them to know what being able to read could mean for people's economic lives and well-being.

With over 2 million committed volunteers, we flooded rural India with information. We set up continuing-education programmes in hundreds of districts. We made tremendous progress. In our initial years we began cutting substantially into the illiteracy rate. In 1989, two years after we established our campaigns, the Technology Mission on Literacy was awarded UNESCO's coveted Noma Literacy Prize. After the first year we understood a good deal about how to communicate to people the importance of literacy, and also how to teach reading to adults. At that point we began exploring how to grow and sustain these efforts.

~

The Edible Oils Mission was one programme where the primary motivation was economic. India had paid 1 billion dollars for imported cooking oils over the previous five years, even though there were significant areas of arable land suited for the domestic production of oil crops—soybeans, rapeseed, mustard seed and others. But Indian farmers weren't growing them. Instead, they were planting wheat, rice and other crops that gave them higher monetary returns. This situation, characterized by unfavourable economics for farmers, was partly due to the fact that the oil industry was controlled by a small number of powerful families and by the exploitative activities of multinational oil interests.

To reverse this situation I called on Dr Verghese Kurien, a legendary figure in the Indian dairy industry. Kurien had done his graduate studies in the United States, then had returned to India and become involved, by chance, in the field of milk production. When he started out, India was importing large volumes of milk and milk powder. By the time I talked to him about the Technology Missions, he had turned the domestic dairy industry around to the point where India was exporting instead of importing milk. He had created a revolution. Under his guidance, some years later, India became the world's largest milk producer, surpassing the United States.

Kurien was known globally as the 'Father of the White Revolution'. He had created this near-miraculous turnaround by organizing farmers into large co-ops that could exert significant leverage on costs and prices, making milk production profitable for the small farmer. Kurien was a straight-talking, take-no-prisoners kind of individual, capable of running roughshod over political and industry obstruction. He simply would not sit still and watch while large interests exploited the Indian farmer. Over time he had become an ally and a good friend. When I asked if he would join in on our effort on edible oils, he agreed.

Our challenge in this sector was to create an environment where small Indian farmers would see the advantages of planting oilseed crops. That meant restructuring the marketing system and making improvements in crop technologies. Kurien brought in some of the same methods he used to revolutionize the dairy industry: cooperative production and marketing, adherence to standards, support for individual farmers and protection against unethical competition.

Kurien was head of the National Dairy Board, which was sitting on large cash reserves. When it was announced that the board was going to throw its weight behind the intervention on oil, the market panicked. Kurien, the Cabinet secretary and I would meet regularly to decide how much oil we would buy and at what price. When that was announced, the market would adjust to our figure, to the benefit of the small farmers.

By 1990, instead of importing oil, India was exporting oilcakes at the rate of 600 million dollars a year. The turnaround was all due to applying appropriate management methods, understanding and information, and giving small farmers a little bit of support. 'We move into areas where there is gross exploitation,' Kurien told one interviewer, 'and try to restructure the marketing system so that the small producer is not fleeced by middlemen or oil kings.'

When we started working on the oilseed mission, Kurien suggested that it would be a good idea to have a mission on milk as well. He had turned the dairy market around through the massive reorganization of producers, but milk production itself had plateaued. A mission on dairy could mobilize the application of technologies to improve breeding, animal health and fodder production. We could significantly enhance milk production. When we launched this mission Kurien invited me to his centre, where I met with 4000 dairy farmers. This was a man who operated on a scale that others could hardly dream of, but which was necessary if you wanted to fundamentally change Indian conditions.

So now we had six missions supported fully by the prime minister. As the missions got under way, all six mission directors—Jairam, myself and a couple of staff—started our crazy, hectic travels as a group. Jairam was my biggest asset. We went to a different state every week. The state's chief minister would be waiting. We'd meet with him and the heads of his departments to go through the missions one by one: What was happening in this state on drinking water, literacy, immunization, telecom, oils and dairy? Then we'd hold a press conference. With the chief minister sitting next to me, I'd announce where we were and what we were going to do. Going public like this meant that everyone was aware of the projects we were undertaking and of our timelines for accomplishing them. This meant operating under scrutiny, with complete transparency and accountability. It meant that the state ministers were publicly associated with these projects and, along with us, would be seen as accountable.

This was a new thing for the local governments—somebody from the prime minister's office coming in to review the situation and making press announcements. The media, of course, loved it and lapped it all up. And nobody could say no, because the prime minister was fully committed to the cause. All the chief ministers and other political bosses were very supportive of the Technology Missions and other initiatives of the Rajiv Gandhi government.

As the Technology Missions work advanced, the UN became aware of what we were doing. The concept of the missions seemed something that might be beneficial to development in other nations as well, and the UN convened a meeting on the subject in Poland. I travelled to Warsaw for this and gave a series of talks, emphasizing on technology as the entry point for widespread development. The upshot of this was a UN report recommending every developing country to consider implementing the Technology Mission concept.

However, not all of our Technology Missions work was successful. We made an important impact in our six established areas—water, immunization, oilseeds, literacy, telecommunications and dairy. But my attempts to expand the missions to include environment, housing, floods and droughts failed to get off the ground. Prime Minister Gandhi was in favour of the plans, but I found that political problems and conceptual differences among the relevant experts were too knotty to resolve easily. I was simply unable to negotiate the problems within a reasonable time frame. I didn't give up on these, but I put off pursuing them until the point where we might be able to marshal more resources.

The Missions also generated substantial political and media controversy. Of the many projects we undertook, some simply did not work out. Critics would say that they succeeded only 60 or 70 per cent of the time—which they deemed a failure and the proof of a mistaken, poorly conceived diversion of government resources.

People take great pride in identifying problems. I always say that you do not need talent to identify problems in India. All you have to do is stand on a street corner and watch the scenes for ten minutes. You will perhaps be able to identify many of the challenges facing India merely in that space. At times, even the solutions are staring

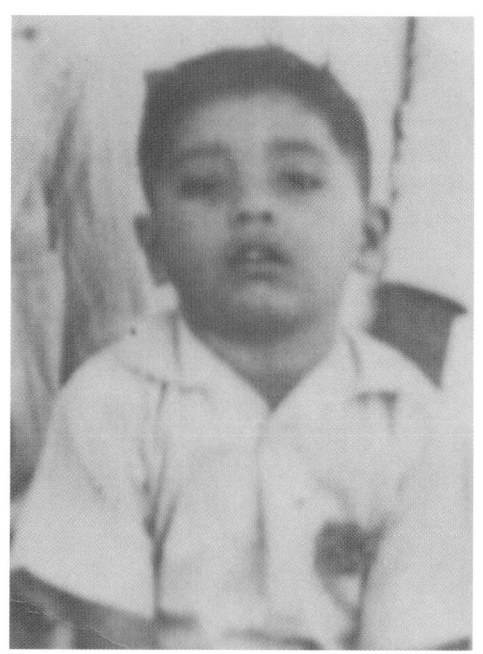

Earliest photo of Sam

Sam at the Gateway of India, leaving for the US by boat, 1964

Shanta and Gangaram, Sam's parents

Sam's first winter in Chicago, 1965   Anu at our engagement ceremony in India, 1965

Sam and Anu at their wedding in Chicago, 1966

Sam with the team at GTE, 1967

Sam and Clint Penny, 1976

Sam signing a marketing agreement with AT&T for Wescom Switching products, 1980

Salil as a baby, 1975

Rajal coming home from the hospital, 1978

Sam with Salil and Rajal at home in Chicago

Sam with the telecom minister Arjun Singh at C-DOT Bangalore, 1986

Sam with Rajiv Gandhi at a conference on the Technology Missions, 1987

The Scienctific Advisory Council to the Prime Minister Rajiv Gandhi, 1987

The National Conference on Telecom Missions, 1987

Sam with Chancellor Helmut Kohl and Mr K.R. Narayanan at a conference in Germany, 1988

PARAM by C-DAC, India's first supercomputer, 1989

Family portrait in Delhi, 1986

Technology Missions' visit by Sam, 1987

Sam visiting Titilagarh, 1992

Sam after his first quadruple bypass in Delhi, 1990

Sam and the WorldTel team, 1995

Sam with the US Secretary of State Madeleine Albright at the United Nations, 1997

Receiving the Lal Bahadur Shastri National Award from
Prime Minister A.B. Vajpayee and President K.R. Narayanan, 2000

Sam and Rahul Gandhi in Uttar Pradesh at an iftar party

Sam giving a speech at the Rajiv Gandhi Institute

Salil marries Arpita in 2007

Salil

Rajal

Barack Obama and Sam Pitroda during the former's visit to India, 2010

Sam and Prime Minister Manmohan Singh at the release of
the National Innovation Council's 'Report to the People', 2011

Sam and Narendra Modi at Vibrant Gujarat, 2011

Sam at the SIES award function, 2012

Aria at age one, 2012

Sam receiving an honorary doctorate from the University of Toronto, 2013

Sam adressing students on video, 2014

Sam as chairman of the m-Powering Development Initiative
of the International Telecommunications Union (ITU), 2014

Signing catalogues for his solo art show in Vienna, 2014

Sam speaking with guests at his solo art show in Vienna, 2014

Aria at age three, 2014

At the opening of the University of Chicago's Delhi centre, 2014

Sam with the replica of an original transistor

Our family photo

right at you, however, we lack men and women with the domain expertise, leadership, ethics and courage to address these challenges against a potentially hostile bureaucratic environment and multiple odds. People tend to shift the blame and believe that the problem lies somewhere or with somebody else, as opposed to looking within themselves to introspect and critique. At times, I found that what people think of as important is really not very important, and that what people think of as unimportant is extremely important.

During one of my trips as part of the Technology Missions, we went to a small village in Uttar Pradesh after visiting a local health facility, a school and a biogas plant. We were escorted to a big meeting organized by the head of the village, with almost 300 people in the audience. In his speech, the village leader started complaining that the village doesn't have a teacher, the doctor doesn't come regularly, electricity is not available, and on and on. When it was my turn to speak, he was basically expecting me to say that I would go back to Delhi and promptly solve all their problems. As opposed to this, I told them that these were their problems and that in a democracy one need to take charge themselves and begin to solve local problems with local resources. I told them to not await the central government's help to solve every local problem. I expect my speech was not too well-received.

I continually tried hard to explain why I thought this kind of criticism was unjustified. My job, as I saw it, was not to ensure a 100 per cent success-rate. We were in the process of building a nation, not a company that needed to maximize its productivity and returns in order to survive and stay competitive. Consequently, I wasn't overly concerned if some of our initiatives didn't work out. I could take responsibility when that happened, but ensuring success was not my goal. I was, if anything, more interested in the process than the product. My goal was to set up processes that were more effective than those currently in practice (which so often moved at a glacial pace, or all too often, not at all).

I was more affected and startled by the criticism of some of my friends, Rajni Kothari, for example. Kothari was the founder of the Centre for the Study of Developing Societies, the person I had consulted when I was first developing the idea for C-DOT. Kothari, a pre-eminent political theorist, was not happy with technologists who lacked what he thought of as cultural and philosophical depth. He also believed that working in partnership with the government was a waste of time that would, as he said in public, 'tie you [Sam] in knots from which you will find it difficult to liberate yourself'. Working in this way would be, he thought, a 'kiss of death'. It was far better, in his opinion, to work from the grass-roots up rather than from the top down.

I thought Kothari was simply mistaken. He and many other leading thinkers were, at heart, anti-government people, which is why they made their intellectual homes in the think tanks and institutes. In that regard I had separated myself from them philosophically. I felt with absolute certainty that partnering with the government was the *only* way to make any real impact on a meaningful scale in a nation the size of India.

I felt very strongly that I had found the right niche for myself. I had certain specific skills in technology, in designing systems, in certain forms of management. I was highly driven and wanted to get things done, and I had developed a thick skin and the ability to project confidence, which helped me bring people along with me on the journey. And through some luck, I had struck up a friendship with Rajiv Gandhi, which allowed me the backing and political will I needed. I also received a great deal of love, affection and support from the media and the public. People were very generous with their praise and appreciated my sincere efforts to help modernize India.

Doing all these things at once—travelling constantly around the country, meeting not just with India's own top leaders but with international personalities as well—was a head rush. I was charged up—there were so many areas where I thought I could make a dent. I knew, too, that time was going to run out at some point, which injected extra urgency into our projects. I could push this button, push that one—and every push could affect a million people, 5 million people. What a romantic thing to do, what a fulfilling thing to do—to make a difference in the fields of education, health, telecom, water and immunization for so many. I didn't know what the future might hold, but for the moment, at least, I had found the right outlet for whatever compulsions were driving me—my need to fix things, my intolerance for political and bureaucratic dysfunction, and my dreams for a more progressive, more humane India.

10

Telecom Commission

Telecom was the only Mission where I truly considered myself an expert. But the telecom sector was experiencing a roadblock despite C-DOT's success. The telecommunications department was the customer for telephone equipment, but they had a long history of buying foreign products, which meant they were enmeshed in a web of personal contacts and monetary relationships with overseas equipment-makers. As a result, they had embarked on a series of manoeuvres that were disrupting the broad-scale manufacturing, acquisition and installation of the Indian-made C-DOT products. They were delaying testing, demanding the addition of unnecessary features and otherwise doing their best to create problems. This had been a challenge with many other ministries including defence. Indigenous development was paid lip service while foreign products were preferred and purchased regularly to favour import lobbies and vested interests. Government policies were designed to encourage indigenous development but not indigenous production or purchase.

When I was unable to resolve these issues with the ministries, I went to Rajiv Gandhi with a proposal to set up a separate Telecom Commission. The commission, as I envisioned it, would include the telecommunications ministry, the finance ministry, the Planning Commission, the Cabinet Secretariat and the representatives from other relevant ministries. High-level decisions regarding telephone equipment, manufacturing and service would be made by the commission, then implemented by the telecommunications department. In this way we could carve a path through these roadblocks.

The prime minister agreed, and we organized a major national conference to help develop consensus. Over 500 people participated in the deliberations, including the prime minister, and various ministers, officers, industry leaders, labour leaders, and others. Then we started preparing the necessary documents. But as this moved forward the ministry went into defensive mode. They delayed processes. They sent the papers back for revision repeatedly. Then they sent back something different that they had purportedly drafted themselves. It was one delaying tactic after another. This went on for seven or eight months until it was crystal clear that they simply were not going to set up the Telecom Commission, whatever the prime minister's office desires.

Finally, I told Rajiv that it was pretty certain that the ministry would not allow us to form a new Telecom Commission. 'What's the solution then?' he asked.

The answer to this conundrum was that I would take on the role of the department's chief executive officer. It seemed to be the only way to move forward. Taking on that job would be a stretch. I was still adviser to C-DOT, even though I had stepped away from any involvement in the operations. I was also, of course, adviser to the prime minister on the Technology Missions. But here too I felt that the projects were well-established enough, so I could move on. As I told Rajiv, I was prepared to take on the secretary's job for two or three years. I could institute new policies, programmes and procedures, train people, and develop an executive management team to move forward.

But when the matter went to the principal secretary to the prime minister, Mr Deshmukh, so that my appointment could be processed, there was seemingly a hiccup.

'I'm sorry,' he said, 'this cannot be done.'

'What do mean "It cannot be done"?'

'There's a serious issue.'

'What's the serious issue?'

'You are already a minister of state according to your role as adviser to the prime minister on Technology Missions. This new job, secretary of the telecommunications department, is one level below. The procedure is that the same person cannot hold positions at two levels at the same time,' said Mr Deshmukh.

'That shouldn't be a problem. Just downgrade me on my adviser role,' I replied.

'I'm sorry. What do you mean?' asked Mr Deshmukh with surprise.

'All you have to do is downgrade me; I won't have a problem with that. I don't need two grades. Just downgrade me,' I said.

For me, any kind of ranking in these things was an irrelevancy and didn't serve any practical purpose. But in India's hierarchical system, holding two ranks at a time was deemed a violation. Having a lower rank might not have meant anything to me—I would be doing the same work, regardless. But it was clear that my request was an unusual one. Mr Deshmukh was bewildered and seemed unsure about what to do when faced with this situation. So he called the prime minister, and the prime minister promptly dispatched Mr Dhawan from his office to resolve the matter.

So it happened. I became secretary of the telecommunications Department and founding-chairman of the Telecom Commission. I replaced Mr Satypal, who became secretary of services at the commission. As a result, I was now able to move ahead and operationalize the commission that had previously met with such dogged opposition.

Telecommunications was a giant department, with 550,000 employees represented by twenty-seven unions. The headquarters occupied a huge multistorey office building near Parliament in New Delhi. The department had around 4 million telephone lines with various state-level telephone operating companies known as 'circles'. It was also home to the international telephone operation facet known as VSNL; wireless service; and manufacturing operations with Indian telephone industries, notably, Hindustan Teleprinters Ltd. However, the department was debilitated by a lack of planning and management discipline, complicated purchasing procedures, manual accounting and a serious shortage of equipment. The challenge was to expand production, substantially improve availability and access, and privatize production and then operations.

Most people who rise to the level of secretary have a lifetime's worth of experience in large bureaucracies. They know the landscape, they're comfortable with it. I, on the other hand, was forty-seven— younger than all the upper-level department officers. I had never in my life been part of such an organization. Now I was going to run one with four other government secretaries in the telecom department reporting directly to me with full profit-and-loss responsibilities.

That first day, a telecom department car picked me up from my home. At the department headquarters, people were lined up in front of the entrance, waiting for me with garlands of flowers. One after another they bowed, their palms together in a namaste. People expected these ceremonies—they were all normal protocol, the customary way of welcoming someone and showing respect. But it was also a reminder for me that I was entering a traditional, formalized culture—one I was going to do everything in my power to change.

Once everyone had greeted me I was escorted to my office by an impressive entourage. There I was met by a person who handed me a key. 'Sir,' he said, 'this is the key to your bathroom.'

'I'm sorry, I don't need a bathroom key.'

'Yes, this is the key to the secretary's bathroom.'

'It's all right. I don't need it. I'll use the regular bathroom.'

'No, sir, you don't have to do that.'

'Why not? I don't need the key.'

The attendant backed away, puzzled. The secretary's bathroom wasn't only private, it was clean. He knew the public bathroom was a different story. When I entered the public bathroom I realized why I had been offered a private key. Based on what I saw, I was convinced that I needed to meet with the janitors and cleaners to improve the building's basic hygiene and maintenance situation.

This was a start. I would go about things the way I did—making the same kind of demonstration I used to make back at C-DOT to dramatize that what I wanted was different from what people expected, that I was not going to be doing things the old way. Of course, at C-DOT I was building from the ground up. The telecommunications department was a colossus with its own deeply ingrained customs and procedures. This place wasn't likely to change easily, secretary or no secretary.

It wasn't just the public bathroom that wasn't clean, the entire building was dirty. I told my office, 'I want to meet with the janitors in the boardroom.'

When I walked into the boardroom there were forty janitors lined up, their backs pressing into the wall, obviously scared to death that I was going to fire them. 'Please sit down,' I said. They didn't sit down. It just wasn't the way things were done. Not only were they janitors, they were at the bottom of the economic pyramid and thus were not treated with respect.

'Please, do sit.' I gestured towards the chairs. They moved towards them tentatively and perched on the edge of their seats.

As soon as they sat the tea arrived, with cashews and biscuits. What was going on now? They thought this man was going to fire them and now they were sitting down and being served tea.

I said, 'Look, we're all spending a lot of time in this place. Can you please clean it better? I don't want to see any garbage on the floor, or have stinking bathrooms, floating papers, cobwebs, falling drapes, dusty files, broken windows or broken chairs around. I don't want to see any paint peeling off the walls. The tiles are falling. I don't want all that. Let's fix this place. This is our home.'

'I'll tell you what I want,' I continued. 'I want you to select two teams. I want to send one team to the Taj hotel and the other to the Sheraton. These are five-star hotels. Go there. See how they clean there, learn what they do. When you come back, tell me what equipment you need. We will get it for you. But I want you to keep this place clean. Tell me what complaints you have. You don't have enough supplies? It's my job to get them for you. You need something else? It's my job to procure it. This is what I want, and I need your support. I'll give you two weeks. If you don't get this place clean, I'll tell you what will happen—I'll come in every morning at eight o'clock and start cleaning myself.'

'Oh, sir,' they said. 'You cannot do that. We are here to do that.'

Their morale shot straight up. They started meeting, discussing who would go to each hotel and how they were going to improve things. The janitors were charged up.

Then I started a little nursery for the janitors and construction workers in the building. We had almost a thousand people, quite a few of them women. I talked to them. 'Whoever wants to bring their kids to work should please bring them. Whoever has toys at home, bring them too. We'll take care of the kids during the day. That's going to be our policy from here on now.'

This was a little thing to do, nothing more than a small gesture. These were poor people, their lives were a struggle. You couldn't *not* see that in their faces. And no one was paying attention to their needs. *Get them some help,* I thought. *How difficult is that?*

I wanted to send a message, a kind of a warning shot across the bows, to the department that there was going to be a shake-up and that I was going to change the way things were done. My real test would be if I could institute organizational changes and begin to rework the culture in a more egalitarian, production-oriented way. The more effectively I could communicate my vision, the better chance I'd have at execution and retooling.

I have found that, many times, in a hierarchical system of work, the people at the top do not engage in the details and articulate vision and commitment that affect the well-being of the people at the lower rungs of the organization. This is very evident at construction sites of big government or office buildings in major urban areas, where women can be seen carrying bricks on their heads. Hardly anyone provides better tools to improve the quality of life for the poor workers. Matters are even more grim for sanitation workers in India. My training in the US, especially in the high-tech field, was undertaken in flat organizational structures that required the top-level management to keep their ears to the ground and listen to the voices of the people at the bottom. To me, this was a Gandhian approach to management.

These relatively minor demonstrations with the janitors made an impact. Word spread, not just to people in the building but through the whole organization. As secretary, my official car was a bulletproof model, earlier assigned to minister Arjun Singh, very heavy, with doors that took some strength to open. Every time I was picked up or dropped off, my driver, Mugliram, would run around to open the door for me, which wasn't necessary and was another of those gestures of deference (and perhaps even subservience) that I found irritating. 'Mugliram,' I said, 'don't do that. The day I lose my hand you can open the door for me. Otherwise you don't have to.'

When I said that, Mugliram had tears welling up in his eyes. 'Sir, why do you say such things to me?'

'No, you sit there. I can open my own door.'

The message went everywhere.

Meanwhile, I was moving ahead with my reorganization plans. My overall objective was to break the department free of its inertia and shift the focus of the entire unwieldy establishment to upgrading telephone service in the country. That meant changing mindsets. It meant creating a goal-oriented culture in place of the frozen-in-time bureaucratic mentality that characterized the department. I was intent on converting the country's telecom entirely into the digital mode, computerizing services and upgrading maintenance and response efforts to users' complaints while privatizing elements of the data and telephone industries, along with a dozen other priorities. I knew all of this would be hard to achieve in the three-year timeline I had set for myself, but my intention was to get things off to a strong start.

I'm not sure how many shared my optimism in 1988; the telecommunications department wasn't going to change easily. There was a great deal of cynical talk surrounding my appointment and the enthusiasm I showed with my direct reports and with the telecom officers. They were brilliant engineers, but were bogged down by old procedures, paper-pushing and a file culture that was designed to block as opposed to initiate change. I had been told that of all the barriers, the most formidable was going to be the labour unions. 'The unions,' I heard, 'are going to eat you alive.'

Of the twenty-seven union leaders who represented department employees, the senior person was one Mr Choudhary, a weathered, old organizer, given to play hardball. 'He's very hard to deal with,' I was told. 'You have to be careful, he's always armed.'

This was a person, a tough nut to crack who, along with the other labour leaders, I could see taking an unfavourable view of my efforts. And I knew they were in a belligerent mood already. By then word had spread that the new secretary was from America. The grapevine was buzzing that I was all for private enterprise, that I was going to break up telecom, that that was the whole reason the prime minister had put me there in the first place. According to the buzz, my entire intention, apparently, was to bring in private ownership and finish off the unions.

I knew that was what they had been hearing. But it wasn't true— not all of it, at least. I wasn't naive enough to believe I could break the unions, even if that had been my intention—which it wasn't. I had no choice but to work with them; I wouldn't be able to get anything done otherwise. Going head-to-head with Mr Choudhary and his friends couldn't possibly advance my agenda. In some way I had to make them my partners.

But instead of an alliance there was a battle shaping up. As soon as I took over as secretary I held a press conference and announced my goals for the department. India now had 4 million phones, double the number we had when I started C-DOT, but still abysmally small. 'We have 4 million now,' I said. 'By the year 2000 I want that number to be 40 million.' (This was in 1988, before the advent of cell phones.) The unions had taken those numbers and made their own calculations. If we had 500,000 employees for 4 million phones, for 40 million phones we'd need ten times that number—5 million workers, i.e., 4.5 million more union members. Their whole attention was on hiring and membership. My whole intention was to cut the number of department employees in half to meet global standards and reduce costs.

The big question was how to do that without inflaming Mr Choudhary and the others to boiling point.

My first meeting with the unions was a highly organized, ritualistic kind of affair. The union leaders took their places on one side of the table, and the other department executives and I sat on the other side. As we started talking, I found that I couldn't understand a word anyone was saying. It was all acronyms: TaDa, CB, JTO, DOTO. *The JTO is this, the CB is that. We won't move an inch off the TaDa.* I sat there thinking, *What are they talking about?* I didn't have the foggiest idea.

Superannuation will take place after thirteen years of promotion from level X to level Y, except for those who are at level Z. What did that mean? And they all had big files with them, everyone except me. At the same time, I was the boss. I couldn't look like a complete idiot. It hadn't been my intention to make this a working session. At this point I just wanted to meet them and initiate some personal rapport instead of dragging on the animosity that seemed to underline our interactions.

Finally, I told them, 'I'm not prepared to discuss contract details now. I haven't been here long enough to completely educate myself on all the issues. I suggest that our next step will be for me to meet with the three senior leaders, Mr Choudhary [the gunman and a strong leader], Mr Gupta [the communist and a great nationalist] and Mr Venkat. Why don't we schedule that? We can meet in my office.'

I might not have known what the TaDa or the JTO were, but I did know that no telecom secretary had invited union leaders into his offices as regularly as I did. It was part of the unspoken protocol governing relations between the two sides. But we set the meeting, and Mr Choudhary, Mr Gupta and Mr Venkat came by.

I understood what kind of preconceived idea they had of me—I was an American businessman who had made a lot of money and was against unions. So the first thing I wanted to do was put those notions to rest. They sat down. I ordered tea. I said, 'Look, I want to work closely with you. Without you, I can't do my job. People matter to me. I want to suggest a few things. I have two simple ideas to start with. Then you give me your ideas and we'll work together. My first idea is that since we'll need to be in close, regular contact, I'd like to set up an office for you here, right next to my office.'

They looked at me, incredulous. 'Are you serious?' Mr Choudhary said.

'Yes, absolutely. We have space. I'll get you an office. Second, all union activity concerns department affairs. Since that's the case, the labour leaders around the country should be allowed to make calls for free.'

'What?' said Mr Gupta.

'Yes. They're my employees, isn't that correct? I'm not talking about personal calls, I'm talking about labour business. I'm not doing it for you, I'm doing it for the department, to make it easier for me.'

We talked. I had thrown them off their guard with my ideas for the office space and the free business phone-calls. They were trying hard to scope me out and weren't sure they could. These weren't people who were particularly susceptible to charm.

'Listen,' I said, 'if we're going to be working together, it's important that we get to know each other a little. Why don't you come to my house for dinner? My mother is there. [She had come to live with us in Delhi four years earlier after my father had passed away from cancer in Chicago.] She'll be happy to meet you.'

That made an impression on them. These three were all older than me. In terms of Indian family culture, it meant something for my mother to host them. They agreed to dinner at my home.

In an organization like the telecommunications department, people talked. And the chatter that now abounded was that the secretary was trying to befriend the union leaders in order to trap them. That I had an agenda and that I was going to brainwash them. That I was educated and smart, and they were naive working people. I had given them tea and biscuits, and now they were going to my home for dinner. It was a perilous situation.

The union leaders came home. Anu and my mother greeted them, both of them traditional women. I might come across at first as some kind of overseas sophisticate (despite the fact that I was from Titilagarh), but Anu and my mother did not give off that aura. My mother was every inch a village woman. And in spite of Anu's years in the US, she had retained her traditional approach to life and her love for the old ways was also intact. They hit it off with Anu and my mother right from the start.

Mr Choudhary, for some reason, especially clicked with my mom. They talked about all things village, about jaggery and the different varieties of rice. 'In my region,' he said, 'we make great jaggery. We grow rice. Next week I'm going to my village. I'll bring some for you.'

And the next week he *did* bring it for her—ghee and rice and jaggery. They became friends, Mr Choudhary, my mother and Anu. Now the whole attitude was changing. Now, I was apparently a decent guy, despite being the boss. That I might think differently about some issues, but at heart I meant well.

When we did sit down to talk business, it was on friendly terms.

'Friends,' I said, 'I need your help. We cannot have such an excessive number of people in telecom. We have to cut down. I don't mean firing people; I don't want anybody to lose their jobs. But I'm not going to be able to hire additional people either. So let's agree on that first.

'Second, I want to make certain that those who have been with the department for a certain number of years will get promotions. The first promotion will come after sixteen years, the second after twenty-six years—regardless of their classification levels or the jobs they are performing.

'Third, I want to retrain people to elevate their skill levels. I want to start an institution for retraining telecom workers.'

What had happened was that if, for example, cable lines had to be laid and ditches dug, the department would hire labourers to do the digging. But because of union rules those people became permanent employees. Once the job was done, they remained employees, even though there was no further work for them. We had employees all over the country collecting pay but not doing enough.

'We're going to put those people to work,' I said. 'We're going to upgrade their skills. Whoever is with us will stay with us. But no more hiring.'

Since the labour bosses weren't dead set against this proposition, I worked out a plan and went to the Cabinet secretary. Then the labour ministry and the law ministry came into the picture. I told the Cabinet secretary, Mr T.N. Seshan, 'This is what I want to do. I don't know all the issues here, you do. Tell me how I need to get it done. Protect me from the legal issues and the inter-agency fights and all that. Please figure it out.'

Mr Seshan was brilliant, sensitive, supportive and willing to go the extra mile. He said, 'Okay, let's do this together. Let's meet with labour together.'

So he called a meeting with labour. He spoke their language—the JTO, the CB, the DOTO. It took eighteen months, but in the end we negotiated an agreement.

~

As of 2015, the telecommunications department has about 200,000 employees instead of the earlier figure of 500,000. This has happened only through attrition and retirement. We had so many people that every year over 15,000 reached retirement age. So we waited and, in ten years, the number of employees reduced by itself to a reasonable figure.

In perspective, that time frame was not a huge deal. You couldn't just get rid of people. Where would they go? It wasn't as if there were other jobs out there waiting for them. This was their livelihood. This was how they fed their families. At the end of the day, they were a part of my telecom family.

After my experience with the labourers and janitors unions, I felt that, if anything, the engineers, bureaucrats and office workers were harder to deal with.

I met with them. 'The system we have is ad hoc,' I said. 'We need to introduce some discipline in terms of strategic planning and annual operating plans.'

That was unheard of in telecom. The telecom department itself was a national entity. Then there were entities in the states and in the big cities. There were different telephone companies in these places. There was a need for greater coordination, cooperation and communication on matters of allocation of resources, plans and priorities.

I said, 'I want a three-year national strategic plan and a one-year operating plan from the bottom up. I want to know how many lines you are projecting for the next three years. Based on that we'll decide how much hardware you'll need, how much manpower you'll need, how much money will be allocated and who will produce the hardware.'

I instituted a planning process to put development and administration on track, with equipment availability and funding. But this turned out to be a painful exercise. Nobody wanted to do it. This step was going to bring about transparency, accountability and visibility. They understood that a rational planning system, with formal projections and a transparent budgeting process, would expose everyone to scrutiny and accountability—a new and deeply unpleasant prospect.

Finally, a few of the younger executives led by Dr Seth supported the endeavour and took charge of the planning process. That was progress. But the complexity of the problems and issues was immense, especially with respect to finance, purchasing, material management, human resources and planning. There were unions and sub-unions for wireless and telegraph as well as for telephones, each with its own requirements and customary practices and issues and personal demands.

It was all too easy to get irretrievably pulled down into all this. So I kept the focus on planning—improving processes, overall management, moral and vision, and introducing a modicum of discipline. I held regular meetings, I gave presentations. I was trying to change an organizational culture that was deeply rooted in a system based on perks, privilege, patronage, personalities, files and antique procedures, more than a few of them left over from the 19th-century British Raj. I travelled around the country to meet employees, view presentations, hold conferences; I even made a series of video presentations to communicate my vision and reach out to others across the country.

The system of files and filing was an exceptional horror. Every small and big thing needed to be approved by someone's superior, and then by the superior's superior. This was called 'clearing files'. After about three weeks on the job I got a call from the prime minister's office. 'We are getting complaints that the chairman [Sam] is not clearing any files.' The fact was that I was indeed *not* clearing files. Piles of them were accumulating in my secretary's office.

I said, 'Look, I'm not here just to clear files. If someone wants a decision made, they have to come and talk to me. I'll make the decision. But someone else has to do the file work.'

They did come. At one point the managing director of Indian Telephone Industries Ltd came by, a big manufacturing operation with several thousand employees. His factory was in Bangalore, but he made an appointment and came to see me in Delhi. We spent half an hour together. We talked, we had coffee, he told me how his business was going. The next day he came again. Then he came the third day. Finally, I asked him, 'Why are you here in Delhi for three days? You're supposed to be in Bangalore running your plant.'

He said, 'Sir, you're supposed to clear my file so I can go to Paris.'

'All right. Why in the world didn't you tell me that the first day itself?'

'Well, I thought maybe you had some objections that you wanted to talk to me about. But you didn't ask me anything.'

'I didn't even know.'

'The file has been in your office for the last two weeks.'

'Nobody told me. I didn't know. But first of all, why should you need permission from me to go to Paris? You're running a multimillion-dollar operation. You're chairman of Indian Telephone Industries.'

'I don't know,' he said. 'That's the way the system is. I need your permission.'

'Okay, I'm giving you blanket permission. Whenever you want to travel, you can. It's your problem, not mine.'

'Sir, that will not be acceptable to my finance person.'

This sort of thing happened with nerve-racking regularity. So I tried to simplify things for people. Then I realized that we had file after file after file—for everything. In our building, in the heart of the city, we had two big floors stuffed with files. Covered with dust. Nobody was going to look at them, nobody was going to open them.

I said to the file keepers, 'Why don't you move these files 50 miles away from Delhi? Clear up the space. This is prime office space in the middle of town. Why do we have files here? If you need a file, send somebody to bring it. No one ever uses them anyway. They're collecting dust. Keep last year's files and send the rest.'

'Oh, sir, we can't do that.'

'Why not?'

'We need these files available at all times.'

'Why?'

'When you review somebody, you need that person's file and records starting from the day he joined.'

This was unthinkable. It just didn't make sense. Several of the employees had been working for the department for years, many for decades. And whenever a review or some incident came up, someone reviewed their file going back to the day he or she was hired.

The file-clearing system was hardly the only problem. Ever since I became the chairman of the department, a variety of national and international business leaders started visiting my office with flowers, small gifts and dinner invitations. I was very strict about accepting anything except flowers. One international company even had the audacity to offer me half-a-million dollars in cash to clear a file to purchase their equipment. I was furious, but I retained my courteousness and said no. I knew about the bribe-and-corruption culture in the country, but I knew I couldn't do much, except to dissociate myself from it completely.

The fact was that a few of the department officers carried on a side business in phone applications. They took 10,000 or 15,000 rupees. Sometimes, they charged a monthly fee, maybe 100 rupees, maybe 400. You could pay a bribe for your phone connection over time, in instalments. I knew what was going on, but I kept my eyes averted. Getting involved in all of that would open a Pandora's box of problems. An anti-corruption campaign would inevitably lead down the road to political people, business people, whole swathes of administrators in national, state and local offices. Just contemplating the possibilities was nightmarish. This wasn't the time to combat the menace. I had other more important things to do.

But every once in a while, I'd get sucked into approving somebody's telephone connection myself. Once, a group of swamis came to my office, unannounced. They just showed up. My secretary buzzed me and said, 'There are swamis here to see you.'

'I don't need to see swamis in my office,' I said. 'Somebody will take a picture and put it in the paper: "Pitroda is seeing swamis in his office".'

'But sir, they've been looking for an appointment for a couple of weeks.'

I hadn't known this. My secretary had been putting them off.

'All right. They're here already? Send them in.'

Five swamis entered the room. The first thing the main swami said was, 'Your eyes are very bright. You have good confidence and energy and knowledge.'

I knew he needed something from me.

'Thank you. What can I do for you?'

'Nothing.'

'Please, you must have come here for something. What is it that you need?'

'No, no. We just came to see you. We heard about you, we wanted to meet you.'

'Would you like something to drink?'

'Yes, thank you. We'll take something cold.'

I asked my secretary to bring in some cold refreshments.

We were sitting there drinking our drinks. He started again. 'We heard about you. You are a great man. You are bringing about many wonderful changes. You are a blessing.'

I thought, *They must want something* really *big.*

Finally, I said, 'I'm sorry. I have another meeting. I'm going to have to leave.'

'No, wait,' said the main swami. He nodded to another swami, who opened a moth-eaten briefcase and pulled out two telephone applications.

They were here to get their applications approved.

I said, 'Swami, you could have called my office. This is for a temple, yes? It's for the public good. Normally, I don't do this, but for a temple I would have done it immediately.' I signed the applications.

The swamis were a minor inconvenience. It was worse when I was flying somewhere, business class, and four or five people would be waiting in the aisle to see me, telephone applications in hand. They had found out where I was going and had booked themselves on my flight for the sole purpose of pleading for a phone connection.

Once, while I was busy in my office, a gentleman walked in and said, 'Sir, I am Milkha Singh.'

I stood up immediately, saying, 'THE Milkha Singh? The high-speed runner that we all admired growing up?'

He said, 'Yes, sir.'

'What brings you here?' I said.

'I am sorry, sir, but I have been looking for a telephone connection for several years and have not been able to get one. I can't pay a bribe, but I need a telephone. I was told that you may give me a sympathetic hearing, and that is why I am here.'

He was so humble, simple and sensible that I felt my eyes moisten as I looked at him. I said to myself, *What kind of a country are we that we cannot provide even a mere telephone to our national hero?* I immediately called member services in the Telecom Commission and requested a telephone connection be obtained for Milkha Singh within the next forty-eight hours.

The phone-connection problem eventually solved itself with the advent of cell phones. But even there I ran into controversy.

When cell-phone technology first made its appearance in India, I blocked it from proceeding. People didn't understand. With landline connections making relatively slow progress, why in the world would I not allow mobile phones? Newspapers and even serious journals wrote articles questioning my judgement and, sometimes, even my sanity.

My refusal to approve mobile technology even ruffled feathers back in the US—that I would rather not have ruffled. Motorola was an early leader in cell phones. Based in Chicago as they were, I knew them well. I was good friends with the owner Bob Galvin and knew his family too. Galvin served as an IIT director when I was a student there. Later, I joined him on the board of IIT. Motorola had helped when I brought C-DOT engineers over to learn from them, and the family had been kind to me in other ways as well.

Now that I was chairman of the Telecom Commission, Motorola wanted to sell mobile phones to India. They had hired former Illinois senator Charles Percy to promote their business, and Percy made an appointment to come and see me. Percy was a powerhouse. He had been CEO of Bell & Howell, and then a US senator for eighteen years. I knew him, of course—everyone in Illinois did. But I didn't connect him with Motorola, so all I knew was that some representative of the company was on my schedule. I was late for our meeting, and when I arrived it was a bit of a shock to see Senator Percy sitting in the lobby waiting for me.

'Senator Percy, you've been sitting here?'

'Yes,' he said. 'I have an appointment with you.'

When it turned out that his wife was with him, I invited them to our house for dinner, which was lovely until he got down to business. 'Motorola,' Percy said, 'could help with India's telecom problems.' He said we should be embracing cell technology and we should be using Motorola handsets.

'I can't do that,' I said. 'I appreciate Motorola, and I don't have to tell you how much I respect you. But I just can't do it.'

Senator Percy didn't like that. Given his background and stature, he thought he'd be able to convince me quickly, that it was more or less a done deal. But I had good reasons, and I wasn't going to change my mind.

The fact was that early mobile-phone technology—Motorola's and others'—was analogue-based. But new standards for digital transmission were being developed. If we went with analogue standards we would be buying into old technology, which we would then have to switch over from. *Much better,* I thought, *to wait a year or two and do it right.* Besides, early mobile phones were so expensive that if we allowed them, only politicians and rich people would have them. They would not even begin to meet the needs of the poor. So I decided to delay the transition—until the new GSM standards were declared we were going to concentrate on rural telecom.

One of my early decisions at the Telecom Commission was to cancel a pending World Bank loan for around 300 million dollars, which was on the Indian government's priority list. The prime minister's office was surprised at my decision and asked for an explanation. Finally, the matter escalated to the point where Mr Barber Benjamin Conable Jr, president of the World Bank, visited India, and we had lunch together with the prime minister. He wanted me to change my mind. In response, I was very firm and said, 'Your loan has too many conditions and you want us to buy something we don't need at this stage. We need to buy components to increase our domestic production and you want us to buy big switching systems from multinationals.' Prime Minister Rajiv Gandhi understood and supported me.

Similarly, there was a proposal to import a large amount of optical-fibre cable from abroad. As opposed to importing forever, I wanted to set up India's first manufacturing facility for optical fibre. Everyone was against the idea and felt India was not capable of producing this locally. I hired a young engineer, Mr Bhagwan D. Khurana, from Punjab Wireless, to lead the project. He was sent abroad to understand the technology, make licensing arrangements, and was thus equipped to launch indigenous production. Today, India has multiple factories producing optical fibre, and we have over a million kilometres in place. In fact, we plan to add another half-a-million kilometres of fibre by 2017 to reach the 250,000 panchayats in rural areas.

~

My tenure at the telecommunications department caused headaches I hadn't anticipated. But at the same time I found myself involved in interesting projects, some of which had profound consequences for India's economy. GE chairman Jack Welch's visit to India was one such instance.

Welch was already a living legend when he came to India in 1989 intending to sell GE products like airplane engines and turbines. He tried to set up a meeting with Rajiv Gandhi, but their schedules didn't match and Rajiv wasn't able to see him. He asked me instead to meet with Welch at his place.

I arranged a breakfast meeting in a private dining room at the Taj Mahal hotel. I had my colleague Jairam Ramesh with me, along with Montek Singh Ahluwalia and Jay Choubey from the prime minister's office. Welch would be bringing six or seven of his executives along. I was a little wary of the cost of this get-together. The Taj was going to charge 8000–9000 rupees, which I thought would not look good on the prime minister's account books. Rajiv was always under close scrutiny, and a fancy meal with foreigners at a five-star hotel, for official purposes, had the potential to generate negative publicity. To preclude this I called one of my public-sector CEO friends and told him, 'Look, you're going to get a bill for a Taj breakfast. Please, just pay it. Don't even ask.'

Welch and his team arrived at eight and we were assembled to meet him. After the pleasantries and coffee we got down to business. Welch knew we were aware of what he wanted, so he asked, 'Sam, what do you propose?'

My answer surprised him. 'Jack, I want to sell you software.'

'I'm not buying software,' he said. 'I want to sell you engines, that's what we are here for.'

'Jack, I'm not buying engines.'

'Strange,' he said. He had come all the way to India, expecting a very different conversation. 'Then what do we do?'

'I guess we have nothing to do,' I said. 'Let's have breakfast.'

There was dead silence. The GE guys just sat there, perplexed. I could feel the waves of discomfort washing over my guys. They felt awkward. I was locking horns with Jack Welch, CEO of General Electric. This wasn't the way to start a conversation. There wasn't any need for confrontation.

After a long silence, Welch broke the spell. 'Okay,' he said, 'tell me what you want to tell me about software.'

I had prepared a 35mm-slide presentation. *India*, the title read, *Country of Snake Charmers, Sadhus and Software*. The slides rolled on. *People think of India as a land of mysticism. But we also make software.* A slide showed a priest praying in front of a computer. *We have a young population with advanced education and great ability. We have a large number of software engineers. GE can benefit from our software talent. India can develop software for GE.*

Welch watched. He listened carefully. 'What, specifically, do you want?' he said.

'Given a choice,' I said, 'I would want a 10-million-dollar software order from you.'

'I'll tell you what,' he said. 'I'll send you eleven top people from my company; you convince them first. I'll send them here in thirty days.'

Thirty days later eleven GE executives appeared in Delhi from their plastics, consumer goods, appliances and other divisions. Our job now was to show them around and give them a sense of our software capability. We had several government-sponsored organizations with software people, including C-DOT, the Centre for the Development of Advanced Computing (C-DAC, our supercomputer operation) and a national informatics centre. But in the private sector there wasn't much, and the GE executives would want to assess our consulting potential.

The truth was that the Indian software-consulting industry was just being born. Tata Consulting had a few people, Infosys had five, Wipro eight or ten. When I called to set up meetings, Infosys called back to say, 'Sam, you've set up this meeting with GE, but we don't even have an office.'

'Don't mention that,' I told them. 'Arrange the meeting at one of the five-star hotels. Say that you will be there anyway for some other meetings. You might as well meet them there.'

While we didn't have the proper organizational infrastructure back then, we definitely had better software engineering talent in India. What I wanted to do was show GE the quality of our people.

It so turned out that the GE executives were very pleased with the visit. At its conclusion, they announced that they would be giving us the 10-million-dollar order.

Today, these software companies have gone global. Together, they have over half-a-million employees and a market cap in the area of hundreds of billions of dollars.

As soon as GE placed their order, I put in a call to IBM to also explore a relationship with them to develop software in India. Before long, things snowballed. At one point, Texas Instruments (TI) came to us with a plan to launch their own software facility in Bangalore. But to do that they needed a satellite link to connect to their Texas facility. I agreed. I had a hard time getting the proposal through, though. 'You want what?' people said. 'You want to give a satellite link to a foreign company?' Getting the relevant approvals and permits took a lot of pushing, but we persevered and in the end TI had a satellite link running between Dallas and Bangalore to help develop their software using Indian talent.

We had the talent to begin with. And after GE we had customers interested in using the talent too. We just had to put the deals together and build some confidence. Most importantly, the government had to be willing to help, willing to bend a little, to compromise and facilitate. Small companies wouldn't be able to talk to GE. But as the government representative, I could. That was our job.

All those years ago, we started with nothing. Now, in 2015, Indian software services bring in about 150 billion dollars every year, year after year. At the end of the day it's a credit to Indian software talent and Indian entrepreneurs that we have been able to build this.

~

As a part of the Rajiv Gandhi government, I was privileged to meet a large number of global leaders and interact with them at official dinners, meetings and social events. The list included people like Mikhail Gorbachev, President of the Soviet Union, Chancellor Helmut Kohl of Germany, President François Mitterrand of France, Prince Aga Khan, the prime minister of Italy, the President of Vietnam, and many others. State dinners at the Indian President's home and at the Hyderabad House in Delhi were special events to interact with not only political leaders but leading global businessmen and intellectuals as well. I also had an opportunity to meet and interact with many distinguished Indian persons like Mother Teresa, Amartya Sen, Jyoti Basu, N.T. Rama Rao, Atal Bihari Vajpayee, L.K. Advani, and so on.

One morning I received a call from Prime Minister Rajiv Gandhi saying that he wanted me to meet with the President of Vietnam while he was visiting Delhi. So that same afternoon, I spent an hour with him, discussing telecom, technology missions and the software industry in India. After carefully listening through a translator, he told me that he would like to send General Vo Nguyen Giap to spend some time with me in Delhi. While studying in America during the Vietnam War, I had heard of the formidable general many times; he was one of those rare few who had fought against the Americans and the French in Vietnam. He was the most prominent military commander besides Ho Chi Minh during the Vietnam War, and led and managed operations until the war ended. He died in October 2013 at the age of 102.

In Delhi, he and I spent a full day at C-DOT talking about our indigenous design and manufacturing efforts, the role of information technology, and the technology benefits available to the people at the bottom of the economic pyramid. He listened carefully, took notes, asked questions, and was keen to learn from the Indian experience. After his visit, C-DOT started exporting rural exchanges to Vietnam to improve their village-to-village communication.

Then, strangely enough, one day I received a call saying that saying Mr J.R.D. Tata, Mr Godrej and Mr Bharat Ram, the leaders of the Indian industries, wanted to come by and have tea with me. I was not mature enough to understand and appreciate the importance of their visit. The trio came and spent an hour with me, talking about population control, liberalization, privatization, education, health, employment, and other important national issues. I was intrigued by their focus on nation-building, the public good and social concerns, especially due to the conspicuous absence of any conversation on business opportunities. These people were the true visionaries and business leaders who had been directly impacted by the Independence movement. Their concern for the country was loud and clear in every conversation I had with them. Later, I learned that they visited me to simply encourage me to continue doing public good. I wish I had videotaped some of our conversations, now that I understand the importance of their generous gift to me.

～

Another high-tech project evolved even before Jack Welch came to visit. We had been negotiating with the Reagan administration for a Cray supercomputer, which we needed for weather forecasting, agriculture development and, more generally, for number-crunching. We had been told that our request was being looked at favourably, and we had every expectation that the deal would go through.

I happened to be with Rajiv Gandhi one day when a call came in from Washington. When Rajiv got off the line he looked concerned. It was Reagan, who had told him that the approval for the Cray purchase was being denied; the Americans were afraid that we would use the technology to develop a nuclear weapon on our own.

'I don't think that's a problem,' I told Rajiv. 'We can build our own supercomputer.'

'What do you mean? How much would something like that cost?'

'We have the ability to do it ourselves. Off the cuff,' I said, 'I'd estimate a cost of about 30 million dollars—about as much as what we'd be paying for the Cray. I think we could get it done in three years at the most.'

When Rajiv agreed, we took the project up with the Scientific Advisory Council and established the Centre for the Development of

Advanced Computing, or C-DAC, in 1988. As with C-DOT, we made it a point to hire young engineers. We worked on parallel processing, and ultimately developed India's first supercomputer, the PARAM. By 1990, we had produced a prototype, which we demonstrated at that year's Zurich Supercomputer Show. Our machine placed second after the United States. Vijay Bhatkar, a leading computer scientist, was our original CEO, and I served for a while as the chairman of the C-DAC board. Today, the centre has over a thousand engineers and is a leader in several fields of supercomputing.

The Soviets collaborated with us for the initial development of PARAM. The fact was that India and the USSR had enjoyed a long relationship, encompassing deep scientific and technological ties. From its birth, India has been a democracy, but Jawaharlal Nehru had admired the centralized economic system of the Soviets and had nurtured ties between the two nations that were still alive and well.

One manifestation of these ongoing ties was that back in 1987, Rajiv Gandhi and Mikhail Gorbachev had agreed to hold science and cultural festivals in India and the USSR. Rajiv was eager to put on the best show possible to showcase India's achievements, and the government had allocated funds to put on a large, wide-ranging science-and-technology exhibit as a part of the 'Festival of India' scheduled to be held in Moscow, Leningrad and Tashkent.

The problem was that the ministries involved told Rajiv that it wasn't feasible to mount the science exhibition on the schedule he and the Soviets had agreed on. They said it was impossible, that there just wasn't enough time for it.

This resulted in Rajiv asking me to do it. He was as frustrated with the country's bureaucracy as I was, and he found in me someone he could use to cut through the red tape and foot-dragging. He asked and I said yes.

The science-and-technology exhibition was going to be huge— the Soviets had allotted about 200,000 square feet for us, which meant we had to fill all that up. The first thing I did was call Air India to book two 747s. Then I worked backwards. Along with Gulshan Kharbanda, a museum technology expert, I designed layouts for the space. Then I called a meeting with the heads of the various science and cultural departments and industries. 'The PM said this has to be done,' I told them, 'so we have to do it well and on time.' I described the overall scheme and the space allocations for each category. 'Aeronautics and space industries, you have 4000 square feet; leather crafts, you have 2000. Drug industry—I want a capsule that people can walk through and be shown the Indian drug industry. The capsule should be 8 feet high and 20 feet long. Technology, I want two robots. As visitors enter they will be able to walk between the robots—a female robot in a sari, and a male one in maharaja clothes, saying: "Welcome, welcome." Delegate this to some institute, they'll design the robots and put Indian dresses on them. Visitors walking in should see a big slide-show—India, a land of deserts and mountains and tigers. Water, dancing, music, a ten-minute show, 150 slides. Everyone has ninety days to produce their exhibits and booths. You don't have to worry about transportation or anything other than designing and producing your part of the exhibition. You just have to get it done in time.'

The Festival of India and the science-and-technology exhibition were a great success. The skills, creativity and talent it displayed were striking. As I saw it, the effort it took to design and create the exhibits was equally exceptional. My role in that effort was simple. The only thing I had to do was lay out the requirements and provide people with the necessary motivation and direction. After that, they were on their own. Once they knew what to do, they did it superbly.

Everywhere you looked, India had a wealth of talented people. All that was needed to propel the country into the highest rank of nations, at least in my opinion, was a modern approach to organization and management. That, and a mindset focused on goals to be achieved rather than on the sterile demands of status and hierarchy.

The festival came at a time when the practices of glasnost and perestroika were the watchwords of Gorbachev's efforts to restructure and open up the USSR. To me, that meant an opportunity to create partnerships that would give India a significantly larger scientific, technological and commercial role in the USSR's development. I told Rajiv that I'd like some private time with Gorbachev during his upcoming visit. I wanted to present some ideas to him along those lines. Rajiv didn't think that would be a problem. 'I'll arrange it,' he said.

Shortly afterwards he called. 'Sam, it turns out you can't meet with him after all. It's a matter of protocol. My meetings with him are devised as purely one-to-one. There's just no opening for him to meet separately with one of my advisers. I'm sorry, you must be disappointed,' he said.

I *was* disappointed, but I knew Gorbachev and his wife were coming to Rajiv's house for a family dinner.

'You could just say after dinner,' I said, 'when you're going to have coffee, that you happen to have Sam Pitroda and a couple of other friends here, and that you'd like him to meet them. Something like that. Don't tell the foreign officer, protocol guys or anybody else anything.'

That appealed to Gandhi. 'Good idea,' he said, 'let's do it.'

That evening while the Gandhis and Gorbachevs were having dinner, I was in another room setting up a slide presentation with Jairam Ramesh and Dr Ashok Ganguly (then chairman of Hindustan Lever) and Dr V.S. Arunachalam (then chief of the Defence Research and Development Organization).

At ten o'clock Rajiv ushered everyone into the room and introduced us. We had a few minutes of casual talk. Rajiv's children, Rahul and Priyanka, were also present. Gorbachev picked up a cardamom pod from a little bowl, and Rajiv started telling him about cardamom. But as soon as I could, I turned the discussion to IT, telling Gorbachev that I believed that perestroika and glasnost, in essence, were about information technology. That might have sounded a bit presumptuous. Rajiv passed me a little note. 'Remember, you're talking to the President of the Soviet Union.'

I read the note, tucked it in my pocket and went into my presentation. The idea was to tell Gorbachev that if he really wanted to take advantage of the Indian relationship, India and the USSR should do some joint roll-outs together. 'We can help you develop IT,' I said. 'We're good at it. We can also provide you with consumer goods, pharmaceuticals, computers, etc.'

Dr Ashok Ganguly talked about what we had to offer in consumer goods. Then Dr Arunachalam told Gorbachev about India's research on hypersonic aircrafts, suggesting how a collaboration on that project could benefit both countries.

We spent an hour with him, and when we were finished, Gorbachev asked, 'What, specifically, would you like to see happen?'

'I would like you to send a team of experts to Delhi,' I said, 'to have further dialogue with us on all these issues.'

'Done,' said Gorbachev. And, sure enough, a month later a group of Soviet scientists and government officers arrived in Delhi—people from different sectors of Soviet civilian and military life. We connected them with people in the right fields and places, and suggested a couple of new programmes.

The Soviet Union, as we all know, was a place where consumer goods had always been in short supply. 'America has big retail stores like Kmart,' I told Gorbachev. 'You have huge consumer needs. We would like to develop Kmart-type outlets in the Soviet Union— I-Marts, which would stock all kinds of Indian consumer goods, like soaps, pharmaceuticals, leather goods, paper products, fashion accessories, and so on. We can build twenty stores. It would be good for Indian manufacturers and good for your citizens too.'

Everybody liked the idea. But Gorbachev said, 'We don't think we have enough management skill to run that kind of operation.'

That wasn't a difficult problem to solve. We could organize a conference. I could send them the best management experts from the US to teach them all they knew—professors and CEOs of Indian origin. When the Soviets agreed to this, I called my friend Dr C.K. Prahalad, a professor of management at the University of Michigan, and he and four other business-school professors of Indian origin went to a conference we set up in Riga (now in Latvia). They gave presentations and seminars on the basic aspects of modern management techniques.

After that I started travelling to the Soviet Union every three months to meet with Soviet scientists and engineers. Among others, I became friends with the then head of the Russian Academy of Sciences, academician Gury Marchuk, who was instrumental in establishing a range of collaborative projects between Indian and Soviet researchers.

I found the Soviets interesting and intelligent, but the Soviet command-and-control economic system had left them in desperate need of help when it came to any kind of market activities. They simply had no understanding of the concept of cost and the relationship of cost to pricing. The people I talked to in the semiconductor industry and other engineering areas had no idea whatsoever of what their costs were. The concept of profit margin was alien to them.

On the other hand, the people I was meeting were well-trained and highly accomplished. I did not, for a moment, foresee how rapidly things would fall apart for them. But their system had been artificially sustained for so long that as soon as the unravelling began, the whole structure collapsed almost overnight like a house of cards.

~

Rajiv Gandhi was a relentless modernizer, a man with great optimism when it came to the prospect of heralding India into the global mainstream of health, literacy, technology and, most of all, economic productivity. He was receptive to new ideas, willing to listen and explore new opportunities. The challenge in all of this was enormous, but Rajiv was focused, creative and energetic. Since I was involved in part of his efforts myself, I saw things from the inside. Given the progress we were making, I had envisioned Rajiv being prime minister for an extended period of time and me working with him in whatever areas my own energies and interests might be best suited for.

At the end of 1989 India held its ninth general elections. Five years earlier, Rajiv had been elected prime minister in a landslide victory. His party, the Congress, held 70 per cent of the seats in Parliament. But as the 1989 election approached, allegations of corruption began to cut into Rajiv's popularity. India had bought a large number of advanced artillery weapons from Bofors, a Sweden-based company. Now it had come to light that Bofors had paid 64 million dollars in kickbacks in order to secure the hefty arms order. It was unclear as to who had actually taken the money, but Rajiv was prime minister and so the suspicion naturally fell on him.

It's typical in India that prior to an election the Opposition will bring up issues of corruption—a perennial campaign ploy. People naturally buy these allegations. The popular belief is that everybody is corrupt anyway. People see little acts of corruption every day, all the time; they're a common part of Indian life. A teacher takes money for grades, a policeman takes money for not charging someone. The assumption is: Why wouldn't everybody be corrupt—people in high as well as low places?

When the Bofors scandal began to rock India, I plucked up the courage to ask Rajiv about it directly. My whole experience with him was that he was an honest person, free from greed. I never saw him do anything for the purpose of self-enrichment, and I knew him well. I was reluctant to broach the subject. I didn't want him to think for a moment that I believed he had done this. But at the same time I wanted to hear the truth from his own mouth. So I mustered up my courage and asked him point-blank.

'Sam,' he said, 'I have not taken a penny, and neither has my family.'

Everything I knew about him said that he was clean, not corrupt. As far as I was concerned, this interaction confirmed my very belief. *Okay,* I thought, *the Opposition is using this as a tool, but it won't stick. The Congress was wounded, so it was probable we would lose seats in Parliament. But in any case we would stay in power.*

But I was wrong. People believed the accusations flying around. I realized that during elections, lies sell well in India.

11

Defeat and Distraction

Not long after the elections I received a phone call from a good friend of mine. 'Listen,' he said, 'take this seriously. They're going to put you in jail.'

For a moment I was speechless. They were going to do *what*? I had no idea what to say. Who was going to put me in jail? For what?

But this statement had some context.

It started after Rajiv and the Congress went down in defeat. I had watched it happen, sitting in the principal secretary's office with the others, staring at the television screen as the election news poured in. As it slowly became clear just how badly the Congress was losing, the principal secretary stood up and said, 'I have to go to the PM and inform him. We need to prepare for the transition.' One great thing about Indian democracy is that the transfer of power happens routinely, without any hassles or bloodshed.

We didn't expect to lose in such a fashion. It came as a big shock to everyone in the room. But the Opposition had used the Bofors scandal more effectively than we had imagined, undermining the popular public perception of Rajiv as a clean, progressive leader who kept the people's interests above all else. I knew in my own heart that a lie had been perpetrated. But that was irrelevant. We were out of the game, and a new government under former defence minister V.P. Singh was coming into power.

I sat there, stunned. I felt as if someone had punched me hard in the chest. I hadn't thought about this. I never expected it. I could see my whole dream falling apart in front of my eyes: C-DOT, the Technology Missions, the Telecommunications Commission and all the plans I was already developing for the future. I was up to my ears in the challenge of restructuring India's telecommunications sector. And now a new team was coming in. There was a chance that they wouldn't support any of it.

I knew V.P. Singh, who was taking over as prime minister. Earlier, he had served as both finance and defence minister for Rajiv before leaving the government to form the Opposition coalition led by Janata Dal, which had gone on to win the election. But our paths had never crossed in any meaningful way. We were neither friends nor enemies. But the backing I had enjoyed for the past five years, that had allowed me to do the things I was doing, that was now history.

I met Rajiv. 'I'm very upset about this,' I told him. 'It's a disaster.'

Strangely, he didn't seem distressed. 'There's no need to take it that way,' he said. 'What's the problem? We'll sit in the Opposition for a while.' I thought he'd be depressed, traumatized even, by the loss. But that was not the case at all. 'It's not that big a deal, Sam. We'll be in the Opposition. Believe me, it's okay.'

Instead of licking his wounds, Rajiv was already thinking ahead. He had every intention of coming back. In his view, the cloak of dishonesty the Opposition had pinned on him was not going to last. He was still the head of the Congress. He'd be a part of the Opposition for a while. Then the fates would favour him again.

My own problem was more imminent. Most of the advice I was getting was that I should resign. That since I was Rajiv Gandhi's man and he was out, it wouldn't be appropriate for me to continue. That I should give the new guy's people a chance. Even Jairam Ramesh, my colleague, was of the opinion that stepping down would be the right thing to do.

I thought about it, then decided not to. I tried to make the most objective assessment I could. *I didn't do any of the things I did for Rajiv*

Gandhi, I thought. He provided the political will, but I didn't do it for him—I did it for India. That's what drew me back here in the first place. I could very well have stayed in Chicago. Resigning now would be cowardly. How was I supposed to reconcile myself to the fact that I went along fine when I was comfortable and feeling safe, but when the tough times came I gave up? Was that the kind of person I was? Of course, if V.P. Singh wanted to fire me, that was his prerogative. If he wanted to bring in his own man, he was free to do that too. But I wasn't just going to give up and walk away.

Prime Minister Singh's newly appointed telecommunications minister was a man named K.P. Unnikrishnan, a former journalist who had entered politics some time ago. As chairman of the Telecom Commission I was required to report to him. But we had never met before. I had no idea even of his reputation, so I had no expectations. But our first meeting did not go well.

Shortly after his appointment Unnikrishnan scheduled a visit to the ministry headquarters. He was supposed to arrive at eleven in the morning, at which point the ministry officials, myself included, would meet him with the usual garlands and welcoming rituals. But his arrival time was revised to three in the afternoon. Meanwhile, I was busy with meetings, but I had left instructions to be informed when he arrived. He didn't get to the building until four and, as it happened, I had someone in my office whom I couldn't just abruptly get rid of, so when Unnikrishnan finally did arrive I was a few minutes late in getting downstairs to greet him.

By the time I got there the outside welcoming ceremonies were completed and he was in the minister's first-floor office already. On my way downstairs someone handed me a bouquet of flowers. When I saw Unnikrishnan, I went up to him, gave him the flowers and put out my hand.

'Mr Unnikrishnan, I'm Sam Pitroda. Congratulations. Welcome.'

I extended my hand. I did not bend and do a traditional namaste, and he didn't look pleased with that. 'Didn't you know I was coming?' he said.

'Yes, I knew. I'm sorry, I had somebody in my office, I got delayed a little.'

He was seething—everyone there could see it. I had breached protocol—whether it was by accident or not made no difference. I was clearly disrespecting him by not observing hierarchy. In his mind what had happened was an 'incident', in mine it hardly merited notice.

The press picked up on the episode though, and the next day it was all over the media. I had arrived late. The minister was angry. What would this mean for Indian telecommunications?

Even back then I dismissed all the hoo-ha. The fact that we had got off on the wrong foot didn't mean things had to stay that way. Besides, I was a political appointee. If Unnikrishnan or Singh really had issues with me and didn't like me, they could simply appoint someone else in my place.

That was why it was such a big surprise some time later to pick up the phone and hear, 'Sam, they're going to put you in jail.'

'*What?*'

'Yes. They're cooking up some corruption charges against you. They're going to put you in jail.'

'That's crazy. I've never heard anything about this. There's no such thing. It's not possible.'

'Well, they'll conjure it up. You'd better take this seriously. We believe that by attacking you, they are attacking Rajiv Gandhi.'

Early the next evening the bureau chief for the *Financial Times* of London rang my doorbell—a friend of quite a few years.

'I need to talk to you,' he said. 'Don't you know what's happened?'

'No, what?'

'I'm just coming from a press conference with the telecom minister. He's alleging that you've abused your office and stolen money—23 million dollars. He claims you diverted C-DOT money from the government to yourself and your family.

My son, Salil, was around, listening to this, very upset. 'Dad, what's happening?'

I said, 'Don't worry. We'll find out.'

'But what are you going to say? How are you going to defend yourself?'

'Salil, my only defence is the truth. Other than letting the facts come out, there's nothing to do.'

I turned the TV on, and there was Unnikrishnan saying that I had done illegal things and embezzled money.

At first I was shocked. But after I calmed down, I wasn't sure how concerned I really needed to be. No one had said anything directly to me—not Unnikrishnan, not the ministry, not the police. I went to the office the next day and everything seemed more or less okay. People were obviously upset, though—you could see the stress and confusion on their faces. 'Aren't you worried?' they asked me.

'What can I do?' I said. 'I don't have anything to do with this.'

Nothing happened over the next few days. Nobody put me on notice. Nobody fired me. Nobody did anything.

But then the backlash began. Unnikrishnan began appearing on television and at press conferences waving a thick file, saying, 'I have in this file all the details of Pitroda's corruption.' His attacks made the papers every day. Headlines constantly screamed: *Unnikrishnan says this. Unnikrishnan says that. Pitroda does not answer.*

I didn't read the papers. The articles were worthless. The Indian press was always shouting about something or the other. The next day they'd be screaming hoarse about something else. That's the way things always worked. *This will pass,* I thought, *as soon as they get hold of something new to create a fuss about.*

I didn't defend myself in public either. If some reporter asked me a question, I answered. But I didn't call any press conferences myself, I wasn't proactive about it. I didn't think there was any need to be. Why would I call a press conference to say that I didn't do anything wrong? *When you respond and counter-attack, the situation escalates,* I thought. *What good would that do?*

Besides, the comptroller general of audit was beginning an investigation, examining C-DOT's books and auditing the transactions. Such investigations were notoriously thorough; their success rate in finding something to condemn was high. But what was there to find? I had cut some bookkeeping corners to get things done faster. No doubt I had violated more than one regulation regarding things like what level person was permitted what kind of expense. I was ready to take on any kind of blame for sins like that. I called the comptroller general. 'If you have any questions for me,' I said, 'I'm available.'

But the attacks were mushrooming. Rajiv had lost, but he was still a force to be reckoned with. In the Singh government's eyes he was still a threat, down but not out, and they wanted to put him out. Since we were so closely connected, I was an obvious target too. Rajiv had appointed me telecommunications secretary, which, according to the critics, was because he knew me—a transgression especially egregious to them since I was technically a non-resident Indian, an NRI. Worse than that, according to them, was that I wasn't just an NRI, I was a foreign national whom Rajiv had allowed to penetrate the government's inner sanctum.

The day this issue was raised in Parliament I received a call from Rajiv. 'Sam, I know you're an Indian citizen. That's correct, isn't it? Are you absolutely sure you are?'

'Of course, I'm sure.'

'Can I send somebody to look at your documents? If there's a problem this could look very bad.'

'Sure.'

Rajiv sent former foreign minister Natwar Singh to my home. 'Sam,' he said, 'Rajiv asked me to check personally to make absolutely certain everything's in order.'

I showed him my Indian passport.

'So why are these people saying you're a foreign citizen?'

They were accusing me because they didn't know and they hadn't bothered to check. I was fairly certain I had told Rajiv at some point that I had revoked my citizenship, but it was possible he wasn't sure either.

'I knew something like this would eventually come up,' I told Singh, 'so I changed my citizenship a couple of years ago.'

What had happened was that some years ago a little newspaper had reported that the CIA had planted a man in the prime minister's office, and had made a reference to me, though not by name. It was a minor article in an obscure paper; I wasn't sure who—if anyone—had even seen it. But I had realized then that the issue of my citizenship would come up at some point and, when it did, it would surely be blown out of proportion.

Besides that, I was aware that I shouldn't be working with the Prime Minister of India day in and day out and not be an Indian citizen. Rajiv had never expressed concern on this subject, so I had written a letter to the US ambassador on my own initiative.

It wasn't an easy letter to draft. I valued my American citizenship more than I could easily put into words. I kept a copy of the letter with me.

I had gone to the American Embassy in Delhi to get this hard task done, but was told, 'We don't know how to do this. Nobody's ever relinquished their US citizenship here before. You will have to wait until we can get information on the procedure from Washington.'

Eventually, two big volumes of citizenship law arrived and the authorities called me. 'To relinquish citizenship you will need two witnesses and you will have to take an oath.'

s.g. pitroda

9TH FLOOR
AKBAR BHAWAN
CHANAKYAPURI
NEW DELHI – 110 021 INDIA
PHONE 676928 604451/901

January 21, 1987

Dear Mr. John Gunther Dean:

The purpose of this letter is to inform you of my decision to renounce U.S. citizenship. I know that this is an irrevocable act and a matter of serious concern. However, after a lot of careful consideration, discussions with family, friends and well-wishers, I have decided to take this painful step.

I went to U.S. in 1964 to learn and decided to stay there to earn. In the last 22 years, I have grown a lot in every sphere of activity. U.S. people and environment have been a great inspiration to me. Because of this, I feel I have been able to contribute considerably to the telecom development in U.S. resulting in creating new jobs and opportunities. In U.S., I have not only learnt technology and trade but also new management methods essential to any entrepreneual activities.

After completing my education, I had an opportunity to build a company called Wescom Inc. which I sold to Rockwell International in 1980. Having made some money, I turned my attention to India.

The status of Indian telecom has been a great concern to all for over a decade. However, no meaningful solution had been offered earlier. This gave me an opportunity to make a meaningful contribution to India's development. As a part of my efforts, I had an opportunity to meet late Mrs. Indira Gandhi for an hour to discuss the programme to modernise India's telecom. At that time, I met Mr. Rajiv Gandhi who took considerable interest in my presentation and involvement. This led to the establishment of the Centre for Development of Telematics (C-DOT) in 1984 and I became the Advisor. One thing led to another and I got more and more involved in other developmental activities and in mobilising young resources in the country.

The encouragement I have been receiving from the Prime Minister Mr. Rajiv Gandhi has been a source of great inspiration to my desire to contribute to India. Having achieved professional success in U.S., I now have freedom to devote my energy to help young Prime Minister to build modern India. Having been working in close contact with the Prime Minister on various developmental issues, now I have got into a point, I feel without having Indian citizenship, I would be a liability for him. I know I can be of immense help to him in bringing fresh thinking from the view point of entrepreneual thrust in many areas of development. This opportunity may never come in the history again. To have meaningful input in the decision making process which will guide the destiny of millions in this nation is a unique opportunity. For this, I have taken this monumental decision.

On the one hand, I feel proud to take this challenge and on the other hand I am sad that I have to give up my U.S. citizenship which I value immensely. I wish I could have had the option of dual citizenship.

I would like to take this opportunity to thank all those who have helped me in U.S. to build my career and reputation. U.S. Government has been very generous and helpful in my endeavour to assist developments in India and help to modernise India. I wish I can put in words the pain and pleasure I am experiencing at this moment.

Look forward to working with America and with the Americans in helping to build modern India.

Goodbye.

S.G. Pitroda

Mr. John Gunther Dean
U.S. Ambassador
American Embassy
Shanti Path
Chankaya Puri
NEW DELHI 110 021

PS: In this connection I am enclosing two articles one published in the International Management and the other in Chicago Tribune.

I went prepared with two witnesses. The official asked me, 'Are you absolutely sure you want to do this?'

'Yes, I am.' I was warned that I would be stateless for a while until I received my Indian nationality. I understood the risk and agreed to move on.

I then had to swear under oath that I was not under the influence of drugs or alcohol. I had to certify that no one was forcing me to give up my citizenship and that I was under no political pressure. Then I had to state that I was sane. After that my witnesses had to swear that they knew me personally, that I was not under undue influence and that I was sane. After this, I signed the renunciation documents and handed over my US passport. It was a traumatic afternoon for me. I remember coming home afterwards with feelings of deep nostalgia and sadness. But I didn't want my decision to affect Anu and the children, so they remained US citizens.

Unnikrishnan's assault was wide-ranging and continuous. He was claiming in press conferences and other public forums that I was corrupt, but he needed to show proof that the charges weren't merely politically driven; he needed other voices to join in. That was why he had the comptroller general initiate an audit of C-DOT; it was something, he believed, that could expose my illegitimate money dealings. He also established a so-called 'independent committee' to investigate C-DOT's record of accomplishments—or non-accomplishments, according to him. The chair of this committee was Mr K.P.P. Nambiar, secretary of the electronics department, someone I had personally been responsible for putting in his job after Rajiv had asked me to vet him. Nambiar was going to be looking into how and where we may have violated our warrants and guarantees regarding the equipment we had promised to produce and what wrongdoings we were guilty of on the technological side.

The idea was that Unnikrishnan would employ the two reports— the comptroller general's and the investigative committee's—to corroborate and use to demonstrate the objective nature of his charges.

Through all of this the C-DOT engineers were getting more and more angry. They knew the situation. They knew I had never taken a salary in India. They knew I had devoted myself to my work to improve telecom and connectivity in India. They remembered very well that when they had gone to the United States on working visits, Anu had received them warmly at the airport with winter coats, that she had cooked for them and looked after them, that she and her brother, Yash, had been family to them during their stay in America. The engineers knew one couldn't be corrupt *and* do those special things. They knew me and knew it wasn't true.

The C-DOT engineers in Delhi got so worked up that they began demonstrating on the streets, marching and chanting and waving flags. That attracted the media. At first there were daily articles about Unnikrishnan's supposed revelations of corruption. Now the papers began running editorials supporting me, one after another. The headlines screamed: 'Fairness for Sam Pitroda'. 'How C-DOT Benefits India'. 'Let C-DOT Do Its Work'. 'Leave Pitroda and C-DOT Alone'.

Things had escalated and this had now become a major national issue. And it was developing in a way Unnikrishnan could not possibly have been happy with.

But he persevered with the onslaught. At some point he decided to go to Bangalore to give a speech in front of the C-DOT hardware-division engineers, apparently believing that delivering a rousing condemnation of me would drive home the potency of his allegations. On stage in front of 300 or 400 engineers he began to wax eloquent on my wrongdoings—that I had taken money from C-DOT for my own purposes, that I had 'looted the exchequer', that I had nurtured a personality cult at C-DOT, which was unacceptable.

As he said these things, the entire audience stood up and walked out—all the engineers. Unnikrishnan was left on stage, facing an empty auditorium. These young people had the guts to simply walk out on a minister—an unbelievable stunt. Who had ever heard of such a thing? And, of course, the press jumped all over it.

It was the courage, conviction and confidence of the C-DOT employees that won the day, however. This was evidenced by the fresh appointment of the communications minister within a month of the submission of the controversial Nambiar Committee report. Although the person at the helm of affairs changed, the attitude of the government towards C-DOT and me did not. The new government directed that 'the Chairman of the Telecom Commission, namely, Sam Pitroda, would not deal with C-DOT', At the same time the government launched a CBI inquiry and special audit of C-DOT, which remained in newspaper and television headlines for some time. C-DOTians were thoroughly demoralized and the main exchange project got further delayed. The export potential of C-DOT products in fifteen developing countries also received a setback.

Finally, with the fall of the National Front government and the formation of the new government led by Mr Chandrashekhar and supported by the Congress Party, the crusade against me ended. Answers to Parliament questions in both the houses clearly indicated that there had never been any mismanagement in C-DOT's finance and purchases.

In all of this fracas, Unnikrishnan never saw fit to say anything to me directly. He never came to me and said anything on the lines of: *These are the discrepancies I've found: A and B and C. This looks like this, that looks like that. Could you please explain these things to me.* He hadn't done that because, as I had come to understand earlier, this campaign was, at its core, not really an attack on me at all, it was an attack on Rajiv Gandhi. This attack on me was intended to demonstrate that not only was Rajiv corrupt himself, the people around him were also corrupt, that corruption pervaded the administration.

It didn't end well for Unnikrishnan. As it became clear that his allegations were false and unfounded, V.P. Singh had no choice but to sack him and appoint a new minister.

~

But the unpleasant affair had taken a toll on Anu, as much as it had on me. As the corruption accusations escalated and the newspapers started spitting out disparaging articles about me, Anu started receiving threatening calls. Once these kinds of things start, they tend to get vicious quickly, and they did. She heard threats about how our children were going to be kidnapped, how Anu herself would be raped and beaten. She began to panic.

'I want to take the children back to Chicago,' she said to me.

In the end I persuaded her not to go, but not long after that, Salil and Rajal themselves decided that they wanted to go back to the US.

I had brought the family to India in 1985. Salil was ten at the time, Rajal seven. It had not been an easy decision. Even then, I was only too aware that with all my travelling back and forth between India and Chicago, I had left them fatherless for too long a period of time. And now I was going to rip them away from the lives they were used to. I had felt so concerned about moving that I had promised I would do everything I could to keep the transition from affecting the way our children were used to living their lives. I knew the sacrifice they would be making so I could follow my own dreams. I was always busy in India with C-DOT, the Technology Missions, the Telecom Commission, and other interesting and exciting assignments. In the process, I had seen my kids grow 'horizontally' rather than vertically—I left early in the day, when they were still sleeping, and came home late, after they had fallen asleep.

Going against the advice of many friends, I had admitted the children into the American Embassy School in Delhi. Then I procured a membership to the American Club so they would be able to have a hamburger or a pizza whenever they wanted. I shipped over all their furniture, their air conditioners, their VCRs. Every few weeks I would have friends airmail videos of the Chicago Bears' football games for them. If one saw my house in Delhi, it was just like being back in Chicago. This might have been a little extreme, but I wanted the children to feel as comfortable as they possibly could. I did all this because I simply felt guilty. I had to come to India, but I didn't want them to have to give up what they enjoyed because of what I had to do. And I told them both, 'Whenever you really want to go back to Chicago, you can go back.'

Now, as the Unnikrishnan affair was winding down, Salil was about to start eleventh grade, two years away from college. 'Dad,' he said, 'I want to go back to the US.'

'All right, but why?'

'Because in India they don't offer enough advanced-level courses.'

I had no idea what he was talking about. He had to explain it to me.

'Okay, if you want to do that, you can go. You'll have a family there with Yash [Anu's younger brother], his wife and your grandfather. The house is intact; we can make arrangements for whatever's necessary.'

While we were having this discussion, Rajal was listening intently. I asked her, 'What would you like to do, Rajal?'

'I want to go back with Salil,' she said.

Anu and I argued about it. Rajal was still very young, how could we send her back?

'She'll have your father and your brother and his family,' I said to her. 'She wants to go back. I have confidence in both her and Salil. Let her do it.' I remembered my parents for a moment, and how they had done the same thing for Manek and me when we were young and sent us on a train to Gujarat to study.

Both the kids returned to Chicago, and we were left with a big empty house. Anu was mad about it. She hadn't wanted Rajal to leave. But the fact was that the children missed their home. Their futures were most likely in the US, and so it made sense for them to start building a foundation there. They had also, I'm sure, been affected by

Unnikrishnan's attacks on me. His assault had made India seem a less welcoming place—not a place they wanted to live and felt comfortable in. Salil told me he wanted to go because of the courses available to him in the US, but had I been more sensitive I would have understood that there were deeper things going on for the children too.

~

Unnikrishnan's dismissal wasn't quite the end of the story. One day Prime Minister Singh's secretary called. 'Mr Pitroda, you have too many titles. You are adviser to C-DOT. Adviser to the prime minister on the Technology Missions. Chairman of the Telecom Commission. Secretary to the Department of Telecom. These are simply too many titles for you to have.'

'Okay,' I said. 'Fine. What do you have in mind? Tell me what you want.'

'We want you to be only chairman of the Telecom Commission and secretary of the department.'

'Fine.'

They thought that if I wasn't adviser to C-DOT, my influence there would be eliminated. I didn't consider that a problem at all. C-DOT had been fully established, and in any event that phase was all but over for me. But in addition they had also removed me as adviser on the Technology Missions. And, sadly, after that, the missions died a slow death. A mission doesn't mean anything unless you have a missionary, and the government hadn't placed anyone in that role.

I was under the impression that I had been handling the stress from all the tumultuous times fairly well. True, my integrity had never been attacked before, but this was hardly the first time in my life where I had been under a lot of pressure. And when I was in that kind of a situation I always thought of Mahatma Gandhi. If I was worried about myself, if I was upset about how something or the other was developing, I would think, *Who are you? Look at Gandhi's life, the scorn and humiliation he faced and took in his stride in South Africa. Look at how he endured, how he was so committed to his cause that he was able to shrug off the hatred and imprisonment. What moral strength the man had!* I tried to use that as my personal compass.

Reflecting on Gandhi had helped me weather this particular siege with what I thought of as decent levels of equanimity. But if I was okay emotionally, the same couldn't be said for my physical well-being.

Anu had just returned from Chicago after settling the children in, when late one night I was awakened by pain in my stomach, as if I had a bad case of indigestion. 'Anu,' I said, 'I'm not feeling well.' I got up and took an antacid. But it didn't seem to help.

Anu insisted on calling the doctor, even at three in the morning. 'Don't worry,' he said, 'take another dose of antacid and see what happens.' I was aware that pain like this could be a symptom for cardiac issues, but I had taken a stress test just a few days earlier and everything had been normal. *Whatever this is, at least it isn't my heart,* I thought.

But Anu wasn't happy with the doctor's advice. 'No,' she said, 'we're going to the heart hospital right now.'

Normally, I had a driver who slept over in the house. But that day he happened to be away. We called a cab to take us to the Escorts heart hospital. The pain wasn't going away. If anything, it was becoming more severe. In the emergency room a flurry of activity started as soon as we walked in.

When the doctor arrived, I told him I didn't think it was anything serious, but that I was in some pain. My stomach was hurting. He had me lie down immediately. He took my blood pressure and listened to my breathing. Then he hooked me up to an EKG machine.

'Mr Pitroda,' he told me, 'you are having a heart attack.'

'No. That can't be,' I said. 'I'm okay.'

'Just wait,' he said. And as he uttered the words, I suddenly couldn't breathe. I tried desperately to get air into my lungs, but I couldn't. I was drowning. I knew I was going to die. It happened in a moment. I had no time to prepare, no time to say anything to Anu.

Then the doctor put a needle in my arm, and just as suddenly as my breathing had stopped, it started up again. The blood clot had dissolved. I felt okay. More than okay, I felt good.

That was so close, I thought, thankful that Anu had insisted we go to the hospital and, in particular, to a speciality heart hospital. Now I felt fine. I had meetings set up in the morning at the ministry, but I thought I probably should give myself a little time to rest. I'd have my secretary push everything back a couple of hours. I could probably get in by ten or so.

In hindsight, I did not understand the gravity of the situation. I believed I could get back to work the next day, but I was wrong.

'No,' said the chief doctor, Dr Naresh Trehan, who had now entered the scenario. 'We're not letting you go back to work for thirty days.'

I thought maybe I had misheard. I felt completely fine. 'What are you talking about?'

'You've had a heart attack. We can't take any surgical measures for at least twenty days. But I'm going to do an angiogram. I'm sure you have blocked arteries.'

They did the angiogram. I had eight blocked arteries.

'Normally, I'd prescribe medications,' Dr Trehan said, 'then have you come back in. But in your case, we can't take a chance. You have to stay in the hospital.'

So I remained in the hospital. I had a telephone installed. I had my secretary come in and see me. I set up a regular office, so I wouldn't have to put off any work.

When Rajiv Gandhi found out he came to see me in the hospital. 'What happened to you?' he said. 'This is just terrible.'

They only waited twenty-one days before they performed a quadruple bypass. I felt quite okay, but the doctors thought they had to take action, and they did.

I somehow didn't understand that the surgery would be so complicated, even though the doctors explained everything to me: Breaking the breastbone, the breathing action performed by the heart–lung machine, the harvesting of other veins, the grafting. When I woke up I'd be wired to this and that. I'd have a tube here, a tube there. Until my bladder was back to its normal function, I'd need a urine bag. It all sounded awful. But the fact was that I had always been healthy; that was how I saw myself—my default. So even now I thought, *Okay, these things will happen, but before long I'll be up and running and as good as new.*

Since the doctors needed blood for transfusions they put out a call. I had no relatives nearby, except my mother. But people came and lined up and down the hallways, C-DOT engineers and others. I was so moved. These people, many of them complete strangers, were helping to save my life. Anu told me that prayers were being recited for me in temples. I had never had much to do with religion at all. Hearing this was almost too much for my fragile emotional state.

At that time—this was October 1990—the techniques for open-heart surgery were not nearly as sophisticated as they later became, in particular the anaesthesiology. After the operation it took me a long time to regain consciousness, which I was informed of later. I didn't know that, but when I did start to emerge from the haze, my face felt strange, deformed, my features weren't in the right place. My eyes, my mouth, my nose—they felt twisted, deranged. No one had warned me about this, but before I had a chance to panic I fell back to sleep. Then I came out of it again for a few minutes, and again I fell back under.

When I finally came around for good, there were all kinds of tubes sticking out of me and blood all over. I was a mess.

Some days later they wheeled me out of the ICU and into a room. Anu was with me much of the time; my mother came, and other relatives arrived from different places.

I had three drivers at the time: my regular driver from the telecom ministry—he was the one who slept in the house—but two others also, one from C-DOT and one from the Technology Missions. I had finished my work at these places, but the drivers hadn't been reassigned to anyone else yet. Every day that I was in the hospital, they would all come to our house and just sit there. Anu told them to go home, it was festival time, Diwali. 'Please go home,' she said. 'You should be with your families.' But they refused to leave.

Anu called me. 'Your drivers are not going home. Tell them to go home. We all feel bad.'

I said to my mother, 'Mom, why don't you tell them; they'll listen to you.'

My mom told them, 'Look, please go home. Your wives are waiting, so are your children. Why are you here? You need to go.'

They finally went home after that. But just an hour later all three were back. 'Why are you back here?' Anu asked. The drivers replied, 'Our wives threw us out. They scolded us, saying, "What kind of a person are you? Your boss is dying in the hospital and you want to celebrate Diwali? Go back."'

When I heard this, I thought, *This can only happen in India.* This was the India I had left on a boat in 1964. This was the India and the people I treasured.

I was in the hospital for almost a month until, finally, I couldn't take it any more. 'You can't go home yet,' Dr Trehan said. 'You're not completely healed, the roads aren't good, it will be too much of a strain.'

I left anyway. I checked myself out and went home. And slowly I recovered my strength and rejoined my work as chairman of the Telecom Commission.

~

It was some months later that I got a call from Rajiv Gandhi asking me to come over to his house. 'Sam, we've decided to pull the plug and call elections.' By now V.P. Singh was out of office; he had resigned only a month after my heart attack. He had been succeeded by Chandrashekhar, leader of the minority Janata Party, whose government was in power with support from the Congress. Chandrashekhar, as prime minister, was very supportive of all my initiatives. But now Rajiv thought the time had come for him to return to the forefront.

We immediately began to plan the election campaign. Three of Rajiv's political advisers were present—Jitendra Prasad, Ghulam Nabi Azad and Oscar Fernandes—as energized and excited as I was. The first order of business was resources: How much of what would we need? The four of us practically ran back to my house to start working the numbers and laying out the details.

We hired a new ad agency. In the previous election, which we had lost badly, we had run a series of negative ad campaigns depicting animals fighting, to convey how the other parties would never be able to create a stable government. If they came to power, politics would turn into a dogfight. It would be utter chaos. Chickens would be clawing at each other.

I hadn't liked that, but I hadn't been one of the decision makers. This time I was. This time I decided we wouldn't have a negative campaign; this time our focus would be on positive things. Rajiv would bring stability. He would bring the people together; he would be inclusive, not divisive. We needed to work together to expand the economy, to create jobs, to reduce inflation, to modernize the country and make it competitive. He was the one who could do that. We created slogans related to progress, stability and growth.

Every day meetings would start at my house at 44, Lodhi Estate. The players included Pranab Mukherjee, Jairam Ramesh, R.D. Pradhan, Suman Dubey, Krishna Rao, and several others. We'd all sit down and lay out a plan for that day, responding to the newspaper headlines, making our own headlines. We planned out all the communication, the logistics, the ads. The advertising expenses were massive, and we decided they needed to be controlled. We were printing campaign posters by the hundreds of thousands and sending them all over the country. There were 560 parliamentary candidates and each one would be given thousands of posters. But the people in charge were using external printing-presses, even though the party had its own press. When I found out about this, I stopped the work being done outside and turned the job over to our internal printer to save costs.

That move caused a ruckus. We had apparently always used an outside printer for this purpose, and those in charge were mad. They went to Rajiv about it. And they weren't the only ones. Many people, insiders and external consultants, wanted to do one thing or another—100,000 rupees here, 200,000 there. They'd go to Rajiv for approval, but he would send them to me. And more often than not, I'd said *no*, which made me the focus of waves of anger from every corner. One famous person wanted to make a movie on Rajiv Gandhi for a lot of money. 'No,' I said, 'we're not doing it,' which was not received well. I became Rajiv's gatekeeper for a while.

Rajiv was campaigning well, giving speeches all around the country. It looked more and more as though our optimism was going to see us to victory. Everyone was charged up. I was charged up. The stars seemed perfectly aligned. During his time in the Opposition, Rajiv had strengthened the party. His adversaries, on the other hand, had not demonstrated any real capacity to govern. We knew that we were doing well, that we would win this time. Maybe not with the massive majority we had earlier, but we would win. We were going to be back in power again.

In late April 1991, we were just a few weeks from the elections, and our momentum was building. I was already thinking beyond the formation of a new government, to the new efforts we could make in telecom, education, technology, infrastructure and other initiatives of national importance. The new digital standards for mobile phones had just been publicized as well, which would open up our own markets to a communications revolution that would change the face of the country. I was champing at the bit to get started.

On the night of 21 May 1991, Anu and I went to bed early. I had just fallen off to sleep when the phone rang. I picked it up, half asleep. It was Mayank Chhaya, a young journalist who had started writing a biography about me.

'Have you heard, Sam? Rajiv Gandhi got bombed, blown up.'

'What? What do you mean?'

'That's what I mean,' he said. 'Rajiv Gandhi is dead.'

I was in shock. I couldn't process it. It was too immense.

The moment I hung up another call came in, this one from the election commissioner, T.N. Seshan.

'Sam, why don't you and Anu come to my house? A lot of people were killed, not just Rajiv. I have more security here. Come, stay with us.'

'No,' I said, 'I think I want to stay at home. I'd rather be at home. I don't think anyone is going to hurt me. Besides, I'm sure people are going to want to get in touch with me.'

Then the floodgates opened. Calls began pouring in from other people Rajiv and I had worked with, from TV and radio stations and newspapers—from overseas as well as within India.

We only had bits and pieces of information to clutch at. It wasn't clear what exactly had transpired, what was going on. Was this solely an attack on Rajiv? Was something far more pervasive in the works? The whereabouts of Suman Dubey, a close friend of both Rajiv and myself, were unknown, so someone asked if he was at my house. Suman's wife was beside herself with worry.

A reporter from the *New York Times* told me, 'No, Sam. Suman was there. But he's okay. I saw him.' Calls kept coming in. I was on the phone continuously. Nobody knew if the assassination was part of a plan, or if others would be targeted too. It was mayhem and confusion all around.

Then someone knocked at the door. It was a KGB agent I knew, someone who maintained contact with political figures for the Soviets. 'I'm here to make sure you're okay,' he said. 'I've been told to take care of you. If you want to go someplace, if you want to fly out, I'll be able to arrange it.'

'No, I don't need anything,' I said. 'I'm okay. Nobody's going to do anything to me. We have to see how this is going to unfold.'

I was surprised that somebody from the KGB would offer to protect me. If anybody other than Indians should have been protecting me, I'd have thought it would be the Americans. But no one from the embassy contacted me. I hadn't thought about it until the KGB person showed up. I wasn't a US citizen any longer, but my wife and children were, and Anu was living here with me. But they hadn't been keeping track, or maybe they were and didn't think that we were at risk.

The next day Anu and I went to Rajiv Gandhi's house. His body was being flown to Delhi from Tamil Nadu where the assassination had occurred. By then we knew that a woman had triggered the bomb. Speculation was rife that it was someone from the Tamil Tigers outfit in Sri Lanka, where India had been involved in ending the civil war.

Anu and I waited for the body with a few others. Eventually, the remains arrived, carried in on a stretcher with a sheet on top. Under the sheet Rajiv's body was laid all in pieces, blown to bits by the force of the explosion.

Anu and I sat together on one side of the stretcher, Sonia on the other side. No one spoke. We sat there in silence. I was thinking about the future of India and all the programmes we had launched to lead India into the 21st century. I was also thinking about the great loss to the country and the time it would take for everyone to recover from this tragedy. I was concerned about Priyanka, Rahul and Sonia, their futures, and the sacrifices they had made for the country. Time passed, feeling like an eternity. Then we stood up and went home.

A massive crowd was at the funeral, flowing rivers of people decked in white—the colour of mourning. Rajiv's body was being carried on a flower-decked gun carriage, the tricolour flag of India draped over him. Overhead, a helicopter released clouds of orange blossoms to rain down on the assemblage below. Then the body was placed on the pyre and the logs set aflame. Sonia, Rahul and Priyanka were visible in white near the fire—an image that will remain etched in my heart and mind for eternity.

～

It seemed to me that the world was coming to an end. Rajiv was gone. Everything I had done was because of his political will and his support. Now he was gone and his support had disappeared with him, evaporated in an instant. My friend was no longer around. My confidence shrivelled up. My future looked bleak and uncertain. My hope and dreams for India were shaken. All the investments we had made in C-DOT, telecom, the Technology Missions and the many other initiatives may never materialize. Maybe India will fall behind by a decade. These were scary thoughts.

Then something else hit me. I was almost completely out of money. It hadn't even dawned on me earlier, I hadn't given it much thought—I was so excited by the possibility of doing more work in India, with Rajiv's backing, that I just kept on with it. Until now, I had not paid much attention to my family, finances and future.

I realized I needed to do something, but what? I had no idea. I had two kids back in the US, Salil was applying to colleges, Rajal thinking about it already, and I was almost penniless. *They were still children only yesterday,* I thought. *How did they grow up so fast? How could I have let this happen without thinking about it, without planning for it?*

The irony of the situation was that almost everyone thought I was a millionaire, which I had been when we sold Wescom—but that was more than ten years ago now. For three years I had gone back and forth from Chicago to India every two weeks, on my own money. I had asked for and received a one-rupee-a-year salary for over ten years in India. The government had given me a house and a car, but I had taken care of the rest of my expenses and my family's from my own personal funds, which were now all but finished.

And now, in India, with Rajiv gone, all I could see was darkness. I couldn't imagine what would come next. All I knew was that to put my life in order I needed to be back home with my family in Chicago.

Part III

Rebuilding, Redefining, Reflecting

12

Personal Challenge

To all of India, Rajiv's death was a national drama. With a prospective prime minister assassinated, it was a political tragedy. To me it was that and much more. It overwhelmed me. I couldn't understand it. It was again the beginning of a different journey, this time being undertaken in darkness.

How does one build with somebody else the kind of relationship that I had built with Prime Minister Rajiv Gandhi? How does one achieve the same levels of understanding, friendship, confidence in each other, commitment, concern, care, comfort, love and respect? It doesn't happen.

Something was taking hold of me, like some dark curtain slowly being lowered over my mind. I began to feel shaky, fragile. I couldn't seem to concentrate. I'd grasp at some thought, some idea, and then it would be gone. *This is not me,* I thought. *How could this be me? I'm the one who makes the decisions, I'm the one who gets things done, the one who solves the problems. I'm the one they look to for help.* One thought entered my head that I couldn't get rid of: *My life in India was finished.* The whole thing was gone. Ten years here. C-DOT, C-DAC, the Technology Missions, the telecommunications ministry. And what was I left with? A ruin. Nothing. A black, empty hole.

Okay, I told myself, *it's done, it's over. You have to move on now.* But how was I to do that? There was no money, no rich uncle to reach out to, nobody in the family or among my friends to look to for advice or guidance.

Meanwhile, the world went on as before. The big question was: Who would take charge of the party now? Sonia Gandhi was a strong woman, but she was in a state of shock, struggling to cope. The elections would be held—with or without Rajiv Gandhi—and the party needed a leader. On my own initiative I called my friend Madhavrao Scindia, the then railway minister and a former maharaja, to my house. I told him that to continue Rajiv Gandhi's legacy we needed a young dynamic leader, someone like him, with vision, values and a commitment to technology and growth. He felt uncomfortable because in terms of party hierarchy he was not senior enough.

Finally, after a lot of discussion the party chose Narasimha Rao, Congress' most senior leader. Rao was a scholar and a long-time party stalwart who had run several ministries for Rajiv. And when Congress won a plurality of seats in the election, it was he who became the new prime minister.

'Sir,' I told Rao, 'I need to leave.'

'Please,' he said, 'you can't leave now. You were important to Rajiv. It would be bad for the party if you quit. Continue as my adviser. Do whatever you want to do, but stay on.'

I understood the political ramifications, so I didn't submit a formal resignation. But I needed to leave. They could keep my name on, but I had to go back to Chicago. I wasn't even up to closing up our house in Delhi. I didn't do that until some time later. 'Sell everything,' I told my assistant. 'Get whatever you can. The car, the washer and dryer, the television. Give whatever furniture to whomsoever. Put the rest in storage. Don't even tell me. I can't look at it.'

On the flight back to Chicago with a heavy and broken heart, sleep evaded me. I tried to make sense of it. *Look at everything that's happened,* I thought. First, there were false corruption charges by Unnikrishnan, then the heart attack. Now Rajiv's death. One of those things you could handle, even two. But three, one after another—it was too much to take.

And now, on top of all of this, there was no money left. All my life I had taken care of people. Now, what was I going to do? How was I going to take care of my wife and children? I didn't know the answer.

~

In our house in Downers Grove the bookcases and shelves were filled with the small curios Anu and I had acquired over the years—things people had given us, gifts from friends, figurines of gods, elephants, Ganeshas, sculptures of wild-eyed Indian musicians. The basement of our house was filled with my own paintings.

Painting had been my one constant pastime for years, ever since college. Painting freed my mind from the compulsions that kept the wheels of work and life turning so incessantly. Sometimes, the rush of ideas made me feel as if I were riding a tiger, that if I got off it would eat me alive. Painting took me away from that feeling for a handful of precious hours at a time. It was my pressure relief valve. It allowed me to escape.

I brought out a new canvas. I mixed the paints on the palette. But not the light colours, the yellows and oranges and bright-reds I usually used. This time, it was all about dark colours, blacks and blues and deep blood-reds. I wasn't sure what I was doing when I began to paint. I didn't have a sketch in mind. It just seemed to come by itself. Ominous black figures looming in the background, a blue-black river at the bottom of the canvas, flowing over another river of blood. Two small figures, a man and a woman, merged with each other like Siamese twins, half submerged underwater. Another tiny figure, a man by himself, staring off towards the edge at nothing. Jagged crimson lines from top to bottom, sharp angles, inverted letters: *SAM*. Sam's life upside down.

Some people examine themselves—they assess their spiritual lives, their relationships, where they've been and who they are. They listen to their inner selves, they judge the state of their souls. But I had never had either the time or the inclination for that kind of thing. Introspection of that sort was not my strongest suit—or any suit. But now I was forced to think about what I had done with my life, and especially how I had isolated myself from the people I loved.

It wasn't that I had estranged myself from them, they were all still with me. But I had walled them off, I had isolated myself. This group included my own brothers, Manek and Pinu; my sisters, Manju, Sushi, Pushpa, Jashu and Indira; and my friends from the old days, from IIT and the India Forum, Bhupen Trivedi, Prakash Desai, Rajiv Desai, Dilip Desai, Ashok Bhatt, Piyush Vyas, Divyesh Mehta, Shiban Ganju, the Dixits, Madhu Mehta and Bharat Thakkar (whose apartment Bhupen and I had lived in when we first came to Chicago). They were as dear to me as ever, but what did I have in common with them now? I couldn't talk about the things they talked about. My mind wandered. Concentration eluded me. I had nothing to say in social circles unless it was about global issues or economies or visions of the future—all the things I had been singularly focused on for so many years. We were still connected, we always would be. But I hadn't kept up with their lives. They were there, but I was gone. How could I have let that happen?

I thought about my brother Manek. Our entire early lives we had been more like twins than mere brothers. We had been each other's emotional support systems at boarding school when we were children, so far away from our parents. When we went to college together we wore identical pants, the same shirts. We were inseparable. We loved the same folk music, the same Hindi movies. When I left for America, no one was happier for me than he was. Manek felt I was fulfilling *his* dream. I felt the same. But when I came back to the US, I felt our connection was strained. I didn't like those movies any more. I didn't listen to that kind of music. I had changed, he said. Why? What had happened to me?

'I don't know,' I would say. 'I had to make a living, feed everybody, support things, bring people over and set them up. I just haven't had the time for movies and music, for normal things. I had only time to work. I facilitated others doing their things, going to school, getting married. And then it was India. All India.'

Manek might say, 'Look at you. You've shut down your family, your friends, your community. What kind of a life is that?'

Even Salil and Rajal, who were eighteen and fifteen by then had, in essence, grown up without me. I had paid so little attention to them. I had never asked them how they were doing in math, what grade did they get on the social studies paper? I was always travelling, always running from one thing to another. I didn't even know what they were studying. I never went to meet their teachers or other parents—I had left all that to Anu. I was not present for them. My idea in life was different. My job wasn't to attend to my children, it was to make a living and see that they didn't want for anything. I loved them dearly, wasn't that enough? I loved them like my father loved us, even though he had spent half his life cutting trees in teak forests. But suddenly Salil and Rajal weren't even children any more. I had missed their childhoods, their youth. They had passed me by. Time had passed me by.

I knew what I was feeling wasn't rational. I hadn't consciously chosen to have things work out like this. Why, then, these waves of regret? I had never had these thoughts before. But Rajiv's death triggered something in me, adding to everything else that seemed to be going downhill. It was the worst with Anu. I had been so deeply in love with her. Never in my life had I loved anyone the way I loved Anu. We had been married twenty-six years then, and I still loved her. She was my friend, my support, the one who took care of everyone, including me. But I had neglected her the most. I had taken her for granted. I hadn't given myself to her. The madness of my life was not her madness. I had left her alone.

I remembered the grand tour we had taken around America right after we were married. We had rented a station wagon and, together with Bhupen, Mahen and my younger brother Pinu, we had set out to see the country. We drove to Yellowstone National Park, the Black Hills, Mt Rushmore, Zion, Bryce Canyon. In California we walked in the redwood forests, we saw Carmel and Point Lobos, then drove down the California coast to San Simeon, then back through Reno, Las Vegas, Boulder, Colorado, the Grand Canyon and the Midwest. We saw the country, its vastness. It opened our eyes, our minds. Anu and I explored it together in the glow of our love, bonding together alongside our closest friends, our companions. I could remember every single day of it clearly.

And now, twenty-six years later, I was by myself, and Anu was by herself. I had done the things I had done, but I had not been the husband that she deserved. I had left her at home and taken myself away. Anu had paid the price. But I had paid it too.

～

I didn't know what to do next. I didn't know how to come out of this. I would sit with Anu and the children, watching TV, but my mind would be somewhere else. I was thinking, *How do I put this back together now? I'm over fifty years old. I have no money. I'm not even an American citizen.* I had to come back home to Chicago on a tourist visa, which meant I couldn't work. I couldn't even go looking for a job.

I did own a little hardware company in Milwaukee called MTI that I had started with some of the money I had made from selling Wescom. MTI had been running on its own pace ever since. But it wasn't big enough for me to get engaged in, and it wasn't throwing off enough money for us to live on.

What was I to do then?

As I was casting around I came across an advertisement for an electronic diary—a gizmo that, upon research, was found to have become popular. Everyone seemed to be using them. Then I remembered that I had filed a patent on an electronic diary many years ago. It was a technology that had occurred to me when I was at GTE. I had filed a patent in 1974 and received it the following year. Patents were valid for seventeen years. I still had a little time left. I still owned the patent, but others were using it.

Major companies were making and selling these diaries—Toshiba, Sharp, Casio, Hewlett-Packard, Texas Instruments, RadioShack. There were six such companies, three Japanese and three American. I could see a light at the end of the tunnel. I wrote to each of them. 'You are using my patent,' I said. 'Royalties are due to me. It's necessary for us to immediately begin discussions regarding arrangements for royalty/ licence and their corresponding payments.'

None of the companies paid any attention. From some I received perfunctory answers. 'Your representation has no validity.' From others I got nothing at all. One responded, 'If your claim had merit, you would have asserted it many years ago.'

When I realized I wasn't getting anywhere I decided to sue all of them in the Cook County Circuit Court in Chicago. But patent litigation is a lengthy, expensive business, and I had no money. So I went to Alan Brown, my former partner at Wescom. I explained the situation to him. 'Let's make a deal,' I said. 'You put in the money for lawyers and expenses, and we'll split the proceeds fifty-fifty.' I think

Alan would have accepted even an eighty-twenty split, but time was passing and I was becoming more and more desperate.

When Alan agreed, we sued.

The six companies boasted an array of pricey, high-flying lawyers. We started the proceedings. The lawyers began to dig into my antecedents—who is this person suddenly appearing out of the woodwork and claiming things. They began checking my background, they explored my private life. One day Anu told me she had spotted people sneaking around looking through our garbage cans. 'They've been coming every night,' she said. 'At midnight.'

'Are you crazy?' I said. 'Why would anybody be looking through our garbage?'

'I don't know,' she said. 'But I see them. They go through the garbage. Right outside the house. I don't like to wake you up.'

I was puzzled. But then during one of the depositions something came up, and I knew that piece of information must have come from my trash. The companies had hired detectives to snoop around.

At first, the company lawyers were dismissive. This wasn't IBM suing them, this was some unknown person with no connection to anyone. But by the time they took my deposition they realized the case was serious. With all their investigating they were reaching the conclusion that I knew the subject and what I was talking about. I had credibility and I could explain things articulately. By then they had understood that I was a bona fide threat to them. They also knew that if the case ever did go to court, a jury would inevitably take the side of David (me) over Goliath (them). In the end, they decided the best path for them would be to settle.

There was, potentially, a substantial amount of money involved in this suit. Electronic diaries had been big sellers for years, with large profits for the manufacturers and sellers. But I was broke, I needed cash immediately. So I settled quickly for a couple of million dollars instead of going through a protracted negotiation that might have given me a fairer, more accurate amount.

What the money did, though, was give me a head start. Now, I had the wherewithal to start rebuilding my life. My depression began to clear. The isolation I felt was still there, but my anxiety was fading. I felt as if the sun might shine again.

~

With the family situation now on an even keel, I could feel myself getting back into gear, thinking about different ideas on how to make money. One day I saw Anu at the dining-room table paying the monthly bills, a stack of statements and invoices piled up in front of her. I asked her, 'How much time do you spend paying these?'

She looked up, annoyed. 'Six or seven hours a month.'

'Six or seven hours? Why?'

'We have a lot of bills. We have a lot of credit cards. We don't synchronize anything. You fill the car at one place, you use one credit card. I fill mine at another, I use something different. Salil fills his somewhere else. Rajal has her own card. We all use different cards all the time. And I have to check all the statements to make sure nobody's cheating us. Then I have to write the cheques and balance the chequebook. This is what I do every month. You never noticed?'

I thought, *This doesn't sound reasonable, spending that much time paying bills. No wonder Anu was exasperated. And if Anu was doing it, everybody else had to be doing it too.* I called my patent lawyer, Eric Cohen, who had won me the electronic-diary settlement, and asked him to send me a list of all the patents issued on electronic money transactions. Two days later I was going through a stack of a hundred or so patents dealing with credit and debit cards.

At home, while the rest of the family was busy watching television, I was scanning patents to understand the concept of 'prior art'. And as I went through the material, I saw that most of the patents were related to inventions for putting magnetic strips or electronic chips on plastic.

While I was reading and thinking, an idea occurred to me that there might be a way to embed a colour liquid crystal display on a card so that if touched in one place, it would become a MasterCard, if touched elsewhere it would become a Visa or an Amex, and so on. Then I'd have all my cards on a single card, instead of having to search around in my wallet for one of them or another. So I started thinking about how that could be achieved. This could certainly pave the way for electronic payment and hugely simplify accounting.

Once I had the basic concept figured out, I called Eric and Walter, my patent lawyers in Chicago, and told them I wanted to file a patent on the idea of a universal electronic-transaction card to enable flexibility, convenience and simplicity while reducing the cost of the transaction.

But while I was working on this, I also realized that mobile phones were going to become a widespread reality before too long. Once that happened it would make sense to put my liquid crystal electronic-transaction idea on to a phone. If I could do that, then users wouldn't have to carry a wallet at all, they would have all their cards on their phones. And not just credit cards, they would be able to carry, at all times, their insurance, health, AAA, airline, loyalty and whatever other cards they usually kept. Phones could be turned into what I began thinking of as 'mobile wallets'. It was the same basic idea I had had for the electronic diary, which had made it possible for people to replace their physical appointment books and day-runners with a convenient electronic device.

The wallet analogy implied that one would have access to software that would function much like an empty wallet. You would load this software on to your mobile phone. Then instead of getting cards sent to you by mail that you would then stuff into your traditional leather wallet, you would get cards issued wirelessly through the Internet. Then you could go to a store and make a purchase by connecting with a point-of-sale device through radio frequency or a barcode. Or you could do a wireless transaction, like buy a book. You could go to the Web via your phone, select your book, select your form of payment, say MasterCard, and pay electronically. You could then receive the receipt for the transaction on your phone and store it there.

Over time, I began to see the feasibility of all sorts of payment-related functions, such as coupons, for example, or special offers, loyalty reward points and airline miles that could be used for payments. Users would have instant access to all of these; they wouldn't have to remember to carry coupons with them to the store, or dig around for crumpled pieces of paper in their pockets or handbags. They could transfer funds between their own accounts or wire funds to a third party's account, all through their phones. And not only would having these functions in one place make the users' lives simpler, it would simplify financial settlements between banks, card companies and merchants.

There were a lot of pieces to the puzzle that still needed figuring out: Wireless issues, proximity transaction issues, security issues, receipt management, point-of-sale devices, the interface with the phone itself as well as with the back-end server.

By 1994 I had resolved the technical problems sufficiently enough to file for a patent on the basis of the concept and design of the mobile wallet. I hadn't worked out the software completely yet, but I had taken the mobile wallet to the point where it met the standards for a patent—i.e., any knowledgeable person in the field could see that it would work. The patent itself was issued in 1996, two years on. Once I had the patent, I asked a group of patent litigation lawyers to look into it for loopholes. They came back to me and said I had to plug about thirty weak spots. I did so, hoping that this invention might someday make enough money for my children to have financial independence, to feel taken care of—and to have more than I ever had.

~

In 1996 I filed a larger patent after I had succeeded in working through the vulnerabilities my patent lawyers had identified. We received that patent two years later, in 1998. Now that I was sure we had thoroughly covered and protected the basic idea, I was ready to set up a business. To help me execute this plan, my friend Dilip Desai's son, Mehul, joined me and moved from MTI in Milwaukee to Chicago.

I had big hopes. I believed I had developed a disruptive technology, something that was going to fundamentally change the way ordinary people managed their lives as consumers of goods and services. The mobile wallet had the potential to make all the cards everyone carries all the time obsolete—the cards themselves as well as the way we use them. The wallet would connect people differently from how they had been connected before and also open up new ways of doing business; it would reshape the way one thought about, used and processed money.

With the patent in my hand, the next thing I needed was a business plan. For that I went to McKinsey & Company. Not long before, McKinsey had elevated one of their senior partners, Rajat Gupta, to the managing-directorship, the first such instance where a non-American national had been chosen to lead the company. Gupta lived in Chicago, and I knew him well. At his house we talked over the patent and my concept for a company, and Rajat put together a team headed by Jayant Sinha to work with us on a plan.

It took six months, but in the end we had a comprehensive business plan that outlined the road map for my potential company, and even defined an entire ecosystem that would be required if the company were ever to achieve the scale I had envisioned for it.

With that we were ready to go. The one problem was that no one could think of a good name, so we finally decided to call it C-SAM—like C-DOT and C-DAC. The new name, C-SAM, stood for 'Commerce—Smart Active Mobile'.

Following my return from India to Chicago, I found myself always thinking about how I might use my experience in India and transpose that on to a larger stage. It was well known that developing nations had little in the way of telecom or IT connectivity. Their networks were primitive and dysfunctional. The inadequacies kept their own business spheres from expanding and discouraged foreign investment. The 'lack of connectivity' was a major element in their backwardness, the same as it had been (and, still in part, was) in India.

Due to my work in the Telecom Commission I knew a great deal about telecom infrastructure issues in developing nations. My tenure at the telecommunications ministry had taught me about an array of organizational issues: Administration, purchasing, planning, project management, and so on. If I could take the approach to telecom that I had formulated in India and apply it to other developing nations around the world, I'd be using my skills to do something truly meaningful.

Privatization was the key here. Governments, especially in developing countries, were rarely equipped to drive change. Whatever monies they had for telecom, they were using to expand landlines for government and security areas such as airlines, military communications, governmental offices, and so on. They weren't improving network access and connectivity for people in rural areas, and they were not doing much to increase the availability of telephones in cities either. Yet, all the technology was readily available to do those very things. In addition, mobile-phone use was poised to explode. But mobile networks needed their own costly infrastructure—the rights of way, towers, base units, power supplies, switches. Without private investment, these things were only going to happen slowly and painfully. As a result, development in these countries was destined to remain badly stunted, especially in comparison to the First World.

What was needed to break this logjam, I thought, *was an international bank dedicated to supporting private telecom and IT projects in the developing world.* The question was: How best to establish something like that?

Since 1975 I have been associated with the International Telecommunications Union (the ITU), a UN agency concerned with information and telecom technologies and standards. The ITU had established a global advisory council in 1993, and I was a member there and, later, the vice chairman. I told the council that I believed this would be a good time to establish a bank to fund telecom in developing countries, with the aim of stimulating privatization and growth.

A similar proposal had actually been placed in front of the ITU twenty-five years earlier, the so-called 'Midland's Commission Report' entitled: *The Missing Link.* It was the lack of telecommunications, the report concluded, that was slowing development in much of the world. Mr Rasswork, who worked at the ITU, was focused on this report and the need to create the right financial instruments for telecom growth in developing countries.

Nothing had come of the Midland's Report—it was too far ahead of its time. But now the council members were receptive to the idea. They first approved a McKinsey feasibility study, *Closing the Information Gap,* which recommended the basic concept, proceeding to then approve our detailed proposal for a bank. Dr Pekka Tarjanne, then Secretary General of the ITU, and Mr Rasswork were my collaborators in pushing the investment-bank idea to the ITU.

At that point I had begun talks with many of the governments that made up the ITU. And in January 1995, the organization officially launched our investment bank, WorldTel.

In 1995, nearly four out of every five people in the world lacked the most basic telephone-service facilities. WorldTel's mission would be to develop and support privately funded telecom projects in nations which most needed them. *WorldTel hopes to break the vicious circle that exists in developing countries,* read the ITU launch announcement. Good telecommunication systems were needed to stimulate economic growth, however, dysfunctional telecommunications were deterring the private investment necessary to improve telecom capacity and capability—a Catch-22 we hoped to cut through. I was named WorldTel's chairman in 1995. I believed we had the potential to make a major impact on communications in the Third World.

WorldTel focused exclusively on telecommunications and information technology to provide direct equity investment raised from private financial investors for projects aiming at improving telecom infrastructure in developing countries. In the process, WorldTel was intended to improve operating skills and provide management support to help productivity and efficiency in the new ecosystem.

With WorldTel under way, I opened an office in London, hired a staff, and began the commute again. I met first with financing institutions—Merrill Lynch, Lazard Frères, Lehman Brothers, Morgan Stanley, NatWest, BNP Paribas—and others looking to raise funds. The World Bank soon got on board and sent a senior staff member to work with us. We finally raised money from AIG, General Electric, NatWest, Intel, and other sources. Their investing in WorldTel meant that they would be on the ground floor of the large projects we were intending to galvanize in the developing world.

As funds became available I began visiting regions that most needed commercial investments in telecommunications. I went to Africa, Latin America, China, South East Asia and the Middle East. I initiated talks with heads of state and telecom ministers about opening up the field to private service providers and equipment makers.

We saw considerable success in some places. We invested substantial amounts in Africa and helped create the first major private telecom enterprise on the continent. In Mexico we put 100 million dollars into Axtel, which challenged the government monopoly and ended up building wireless and landline infrastructure throughout the country.

But at the same time, in many places we encountered an astonishingly brazen environment of corruption that often made it impossible to do business. I wasn't naive about corruption, but I can't say I was prepared for the way it operated as a completely normal way of life in some places. In the countries I visited, I usually met with the prime minister, the communications minister and other high government officials, who very directly made unabashed demands for gifts and money in exchange for a way in. In one of my first meetings, I remember a communications minister once said to me, 'My daughter is going to college in England. Can she get a laptop from WorldTel?'

'No,' I said, 'she can't get a laptop from WorldTel. I can give her a laptop myself, but not from WorldTel. From me, personally, as a friend.' In hindsight, that was still perhaps a bribe of sorts, though I thought of it as more of a goodwill offering.

'Okay,' said the minister, simply. 'You do that.'

That was the mentality. They made no bones about it. No embarrassment, no awkwardness. Of course, a laptop was a small thing. Most often, they wanted only money—and no small amounts at that, not 15,000 or 20,000 dollars. That would be candy. They didn't want *candy*; they wanted the entire candy shop. The corruption was so rampant in these countries that, in one instance, one of our partners forged my signature (in my capacity as the chairman of WorldTel) to mortgage a WorldTel licence, and took loans of tens of millions of dollars for personal use from local banks. I was aware of my duties and responsibilities as the chairman, and had no intention of getting involved in any corrupt practices.

At this time, steady progress in the cellular realm was making a development bank like WorldTel less crucial as a catalyst for private investment. In particular, governments realized that they could make serious money by selling airways to private companies. Thirty years ago, no one had any idea about doing this. Governments allocated frequency spectrums for radio and television without charge, sometimes to government monopolies, sometimes to private operators. After all, it was only air, and air was free.

But with the explosive growth in cell-phone use, the airways turned into gold mines—like real estate in the sky. Governments exploited this potential and auctioned off spectrum licences for billions and billions—an amount mobile operators were willing to pay since they could perceive the fact that putting in many millions of cell phones on a spectrum would bring in monthly fees from users that would dwarf the initial licence costs. So cell-phone growth itself began to fuel privatization.

I worked as WorldTel's chairman and CEO as we made our own groundbreaking investments, while, in the background, cell phones began to transform the investment environment. I stayed on until 2003, when I brought on board Sweden's Par Ivar Eriksson as WorldTel's new CEO.

Once I was in Beijing for a WorldTel-related meeting, when I received a call from my family friend Dinesh Trivedi asking me to come to India to discuss telecom opportunities with the railway ministry. I immediately flew to Delhi to meet with the then railway minister, Ms Mamata Banerjee, along with Dinesh. We discussed the benefit of the 'right of way' that railways enjoy, and the role it can play in Indian telecom development. Based on our conversation, we decided to hire McKinsey & Company to prepare a business plan for the RailTel operation. I also met the then telecom minister, Mr Pramod Mahajan, to discuss my vision to help build a nationwide fibre-optics network and infrastructure for the information highways of tomorrow's India. In subsequent visits I started meeting the chief ministers of West Bengal, Karnataka, Tamil Nadu, Andra Pradesh, Gujarat and other states to help build statewide fibre-optics networks to handle e-governance and to manage the ever-increasing mobile-phone traffic in rural communities. This was perhaps the beginning of my second innings in India.

∼

In the meantime, Salil and Rajal were growing up splendidly. Salil had graduated from MIT with a dual degree in electrical engineering and economics. He worked at the Boston Consulting Group and at General Atlantic. From there, he decided to go to Harvard University and get an MBA. He then moved on to work in the venture capital and private equity business. Rajal, on the other hand, had graduated from the University of Michigan with a degree in economics. She moved on to working at C-SAM and helped me for several years. Later, she moved to India for two years and worked with CII to help build their film division. Finally, she moved to Hollywood to work in the film industry. I was very happy looking at the progress Salil and Rajal were making. However, both of them, like Anu, were always very worried about my health.

As part of a routine annual check-up in 2000, my doctor Surjit Patel found that I had elevated PSA levels, which reflected some issues with the health of the prostate gland. Immediately, we decided to go through a biopsy procedure and, to my shock, we found that I had prostate cancer. I started educating myself to understand the implications of the disease and the alternatives in treatment methods. Fortunately, by now, a huge amount of information was available on the Web. After consultations with several cancer experts, I decided to take a drastic step and go through surgery to remove the prostate gland altogether. General wisdom advised one to go through radiation therapy and other simpler alternatives. But I did not want to take any chances. After discussions with my doctor friends and family members, I went through a major surgery to remove the cancer, and started actively working again.

~

In 2004, not long after I had left WorldTel, the general elections started afresh in India. By then the Congress had been out of office for eight years. India had been doing relatively well in recent times, building on the liberalization policies established under Rajiv Gandhi and taken to further heights by Narasimha Rao (who had succeeded as prime minister after Rajiv's assassination) and his finance minister, Dr Manmohan Singh.

For the first time in years I found myself taking a pointed interest in the Indian political scene. Indian TV channels were just being introduced on American cable. I was following the election developments avidly and also receiving news on the Internet and from friends in India. 'India Shining' was the election slogan for the Opposition party—the BJP. According to them, nothing had been done in the last fifty years before they came into office. The Congress might be challenging them in this election, but the Congress in the past had done nothing to improve Indian lives, they claimed. If the Congress won, they would continue their long record of doing nothing. Sloganeering was evidently rife.

I didn't mind the 'India Shining' slogan, but listening to BJP politicians go on about how nothing had been done in half a century was incorrect and simply insulting. And I took it personally. Worse, no strong Congress spokesman was out in the field rebutting the charges. *How can we let this go on?* I thought. *Somebody has to do something about it.* When I left India thirteen years earlier I had been a wreck. But that felt like the very distant past. Once again, I was full of energy. I told Anu, 'We need to go back.'

13

Knowledge

Over the years, I had thought a lot about what I wanted to do in India. At the very outset, when I was thinking about how to fix the telephone situation, I had considered the idea of starting a business. I considered my career milestones—I had built Wescom; I had inside experience at Rockwell.

I believed I had the knowledge to launch a company. It wouldn't have been difficult to raise the seed money. I had thought about my own business, but only briefly. I had already made my money—at least I thought I had. I had the know-how to build a business, but what excited me was the idea of doing something for India rather than just for myself. This was my American Dream. *If I do get involved in public life in India,* I thought, I should do it with as few attachments as possible. Mahatma Gandhi had no attachments at all, no personal needs. His independence had been the source of his power. But businessmen need things: Tax concessions, government benefits, personal favours, competitive advantages. I didn't want to 'need' things, or be obliged to anyone. I just wanted to work to help modernize India for 1 rupee a year for as long as I could. I wanted to give and not take.

In 1991, when Rajiv brought up the idea of my running for the Lok Sabha—the Parliament—I thought briefly about that too.

'I don't want to run,' I told Rajiv. 'I'll be more useful to you, the party and the country by working from outside the political arena. I can see things from the outside that I wouldn't be able to from the inside. There are hundreds of guys in politics. I'd be just another face. But by being on the outside, I'm also inside. I'm close to you, I'll be able to get things done. But I don't have to be an MP for that. I don't want it. I don't need anything. I don't need money, power and/or position. I just want work that I love and I know there is enough interesting work in this world, especially in India, for the next fifty years.'

I had turned Rajiv down, but I had worked hard for the party for the 1991 elections, right before his death. Now, in 2004, I was feeling the pull again. I met Sonia Gandhi. 'I would like an opportunity to campaign for the party.'

Anu and I flew to India. At Sonia Gandhi's house we all enjoyed a leisurely tea and spent time together. She told us family stories about Rajiv and about her mother-in-law, Indira Gandhi, who had been assassinated in 1984, only seven years before Rajiv. I had known Sonia for years, but I was moved by her strength and the generosity of her spirit.

When we finished talking, she stepped out of the house with Anu and me towards a crowd of newspaper and TV reporters. I said in a written statement:

> I first started working with Rajiv Gandhi over twenty years ago. Two decades later, it is time for me to repay a personal debt to a friend who was so generous with his time, goodwill and support—a friend who gave new meaning to my life.
>
>   It was during Rajiv Gandhi's tenure that many seeds were planted, seeds that grew into strong trees that gave India strength and confidence. He had begun the process for the liberalization of Indian industry. He discovered the essence of the Panchayati Raj. He ushered India into the electronics and computer age. He established the foundation for our success in IT and telecom. He gave a new social dimension to Indian science and technology by launching the

Technology Missions for drinking water, immunization, literacy, oilseeds, telecom and dairy. If there was one programme that revealed Rajiv's greatness and vision, it was the computerization of railway reservations. I was fortunate to be part of those exciting times.

Yesterday's critics have become today's champions. Those who vilified us now want to usurp the credit for all that was accomplished under Rajiv's leadership. I find it appalling when people say things like how the Opposition has done more in five years than what the Congress has done in fifty. I cannot understand how people can lie blatantly like this and live with themselves.

I'll be campaigning for the Congress Party in the Lok Sabha elections. My objective will be to replicate the successes of Rajiv's time and reclaim what the Congress represents. More than science and technology, it is respect for social values and India's social diversity that lies at the core of what Rajiv and other Congress leaders have stood for. In many ways, the Indian diaspora in the US and the professional classes in India are the prime beneficiaries of Jawaharlal Nehru's vision and unparalleled commitment to institution building, a commitment that was taken forward by Rajiv.

I feel it's important for me to campaign. Rajiv Gandhi's agenda is unfinished, and now it needs to be seen to fruition. If Rajiv were alive, I wouldn't have needed to be in the picture. But unfortunately he is no longer here, and I feel it's my moral responsibility to carry on. We, the Congress Party, will not let the work that he began be hijacked by those who repeat endlessly that India is shining and that we ourselves have done nothing. That is a lie that we cannot and will not allow to stand.

India's electorate comprised over 670 million people, most of them living in rural areas. But I knew I could maximize impact by appearing on TV and the radio and giving speeches to large audiences in big cities. I did that. I went to Ahmedabad, Baroda, Bangalore, Delhi, Mumbai, Pune and Hyderabad. I spoke at universities, business associations, press clubs, Rotary and Lions Club meetings—anyplace we could muster a decent-sized audience. The press covered me; I was something of a story for them—Rajiv Gandhi's ex-telecom and technology guru coming back to India after years of silence and being absent from the scene.

I campaigned for six weeks straight. My message was clear. *We—the Congress—did get things done. We opened up the telecom and IT sectors. We liberalized the economy. We made great strides in education, health, agriculture, water, nutrition. We had a strong track record in building an inclusive India. We accept that there is a lot more that needs to be done.*

'You have to realize what the Gandhi family has gone through,' I said in my interviews to the media and in my speeches. 'The grandmother, Indira, was murdered, then the father, Rajiv. But the family has stuck with the party, they have stuck with us, with India. It would be so easy to just walk away. But that's not what they are made of. They are people of character and responsibility. Sonia Gandhi, an Italian lady—look at the defeats she has faced. But she is still here, genuinely believing in Indian development, believing in India. What a remarkable thing. At the end of the day you need to have immense inner strength to be able to do this. She and her party have done great things for India in the past.'

All the polls indicated that the BJP would win, but the polls didn't count on the poor, the disenfranchised and the rural voters. 'The core of the Congress Party,' I said, 'is respect for secular values and India's social diversity. Those were the key elements that drove our founders to build our institutions, those are the values that Rajiv Gandhi embraced and nourished. Those are the values that will take us forward.'

In the end the Congress and its coalition scored a stunning victory, winning 325 out of 523 seats in the Lok Sabha. As leader of the party, Sonia Gandhi was expected to become prime minister, but in a surprise move she declined the position, and the Oxford-trained economist and former finance minister Dr Manmohan Singh was sworn in as prime minister on 22 May 2004.

Although I had been part of the victory, I wasn't interested in taking an active role in the government. But then I received a phone call from Mrs Sonia Gandhi's office. There were plans to form the National Advisory Council, with her as the chairperson. And they wanted me to become a member.

I said, 'Of course, it's a privilege.' And so I became a member of the council.

The council consisted of twelve people in addition to Mrs Sonia Gandhi—academicians, social activists, NGO leaders and industrialists. The idea was that the council would advise and provide inputs to the prime minister on crucial civil society legislation dealing with poverty reduction, economic growth, rural development, labour and other efforts to ameliorate the lives of the poor.

As I drew together my thoughts on this general subject, several basic facts about India and its relationship with the rest of the world assumed fresh significance. The first point was regarding demography—India was a giant nation of over a billion people, and it was a young giant. Most of the world's populations were ageing, while India's was growing younger. Second, we were living in an information age, where knowledge and the innovations based on knowledge had become the most critical resource in nation-building and in the competition among nations. Third, knowledge in terms of education and skills was the only pathway out of poverty and into relative well-being for those at the bottom of the pyramid. I was an example of a person who had benefited from low-cost higher education in India.

Since the initiation of the economic liberalization process in 1991, India's economic progress has been accelerating. But we did not have enough educated, skilled people to maintain the growth we needed. We had shortages in every sector: Teachers, doctors, scientists, engineers, nurses, plumbers, carpenters. We needed to produce much larger numbers of qualified people. We had the youth and we had the innate talent. What we didn't have were the adequate means to capitalize on these advantages. Education and knowledge had to be the key for us. If India was going to prosper among the world's nations, we needed to develop what I began thinking of as a 'knowledge edge'.

The question was: How were we going to accomplish this? It obviously was not about starting one college or one university. But how did one take a country of 1.2 billion and develop society-wide plans to bring education into the 21st century?

I started thinking about university reforms. But universities were only one part of the picture. Vocational education was equally important. We didn't just need professionals, we needed skilled people occupying the trade and service sector. And we needed to excel too. Apart from the top 5 per cent of the universities, the quality of Indian education was, to put it bluntly, just not good. Also, there was a need for equity. The poorest of the poor needed to have access to the best—or at least halfway decent—schools. We needed trends of expansion and excellence, but just as important, we needed equity and inclusiveness.

Thinking about all this: Growth, education and inclusiveness, I began to understand that in order to accomplish these things on a countrywide scale, we needed to create a countrywide platform—and that platform was knowledge.

I did some research and found that nobody had put together a big national platform on knowledge before—no country, ever. The world was moving fast towards transforming itself into a global knowledge community, but no nation had looked at the challenge in a comprehensive manner. The next question, then, was: What would a comprehensive knowledge platform look like?

As I read more and more literature on the topic, I began breaking down the problem. After a while I concluded that that there were five essential areas we should be focusing on—a knowledge pentagon with five points—namely, access to knowledge; knowledge concepts; knowledge creation; knowledge application; and knowledge services.

Access to knowledge meant making knowledge as widely available as possible. However, this didn't happen automatically, it had to be a matter of state policy. To begin with, in India, the translation of languages had to be a priority. It is often the case that people—young people and poor people especially—know only their local languages. One also had to consider places like libraries. Knowledge-sharing institutions had been in decline for years, a trend which had to be reversed. India has 53,000 libraries, and we needed to modernize, digitize and rejuvenate our large libraries and build small local libraries, incorporating Internet and broadband facilities. Then there was the matter of content—what *kind* of knowledge? We needed open access to government functions. Accurate information about what regional and national governments were doing in sectors such as agriculture, health, education, food distribution, disaster relief, and so on, had to be readily accessible to everyone. We needed to establish Web-based portals that would be one-stop sources of information on vital issues such as water, sanitation, health, housing, nutrition and employment.

The second point on the pentagon was *knowledge concepts*. Where are knowledge concepts taught? And what do we need to do to upgrade our teaching institutions, to make more of them world-class? What were the specific reforms needed in elementary and secondary schools, vocational education centres, colleges and universities, distance-learning centres, continuous-learning centres, teacher-training institutions, and professional training centres for engineers, doctors, lawyers and others; and how did one access open-source courseware? How do we send more of our young people into PhD programmes? How do we get more of them into the math and science streams? How do we reduce and eliminate adult illiteracy?

The third point was *knowledge creation*. Knowledge is created by those who work in science, the arts and humanities, but in order to grow economically, to create jobs, modernize our industries and lift the masses out of poverty, we needed to focus on science and technology. India had some of the world's leading scientists and technologists, but our institutions lagged behind both the West and developing nations such as China and Brazil. We had to find more effective ways to promote and fund research. That meant, among other things, encouraging private investment, both domestic and foreign, and nurturing private/public partnerships. We had to be able to link research with the needs of industry and foster a mutually productive relationship between the two spheres. We had to augment our R & D infrastructure and stimulate innovation by creating a culture of entrepreneurship. And we had to strengthen our protection of creators and inventors by establishing a more robust intellectual property rights and patents regime, which would earn the confidence of global leaders and encourage investment and licensing.

A fourth point on my pentagon scheme was *knowledge application*. What are the most effective ways to make knowledge practical and useful? In what areas would the application of knowledge have the most impact? Education was an obvious example—the Internet and e-learning would be able to enhance and complement classroom learning and continuing education. Agriculture was another area. Agricultural research needed to be expanded and brought to bear specifically on farmers' needs. Farmers had to be able to capitalize on new technologies and techniques; they needed access to the most updated information on prices, distribution channels, weather, water, power and livestock management. Rural areas were peppered with small- and medium-sized industries. These needed access to market information, credit and insurance information, training opportunities and advances in manufacturing processes. Another immensely important area was India's almost unfathomable richness of traditional knowledge in medicine, arts, architecture, crafts, food, culture, and more. So much of this was scattered and inaccessible, so much was falling into desuetude and was fast disappearing. But modern technology gave us the ability to preserve and document and disseminate and utilize this national treasure trove.

Knowledge services was the final point in my pentagon. By this I primarily meant e-governance. India was a country where the citizens' interactions with the government were commonly a source of frustration, fear, and a door to corruption. Everything from driver's licences to birth certificates, land titles, business approvals, voter registrations, students' stipends, passports, pensions and other social payments—all the procedures for these kinds of interactions were antiquated, unnecessary and complex, and vulnerable to the nuisance of venal clerks and administrators. People trying to access public services were at the mercy of those who controlled the services. Court, police, prison and other public records were in a state of disarray, and were often inaccessible. But information technology was readily available to simplify and facilitate these services. ICT—information and communication technology—could streamline all the processes, make them transparent, reduce their costs, help eliminate dishonesty, and ensure overall accountability on the part of the public servants. E-governance and ICT were poised to usher in a new era in government functioning. All that was required was the effort to put it in place.

That was my Knowledge Pentagon—Access, Concepts, Creation, Applications, Services. I did my best to put the main ideas into digestible form and made a PowerPoint presentation to Prime Minister Singh and his staff, including Mr Nair, his principal secretary. 'Here's what we would like to do,' I told him. 'This is where we think we should be going. Right now we just do bits and pieces of what's necessary. A National Knowledge Commission will enable us to structure a comprehensive platform and push a truly national agenda.

Singh grasped the idea immediately. It had as much cogency for him as it did for those of us on the council. 'Sam,' he said, 'we're going to do this right away.' I received substantial support from a brilliant secretary, R. Gopalakrishnan, in the prime minister's office. He had worked with me as a junior officer on the Technology Mission on Water in 1987.

I gave the proposal in December 2004. The prime minister wanted to make an announcement regarding this in January 2005. I requested him to wait until we had done some more work to internalize the concept.

~

While in Chicago, I was busy learning about the different knowledge-related initiatives in the US, Europe and Japan. I was meeting leading experts at major universities and scientific laboratories apart from my friends in the field. I am lucky to have some great friends all over the world, especially the doctors in Chicago, to educate me on various health-related technologies. They also take personal interest in my well-being. These friends include Dr Prakash Desai, a psychiatrist; Drs Dinker Trivedi and R.K. Patel, both cardiologists; Dr Piyush Vyas, a radiologist; Dr Divyesh Mehta, an oncologist; Dr Shiban Ganju, a gastroenterologist, Dr Nikhil Bhatt, an ENT surgeon; Drs Surjit and Dilip Patel, both general practitioners; and a few others, who graduated from medical colleges in Baroda and Ahmedabad in the 1960s and 1970s.

Ten years after my first quadruple bypass in 1990, Dinker Trivedi, my cardiologist, had put four stents in my body to force open my blocked arteries. During a routine check-up, he became concerned and asked me to do another angiogram, after which he said, 'I'd like you to go through a second bypass surgery.' This was 2005, about fifteen years after I had undergone my first bypass in Delhi. I had been informed that the first bypass would last around fifteen years and that the possibility of blockage after that would be significantly higher if I continued with my present lifestyle. A second bypass was a scary thought. For the first time, I was really worried about going through another major intrusive operation.

Normally, I look at every surgery as a process where I am an object, placed in the hands of my competent doctors, who take me through a production line and perform all the necessary tasks with great care for the best results possible. I go in with my eyes closed and with full trust in the doctors' abilities, and through their competent craftsmanship I come out with my eyes open, well and fine. However, this time the thought of having my ribs cut open again to access my heart was more frightening. After consultation with the family, a date was fixed; Salil, his fiancée, Arpita, and Rajal, all came home along with other family members and friends—almost twenty of us went to the hospital early in the morning. However, that night, somehow, I felt that this could be the last night of my life. I called my children in to sleep in the same room with me, so I could feel a little more safe and comfortable before I went to sleep.

Something like this had never happened to me before. I had been close to death several times during the course of these surgeries—the first bypass, the prostate cancer scare, the removal of my saliva gland and my two hernia operations (the left and right side). Once I was in the hospital, I was still not completely without fear and requested the doctor to give me a tranquilizer shot to relax before they took me in for anaesthesia. Dr Papas, a well-known heart surgeon who specializes in second bypasses, came to see me and assured me that everything would be okay. A couple of weeks before that, Dr Naresh Trehan from Delhi had come to Chicago. He said he was there to take me to Delhi for the second bypass, and that once I got well, he would bring me back home to Chicago as well. I was very touched by his gesture of love and affection. I told him that my family had agreed to my first bypass in India, because then I had been consumed by the thought of championing indigenous development and local capabilities in India, and would need to remain there. But now that I was in Chicago, I didn't think my family would allow me to travel to India for a second bypass there.

After four days in the hospital, I was back home from my second bypass. Dr Papas told me not to travel for at least thirty days. I was very anxious to go to India to launch the Knowledge Commission. I was in touch with the prime minister's office, and we fixed a date in June 2005 for the launch, as soon as I was allowed to travel. The prime minister came to the Planning Commission to launch the National Knowledge Commission in the presence of the members of both commissions and the media. The prime minister even made a special reference to the fact that I was so eager to start my work in India that I had flown in immediately after my second bypass. And so the world's first National Knowledge Commission was formally launched.

The Knowledge Commission comprised several distinguished members from industry, universities and the scientific community, including Dr Ashok Ganguly, Nandan Nilekani, Dr Jayati Ghosh, Dr Sujatha Ramdorai, Dr Mashelkar, Dr Bhargava, Dr Balram, Dr Pratap Bhanu Mehta, Dr André Béteille, Dr Mattu and Dr Deepak Nayyar. To begin operations, we established a small office in Delhi with a staff of around ten young enthusiastic analysts. We used the C-DOT–model of egalitarian management and established low-budget infrastructure and a self-supporting team, equipped with digital tools for research on various areas. Throughout the process R. Gopalakrishnan, from the prime minister's office, helped us coordinate with the various ministries and managed our discussions at the appropriate levels.

After a few meetings of the commission, we set up working groups in twenty-seven areas, where each group included domain experts in that field. We flagged most of the groups off and presented a basic vision and our approach. The members, of course, always had their own ideas and added their advice gleaned from experiences, and provided support. We gave each working group a year or so to consult with the stakeholders and develop consensus. I directly monitored the progress of all the groups and attended as many meetings as I could. Other members along with advisers from the Planning Commission and the secretaries of the various departments actively participated in the working groups. All the members of the National Knowledge Commission were distinguished leaders in their own fields and devoted all the necessary time and energy to mentor, guide and support working groups and our young research associates on a day-to-day basis. In the process we all became close friends, collaborated on multiple initiatives, learned from each other, agreed to disagree and collectively developed a national knowledge agenda. As a group we met with the prime minister on a regular basis to brief him on our progress.

When the working groups in these twenty-seven subject areas were satisfied with their conclusions, they each produced a white paper, which we then discussed and debated on at the Knowledge Commission. The output of the Knowledge Commission comprised a three-page 'letter' on each working-group area written by me and addressed to the prime minister, with recommendations for action areas, which we posted on the Internet. The commission dealt with twenty-seven major subjects and submitted almost 300 recommendations to the government in the form of 'letters to the PM', annual reports, as well as a final report brought out at the end of three years. These reports were sent to all the members of Parliament, chief ministers, media houses and universities.

~

The National Knowledge Commission was established to conceptualize, plan and recommend changes to India's knowledge infrastructure, which would enable the leapfrogging of social and economic development. We had designed the commission to function for a period of three years—which seemed about the right amount of time for it to do its job and provide the government with a blueprint for accomplishing the transformations we had envisioned.

At the end of the three years we closed the commission down as planned and issued a final report addressed to the prime minister and the Indian people. I then spent the following six months publicizing our ideas and selling them to the various ministries. The National Advisory Council first entertained the Knowledge Commission concept in 2004, shortly after the general elections. By the time implementation was decently under way, it was 2009. Five years had elapsed. It had taken that long a time to lobby and create an understanding for what needed to be done.

Even then the ministry bureaucracies took their time to respond. Secretaries changed. Administrators sometimes weren't eager enough to make the necessary effort. We had to reconcile ourselves to the reality that there were not enough change agents in the government and our priorities were not necessarily theirs. Unfortunately, even the student community directly affected by the Knowledge Commission recommendations never organized themselves, nor did they agitate to demand change in the education system. Similarly, teachers also had little interest in a new approach to education. It is difficult to institutionalize change in a democratic system under these circumstances. But the work began.

As a result of the Knowledge Commission push, the government, as part of the Eleventh Five-Year Plan (2007–12), allocated 70 billion dollars to education as opposed to the usual 14 billion. When we had started out, only about 10 per cent of Indian children were recorded as going to college. Today, ten years down the road, we have 20 per cent of children getting a college degree, double the number. The quality of many schools still isn't what it should be, but I believe over time that will change.

Vocational education is a key area that needed—and still needs—special attention; our vocational institutions have simply not done their jobs well. But we have now set up a national mission on skill development headed by the former CEO of the international giant, the Tata Consulting Company. Transformation here is a long-term prospect, but we can take comfort in the fact that it has taken flight at least.

The traditional-knowledge working group had one of the richest fields to mine, a whole historical culture—some of it still vibrant, some all but lost, some of it in museums, some in somebody's house, some handed down from generation to generation of craftspeople and some written on banana-leaf parchment in extinct scripts. Finding and preserving India's traditional knowledge is a critical, prodigious task. We have documented over 1.5 million manuscripts, catalogued several thousand medicinal plants, and taken several other major steps towards supporting this heritage and making it available. However, a great deal still needs to be done in this area.

Another enormous project was catapulted into action by the knowledge-network working group headed by Dr Chidambaram and assisted by Dr Gairola, Dr Raghavan, Dr Y.K. Sharma and Dr Mani, which recommended connecting all of India's universities, colleges, R & D institutions and libraries via optical fibre at an investment of around 2 billion dollars. Because of the growth of telecom we already had a million kilometres of fibre optics in place, some of it lying unused and dark (meaning, not activated, nor energized). The government funded the group's recommendation; we lit the dark fibre up and laid more, connecting over 20,000 institutions from one end of the country to the other. All research today is multidisciplinary, requiring a great deal of collaboration, and the process is happening at a faster pace than ever before. As a result, modern research requires real-time collaboration, high-speed computing, resource sharing and an international context. The knowledge network will not only connect Indian scientists to each other but will also bring global science to Indian doorsteps. There has been a great deal of debate on the issue of brain drain in India and many developing countries. I firmly believe that because of the extreme prevalence of the Internet and globalization, the challenge today is not about brain drain, but about 'brain gain' (meaning, the ability to gain from brains around the world) and 'brain chain' (meaning, to network brains globally).

The knowledge network is fully operational today. It can instantly connect a professor from Bangalore to a professor from Guwahati. A student doing research now would be able to access all our scientific laboratories. Michael Sandel, a world-famous Harvard professor teaching justice and philosophy, came to India, and we decided to speak to the Indian university community together using this very knowledge network. He and I held the talk in a large auditorium at the University of Delhi, with maybe 700 students and professors who physically attended the talk. But there were half a million others in lecture halls all around the country in Indian universities who watched and listened too. And since the connection was interactive we opened the forum up for questions. Sandel was accustomed to speaking to large audiences at the world's leading universities. But he'd never experienced anything like this before. It left him wondering, 'I've never in my life talked to so many students at a time.'

These are all significant accomplishments. We will be able to see the results ten or twenty years down the road. This work is all about planting seeds, not being concerned with the fruit. By the time you get fruits you may not even be around to see them. But this is the kind of thing that has to be done. Michael Porter, the world's leading thinker on international strategy and competitiveness, makes the point that the United States today is such a leader economically because of the commitments made to education, communication, health, access to information, and other sectors, about fifty or a hundred years ago. Many other nations have, in recent times, caught up with and surpassed the US to some degree or in some area, but America's earlier investments made the country the global powerhouse it remains today. With the broad-scope knowledge platform we have now put in place, we hope to see India in a world-leading position itself as the 21st century advances.

~

The Knowledge Commission was an immense, inspiring endeavour that inevitably expanded my views and thought process regarding India. I began to grasp, among other things, the progressive nature of the development I had been involved with since I first came back to the country in 1981.

The way I saw it, the first phase of the telecom revolution was over. The foundation of that revolution was connecting rural India to the rest of the country and the world, giving the villages access to the grid of modernity. We achieved this through privatization, liberalization, corporatization, deregulation—and the systems that C-DOT pioneered. Then, once international standards had been promulgated, we opened India up to mobile telephony. I had put that platform in place just before my return to Chicago, after Rajiv passed away.

After that the private entrepreneurs took over. The entrepreneurial spirit and the prospect of making money drove big and small mobile operators to go into all parts of the country and find interesting ways to sell telephones. They borrowed money, they leased, they leveraged— they found creative ways of financing their augmentation. They advertised and promoted, and they sold the idea. The result was that in 2014 India had over a billion mobile phones in use.

That first phase took twenty years.

The next question was: Now that we had this connectivity, how could we best use it? The answer to that lay in the fact that connectivity enables the transfer of information—or in other words—knowledge. People connecting with each other, exchanging views and conveying information—personal, business, technical, academic, practical, social, all of it. Connectivity is the vehicle, and knowledge is the content.

While the political system was working on the Knowledge Commission's recommendations, I found myself thinking about the overall goals we wanted to accomplish with this connectivity revolution that had taken place—which was still progressing at breakneck speed.

The ultimate goal, as I saw it, was to ensure that India would become a thriving democracy, a place it had been moving towards clumsily, in fits and starts, since Independence. *Could we,* I thought, *rationalize that movement and accelerate it?* That was the goal. And the key value at the core of the goal was inclusivity. A thriving democracy *had* to be an inclusive democracy. Growth *had* to benefit those at the bottom along with those flourishing at the top.

I had been saying for years that the best brains in the world are busy solving the problems of the rich—who actually don't have any real problems to solve. As a result, the difficulties of the poor don't get the right kind of attention, or the right talent to help them get through it. Whenever I discussed this, in my mind's eye I pictured Tara and Budhwari, the two tribal women who had raised me as lovingly as my own mother had. If we enabled the wealthy to become richer and expanded the middle class, how could we, in good conscience, leave them behind? Inclusiveness, as I saw it, was inseparable from democracy. You needed to carry people with you. You had to include them in the national political body and you had to improve their lives along with everyone else's.

Bringing the poor into the mainstream meant making the nation's government inclusive, open and transparent. It meant providing information to everyone. Then there was the matter of growing the economy—and that meant innovation. The facilitator of inclusive democratic politics was equal access to information. The driver of inclusive growth was innovation. And technology was at the root of both.

We knew we needed to build a public information infrastructure in order to democratize information. And we needed to galvanize innovation in order to energize growth. I saw both these endeavours as the next phase of the technology revolution we had begun shepherding with the Knowledge Commission. To me, five phases were critical to India's development: Telecom, the Technology Missions, the Knowledge Commission, the democratization of information, and innovation. I had a series of discussions on these with R. Gopalakrishnan in the prime minister's office. Three of these were under way, and we still needed to launch the next two. With this concept firmly in mind I went to see the prime minister.

Manmohan Singh was pleased with the way the Knowledge Commission had gone about its work, and he had invested himself in the recommendations of the working groups. When I described how I envisioned the next phase, he was immediately supportive. In the end he established an 'Office of the Adviser to the Prime Minister on Public Information Infrastructure and Innovation', and I was bestowed with the rank of Cabinet minister.

The official announcement of the new adviser's office noted that India's inclusive growth agenda and its global competitiveness would depend on its ability to give citizens access to information and public services. To accomplish this, the country needed 'a comprehensive

Public Information Infrastructure and a road map for innovation geared towards meeting the challenges of the 21st century'.

~

While all this was going on in India, I was working in tandem to build C-SAM up as a successful business with what I hoped would be a bountiful future.

In spite of my extensive technical background, I had seriously underestimated the complexity of the ecosystem the mobile wallet would need to operate in if it was going to attract customers. So instead of creating an income-producing product, I found myself climbing a very steep learning curve. Since I had been immersed in WorldTel since the first part of C-SAM's existence and, after that, with the National Knowledge Commission, Mehul had to take charge of day-to-day operations.

In particular, what we discovered was that in order to create a mobile-money platform that consumers would actually be interested in, we needed three major industries to come together—first, the mobile service providers in the US, namely, Verizon, AT&T, Sprint and T-Mobile; second, the credit card companies and bank; and, finally, the merchants—the bricks-and-mortar merchants like Walmart, Macy's and McDonalds, and the online merchants like Amazon.

So in order to create a mobile wallet that consumers would adopt we needed, first of all, to integrate ourselves with these three entities. They had to accept that it was important for them to possess the capability we were offering the consumers. That was the prerequisite. Then we had to make the system easy, convenient and secure for the customers to use. And beyond that there was the question of unpredictable consumer behaviour.

I was excited by the concept of the mobile wallet, and I had confidence in it. I thought the chances were excellent that we'd have a ready market soon enough. The Internet was booming, smartphone technology was gathering steam, and market caps were skyrocketing. We had clearly entered a new world, an electronic world, encompassing not only knowledge, but buying and selling and all kinds of commerce and money transactions—exactly the environment C-SAM needed in order to succeed. The stars seemed to be aligning themselves in the most auspicious order.

Then, suddenly and unexpectedly, the Internet bubble burst in 2000. Everything shuddered to a halt. Market evaluations of the new dot-coms had been wildly speculative, fuelled by raised eyebrows and hopes for and talk of future profits rather than being based on anything like actual earnings. All the 'irrational exuberance', as Alan Greenspan put it, was followed by widespread, and often spectacular, bankruptcies, as many of the new companies burned through their seed money and failed to generate income.

The Internet companies triggered the stock market collapse of 2000, but it affected telecom too. With the market plunging scarily, semiconductor companies slowed down their chip development and production work. As a result the telecom industry decided that the plans for smartphones needed to be postponed. New models were put on hold. The world slowed from full speed ahead to a sluggish pace. Interest in innovative ideas—our idea, for example—dried up. We found ourselves going into crisis mode in the blink of an eye.

I still thought that we could make it, that it was going to happen. But now it was going to happen three or four years later than I had initially thought, and my funds were nowhere near sufficient to see us through. And to add to that I had to keep C-SAM alive. I had put all the family money into it. Shutting it down and walking away simply wasn't an option.

We knew the only way we could go on would be by obtaining the support of a big-name strategic partner. Happily, at the same time, all our missionary work had paid us dividends. Our electronic-money-transaction platform was well known and appreciated. Our security software commanded attention. Other companies working in our sphere had burned through their venture capital and gone belly-up in the dismal market. We were at least alive, and our work was gaining more and more recognition.

In 2011 Discover acquired a minority equity position in C-SAM. This provided us the backing we needed to close a large licensing agreement with the AT&T, Verizon and T-Mobile ventures. With the investment locked in, we hired a professional management team, headed by Felix Marx from Vienna as CEO, to help build the organization for growth.

At the same time, however, the market was evolving quickly. PayPal and Google were in the game now with their own mobile-wallet technologies—big players with deep pockets. There was news that Amazon was developing its own payment system, as was Walmart. While discussing our strategy it became clear that we would need to build up fairly dramatically if we hoped to compete for the big licensing deals that were going to be out there (or were already out there). But as we debated our strategies, the market continued to change swiftly.

Based on these developments, I went to New York for an important meeting with MasterCard. This started the ball rolling and, after a year of discussions and due diligence, MasterCard decided to make a strategic investment in C-SAM.

The C-SAM journey was far longer and rougher than we thought it would be. We were the pioneers in the field, and had enough arrows in our backs to prove it. We conceived of the mobile-wallet concept all the way back in 1994 when no one had even heard of smartphones or the digital wallet. Only ten years and over fifty patents later has the mobile-wallet idea surfaced in the market. Now, with the entry of Apple Pay and MasterPass, mobile payment is becoming a reality. We've finally arrived.

In the end we closed a deal with MasterCard to buy the entire company for a substantial amount and take under their wing around 300 employees and offices in Chicago, Tokyo, Singapore, Vienna, Baroda and Pune.

While all of this was going on, Salil and Rajal were busy on their own journey. We were a virtual family, living in three different parts of the US. Salil in San Francisco, Rajal in Hollywood, and Anu and me in Chicago. However, I always made it a point to speak to my children at least once a day on the phone no matter where I was. In 2007, Salil married Arpita Patel, an endocrinologist from New York. Rajal decided to go to London Business School for an MBA.

After my first heart attack in the late 1980s, I had arranged to transfer all my business and other assets to my wife and children. In 1998, we sold a piece of MTI to enable us to buy a bigger house and a few fancy cars, and to pay for the children's educations. It also allowed us to fund C-SAM, which was essentially owned by both the kids. By selling off C-SAM, I felt comfortable that Salil and Rajal's financial futures were secure. I heaved a sigh of relief.

14

Digital India

I was finally coming to terms with the next phase of India's ICT revolution. In particular, I was now thinking more comprehensively about the impact and benefits of the Internet which would help make Digital India a reality.

In that regard, my own fundamental beliefs centred on the concepts of democracy, globalization, free-market economy and privatization. But the enabler here, in my view, was democracy. The democratic ethos, its values, its mores, its procedures and its spiritual characteristics allow for the attainment of what it means to be human—to a far greater extent than any other political system. And the essence of democracy, again, in my opinion, is that it recognizes the humanity of each person, which includes empowering all people as full participants in the national community. This is another way of saying that democracy is inclusive. I am a firm believer in democracy, and I am a firm believer in inclusiveness. They are two parts of a whole.

'Inclusiveness' means that I cannot worry simply about my own well-being, I have to worry about my neighbour's well-being as well.

In the last two decades India has done an immense job of raising the standard of living for several hundred million people, but we still have almost 200 million surviving in the 'subsistence' bracket—the largest number of poor in the world. As I see it, the task of public information and innovation is to bring those at the bottom (out of subsistence and) into a plane of well-being.

Around the world, poverty is typically linked to the lack of knowledge. To me, that meant we needed two complementary efforts—one, to give people a way of accessing knowledge and, two, to make sure the knowledge they needed was accessible and useful.

The first order of business was to create the Right to Information (RTI) bill. The National Advisory Council headed by Mrs Sonia Gandhi, president of the Congress Party, drafted the fundamental document on the right to information. Several distinguished members of the council, including Aruna Roy, Jairam Ramesh and Jean Drèze, actively participated in the exercise. To me this was a landmark bill designed to create a more open society and give people a real voice in the system. I have repeatedly stated that information brings about openness, accessibility, connectivity, networking, democratization and decentralization which, resultantly, leads to substantial social, political and economic transformation. I firmly believe that information is the fourth pillar of democratic government in the 21st century, in addition to the legislative, executive and judiciary. Without this fourth pillar of information, ordinary people are unable to participate fully in the democratic process. To achieve this, information has to be democratized.

In most countries, government information resides in silos that are under the direct control of the government. But with the RTI Act of 2005, like America's Freedom of Information Act, information is far more extensive in the sense that all non-protected information is mandated to be readily available and accessible upon request. We believe that every citizen has the right to ask the government about anything. What happened to the road in my district that was supposed to be built? What about the health centre, the sewer system? How much money was spent, what was accomplished, where is the accounting? None of this sort of information had ever been made available before—a direct legacy of the British Raj where no government information was ever made privy to the public. But India, today, has the most progressive right-to-information law in the world, because we took the best from everybody's legislations and policies while we were drafting our bill.

Of course, despite the RTI Act, the fact is that all information is not really accessible. It isn't accessible because the information is locked up in the government's *nadawali* files (literally translating to 'files tied in red tape') in reams of physical forms. The present national organization system comprises thirty-six states and union territories, fifty central ministries, sixty departments, 100 commissions and 4 million employees with multiple establishments and multiple channels for delivery of public services. It is full of fragmented structures and archaic processes, and there is a glaring lack of transparency, accountability, clarity, and it is also plagued by duplicate files, conflicting priorities, inadequately trained manpower and poor infrastructure.

During the late 1980s the Rajiv Gandhi government planted the first seed for Digital India by creating the National Informatics Centre for computerizing government by building a national communications network (NICNET) with data centres in Delhi and a few other states. This was the beginning of an effort to computerize government information and digitize India for the 21st century. In the last thirty years, the centre has done a remarkable job of building human capacity and the necessary institutional frameworks and programmes in order to help computerize all major government departments for e-governance functionalities. However, the technology then was very different.

Now, with low-cost computers and terminals, cloud computing, open-source software and tablets and smartphones, the entire landscape has transformed completely. Now e-governance is required to be on the cloud with prescribed standards for all states to follow to access the common software and applications and maintain interoperability. To examine this issue further, a committee headed by Nandan Nilekani was set up by the Knowledge Commission to review the status of e-governance in India.

The Knowledge Commission committee established in detail that e-gov is more about an opportunity for administrative reforms than being merely about technology and infrastructure. The commission also stated that at present the efforts in the area are primarily based on computerizing age-old processes left behind by the British Raj and further complicated by the Indian bureaucracy with department boundaries, more paperwork and pet priorities. As an end result we end up computerizing pointless processes and hence do not commensurately benefit from it. The Knowledge Commission felt that there was now a unique opportunity in the history of India to put to rest this colonial hangover and re-engineer and modernize government processes to build a new India of the 21st century. Hence, it is essential to first redesign the government processes keeping the citizens' interests firmly at the centre, providing for the benefit of citizens, businesses, consumers and producers, and replacing the old mistrust and controlled regime that plagued our colonial past.

For there to be an immediate impact on citizens it is critical to identify and simplify ten to twenty important processes and services that are currently burdensome, bureaucratic and prone to unnecessary delays and corruption. At present, various state governments are still choosing their own way of selectively computerizing their processes to provide e-gov. Many of these programmes are vendor-driven and not scalable. It is extremely critical to develop and enforce standards uniformly over all states and central ministries on issues such as voting, taxes, certificates, law enforcement, welfare and land records. These yardsticks, templates and data formats must be designed by teams of domain experts carefully drawn from the government, IT, the academia, R & D institutions, and users who understand the latest trends, technology, software, interoperability and user interfaces.

A great deal of work has already been done in various central ministries and state governments. The key is to learn from these and design best practices. At the same time, data collected by one agency should be made available across all agencies as well as to the public, subject to security considerations. It is important to provide secure broadband infrastructure and associated hardware, software and hosting facilities nationwide, with easy access at all levels. It is also important to provide Web-based services, use open-source software and appoint chief technology officers with relevant expertise and skills in the domain and in IT. For national e-governance to succeed it is important to create a government organization at the national level with structures that can operate in mission mode with full accountability and autonomy.

For the RTI model to function sans hiccups, and for the government to improve transparency and accountability, it is critical to build a public information infrastructure with the focus firmly on democratizing information at various levels in the government and public institutions for citizen services and support. The public information infrastructure required four key elements: Connectivity, platforms, applications, and data centres and security.

To take on the challenge of connectivity, we had already established the National Knowledge Network to connect our universities and research facilities with a dedicated Internet bandwidth of 1 gigabit (expandable to 10 gigabits). This network was already operational and had been connected to around 1500 nodes by the end of 2013. The network was designed for managing applications related to enabling countrywide virtual classrooms, virtual libraries, grid computing, high-speed networking, e-governance, collaborative research and the sharing of computing resources. However, we needed the set-up to go far beyond the Knowledge Network's reach to village panchayats and rural areas.

This was the same idea I had advocated years earlier—connecting the villages and rural areas of India first, not last. Our identity as a country starts with the villages. I always remember the words Gandhiji said: 'I would say that if the village perishes India will perish too. India will be no more India. Her own mission in the world will get lost.'

I personally started putting a plan together with the help of the team at the National Informatics Centre and the telecommunications and IT ministry. We already had around a million kilometres of optical fibre running through the country. We now had to systematically map out each individual panchayat with the existing fibre network using GPS to estimate the additional fibre length required to connect the last mile. This task took us two years, from 2009–10. Finally, we put together a Cabinet note for the government asking them to add approximately another 500,000 kilometres to connect all panchayats and to also provide all necessary equipment for the network.

But cost estimates for the system ran into 7 billion dollars, a price tag that brought much consternation. For an administration strapped for funds, where were those billions supposed to come from? By chance, we had almost exactly the same amount, 7 billion dollars, in something called the Universal Service Obligation Fund. This fund had been set up to encourage telecom companies to go into rural areas (which they might have been disinclined to do because less population density meant less profits). The rationale behind the law was that service providers had a moral responsibility to bring service to remote areas. If they didn't meet their rural obligations they were charged a penalty of 2 per cent on sales. These penalties were channelled into the Universal Service Obligation Fund, which I now clamped my hands on. Fortunately, everyone involved agreed, so we had access to the money.

The project, called the National Optical Fibre Network (NOFN), meant to connect 250,000 panchayats, was finally approved by the government on 25 December 2011. The plan was to use government-owned-and-run Telco, BSNL, RailTel and Power Grid to implement the Fibre Network project. RailTel and Power Grid had the right of way to lay their own fibre-optic cables.

To understand the challenges of fibre-based connectivity at the panchayat level, we launched three pilot projects in Rajasthan. We verified Internet connectivity and the relevant applications that benefit the local population.

In India, connectivity on the scale we were perceiving would have huge implications for our citizens' lives. Many interactions between individuals and government will be vastly simplified. Applying for drivers' licences, vehicle registrations, passports, birth certificates, proofs of residency, business licences, scholarships, tax and fee payments, etc., will no longer require visits to agencies and lead to interminable delays. Government welfare programmes, notoriously prone to corruption, would become efficient and transparent.

A public information infrastructure also needs two fundamental platforms to identify people and places—the Unique Identification Number (UID) and Geographic Information Systems (GIS). In 2005, the Indian government launched the world's largest public works programme on rural employment to guarantee work for over 180 million of the nation's poor and provide them with a social security net. But often these life-sustaining payments don't arrive for many months. Books aren't up to date. Corruption eats into the amounts. On the other hand, computerization and connectivity allow for direct cash transfers. People can automatically check their bank accounts. It would be possible for payments to be directly channelled to women, specifically, to buy food and household rations (in order to pre-empt and preclude diversions for alcohol and non-necessities).

Nobody in the world has ever done anything similar on this scale. In a country with such an immense population, 1.3 billion and counting, the only way to accomplish these kinds of transactions and exclude or minimize corruption is to issue each citizen a permanent identification number that allows access to all government services and information as well as to private transactions such as mobile banking. Such a number provides instantly verifiable paperless identification. Internationally, this is known as a 'UID'.

In order to enable the government to set up a Unique Identification Authority of India, headed by Nandan Nilekani, former CEO of Infosys, the process is that each person's face is photographed, as well as the fingerprints and iris images recorded for biometric identification. Once that is done the individual is issued a twelve-digit number that stays with him or her for life. By now, in 2015, 800 million Indians have been issued UIDs, known in India as 'Aadhaar' numbers. By now, everyone in India who is entitled to have one should have been allotted such a number. The Aadhaar programme is the largest national identification programme in the history of mankind.

The idea of a national identity number has met with serious resistance in the US and elsewhere, because of fears that this sort of universal registration is insidious and can be used by governments for nefarious purposes. Those fears have cropped up in India too.

I do not share these fears. The fact is that the government already has all the information about us that it needs, at its disposal, as do many commercial companies. It's simply naive to believe that one's information is confidential. Every time I use a credit card, a computer or a mobile phone, others know who I am, where I am and what I do. The whole business of privacy is complicated, confusing and controversial.

The Unique ID or UID programme verifies each citizen and gives him or her access to a variety of services like telecom, banking, entitlements, pension, etc. A second, complementary platform we launched was GIS mapping. GIS uses geospatial-mapping technology to locate each geographical and structural location in the entire country. Just as the UID identifies a country's citizens, GIS identifies a country's physical assets—its water resources, land configurations, infrastructure of roads, bridges, railways, power lines and buildings. GIS tells you where the nation's schools, clinics, hospitals, libraries, factories and farms are located. The GIS platform will help execute environmental and city planning, land management, water projects, road building and healthcare facility construction in a vastly more sophisticated and effective way than has ever been possible before. It allows public health officials to track disease patterns, security officers to monitor crime outbreaks, and environmental scientists to understand the dispersion of pollutants. If a company is funded by the government to build a road or a clinic in some inaccessible area, one would be able to monitor its progress remotely and check whether the work is being done at all.

We spent almost two years lining up everybody from the various ministries and convincing them that we needed one standardized, digitalized, nationwide set of maps instead of the tens of different manual maps they had been working with. Traditionally, each government department has their own map. For example, departments of water, telecom, power, revenue, etc., will all have their own maps, and most of the time these maps are not standard and don't tally. This process is a hand-me-down from the days of the British Raj and has continued till today. GIS offers a unique opportunity to consolidate and standardize all maps on to a common platform for everyone to use. GIS, like UID, fosters transparency and accessibility. It supports effective public service and good governance. It enhances the efforts to further Indian democracy.

These ideas are new. Once everything is fully operational, people will learn to use the new processes and systems. We will train experts to manage them effectively. We will make mistakes, no doubt, but I believe our work will transform the country. These innovations will radicalize our democracy. I'm very hopeful about that.

At the conference of chief ministers and chief justices held on 16 August 2009 the prime minister described the staggeringly high arrears and case backlog as the 'scrooge' of the Indian legal system. Today, India has 32 million pending court cases; sometimes it takes ten to fifteen years to settle a court case. I personally know of many court cases that have been pending for the last twenty years. To address this, the National Mission for Delivery of Justice and Legal Reforms was set up with the objective to reduce the pendency of cases from fifteen years to three. Leveraging ICT in the justice system can help reduce errors and enable citizen-centric services. Since October 2009, as adviser to the prime minister on public information infrastructure, I have been personally engaging with various stakeholders in the justice system—judges, police officers, prosecutors, civil society, lawyers—and I have set out our preliminary thoughts in a report titled, *The Courts of Tomorrow*. We believe it is time to develop an integrated solution where the courts, the police and prisons are integrated and standardized across the country.

For a period of five years, every time a new chief justice was appointed, I went to meet him immediately. Each one was welcoming and receptive to what I was saying. Each said something along the lines of, 'It's an important idea; we want to computerize courts. We support it.' But then they had to figure out how to do it, and they had other priorities. Then, because of India's antiquated, maddening, bureaucratic seniority system, eight months later that person would retire and someone new would come in. And I would have to pitch our idea to them all over again. It was like *Groundhog Day*, the same thing on repeat. Similarly, I had several meetings with the home affairs ministry and the law ministry to discuss the computerization of the police and prisons. Their response was that they were already doing what needs to be done on their own. They were not really concerned about integrating the police, prisons and the judiciary at this stage. I kept emphasizing that if you do not integrate now, you will essentially lose the opportunity and waste all the investments in developing stand-alone software. In spite of all the good intentions and promises from everybody, nothing really happened.

If you go into a court-records room, you will find wall upon wall of files. To retrieve the records of any given case, a clerk has to climb on to a ladder and search for the right file, which he may or may not eventually find. The scene is right out of the 19th century. I have personally visited Delhi courts to witness room after room of prime real-estate stuffed with legal files and documents. When Delhi successfully computerized its courts, it was possible to fit all of these documents into a hard drive no bigger than a briefcase. I sincerely believe that the computerization of courts will not only free up prime space in major cities (which can be utilized for better purposes), but it will also provide jobs to people in rural areas (when they can be gainfully employed to digitize old files).

While we were exploring the computerization of prisons, we learned that a large number of prisoners do not have adequate documentation for their offences and are still languishing in jail. Most of these people are very poor people and have no money to spare for bail or expensive lawyers. We had a series of conversations on this issue with the then law minister Mr Veerappa Moily. He was very supportive and decided to write letters to all the chief ministers and appropriate persons in the judiciary to identify and free those people who were stuck in jail without proper documentation. To our happy surprise, we learned that over 170,000 had been freed from jail as a result of our discussions with Mr Moily.

The Indian government essentially runs on the nadawali-file system, appended with green sheets of paper and handwritten notes on the sides by officers and ministers. These files move at a snail's pace, in keeping with all the levels in the government hierarchies. I have been very interested in computerizing this system for quite some time now. It is unfortunate that very few people in the government use digital files or digital signatures for official government work. The National Informatics Centre has done a fair amount of work to computerize the nadawali-file system. When I looked at NICNET's user interface—e-Office—I realized that most of the government officers would most likely be intimidated with an interface that looked like a real computer screen. Some of these people would never even have used computers before. As a result we decided to create a user interface that mimics an exact office-desk scene with a telephone, clock, calendar and a stack of incoming and outgoing files. We even created an interface for them that animates the physical opening of the nadawali files to ensure that the transition from old to new is as comfortable as possible. Now, e-Office has been implemented at almost forty locations in central and state government departments, including the prime minister's office, the Cabinet secretariat and the Planning Commission. There are many benefits provided by e-Office including parallel transmission to substantially improve productivity and efficiency. We had dozens of meetings with various government secretaries to convince them to use e-Office for their daily work. However, most of them are so used to the traditional nadawali-file system that they are afraid to move into the information age. I am waiting for the day that will signal the definite death of the nadawali files.

If you look at Digital India in the broader framework, it's all about openness, transparency and accessibility. It's about re-engineering the government, and breaking entrenched conventions and conditioning. In that sense, it's not just a technological exercise, it's a fundamental psychological reorientation. This is, of course, a major national infrastructure endeavour, where the time frames are considerable. Think, for example, of the American interstate highway system, a national infrastructure project that took thirty-five years in the making and is still under way.

~

During the visit of US President Mr Barack Obama to India in 2010, the two nations agreed to exercise global leadership in support of open government and democratic values. Consistent with their commitment, the leaders launched a US–India open-government dialogue with a view to promote access to information, energize civic engagement and share expertise with each other.

Afterwards, it was agreed that India and the US would work together to create an open government platform that other countries could use, the idea being that it would stimulate democracy by promoting transparency and greater citizen engagement. The American President's chief technology officer, Aneesh Chopra, and I planned the way forward and brought together Indian and American teams of software engineers who designed what is now known as the 'Open-Government Platform', which combines features of the Indian gov.in and America's data.gov domains.

We launched the Open-Government Platform in a combined press conference, with demonstrations from New Delhi and Washington, in early 2012, offering the platform for use at no cost—as a gift from India and the US. The first takers for this technology were Ghana and Rwanda.

When President Obama visited India in 2010 I was approached by the American Embassy to show him what we were doing about opening up government information. I set up a little demonstration for him in Mumbai, constructing a number of booths where people could talk to him about one aspect or another, intending to show him what we had opened up in that particular area. I connected him via our new fibre-optics system with a tiny, remote village in Rajasthan. He interacted with people from the village, a crowd of neighbours standing around applauding in delight. The whole thing was televised and made one feel warm in the heart.

The next day I had dinner with President Obama at the prime minister's house. He told his wife, Michelle, 'You know, Sam's from Chicago, and he's doing some interesting things on the democratization of information.' He had liked the idea and the term of choice—'democratization of information'.

Once we launched the platform we realized that no one in the central government was coming forward to open their data sets. We had most of the data, but no one was willing to share. Finally, I had a meeting with Dr Montek Singh Ahluwalia, deputy chairman of the Planning Commission, on the subject, and he readily agreed to share all the available public data. Some people in the meeting went so far as to say that what we were dealing with was 'government data'. I had to remind them that there is nothing wrong in sharing data on infant mortality, female literacy, health, education, agriculture, and so on. I reminded them that a lot of this data belongs to the people, and they are entitled to access it. Right after that meeting, the secretary of the Planning Commission set up a committee to look into opening data up to the public. The collective fear came from the thought that the data needed to be sanitized.

In the meantime, I had a series of personal meetings with the principal secretary to the prime minister and the Cabinet secretary to push various departments to open up their data. It took almost six months of strong lobbying in the background to convince people to share their data with the public. Now, we have thousands of data sets on open government platforms for our young to pore over and analyse; they will now be able to use all this information as a tool to create new markets and new businesses.

People do have an understanding of how this new system works, but every one of these initiatives takes two or three years to properly begin in earnest. When we launch a platform, I typically have to meet with the relevant minister and the secretary. We engage in protracted debates and discussions. We bring in domain experts, and we have more meetings and debates. I steadfastly push my point. Earlier in my career I might have become frustrated at the pace at which things seem to progress. Now I know that these are slow processes in essence and that it takes time for people to rearrange their customary ways of thinking.

In effect, the public information structure, at least as I see it, will change the Indian mindset on how to conduct governance and how to access and use information. A disruptive transformation of this sort never happens quickly, and young people adapt to it far more readily and quickly than those conditioned by earlier practices and old habits. But it *does* happen. We have now completed the groundwork for a different psychology to take hold of the beneficiaries, and we believe that the benefits in health, education, nutrition and welfare will inevitably follow. New media like Facebook, Twitter, LinkedIn, Google Hangouts, Skype, WhatsApp, and so on, all driven by young people, are accelerating our understanding, and expanding the utility and benefits of Digital India to the masses.

The support we received from Dr Manmohan Singh's government on Digital India was phenomenal. In particular, new initiatives relating to UID, GIS, the National Knowledge Network, the National Optical Fibre Network, and the computerization of courts, the police, prisons and various other government applications, required substantial funding commitments estimated in the region of around Rs 1 lakh crores. The mammoth effort also required significant human resources. For example, the National Informatics Centre had around 10,000 software people working on Digital India, including 6000 software engineers from local private industries. Based on all this, I am confident that Digital India, initiated decades ago, will finally begin to show substantial growth and translate into benefits in the coming decade.

15

Innovation

It is commonly recognized and accepted today that the key driver of growth is innovation. Innovation is on everyone's agenda; the government, industries, businesses and universities, all aim to improve productivity and efficiency, fulfil unmet needs and reduce costs. It is also essential to build new products, provide new, better services and access new markets. Innovation is the most basic requirement for global competitiveness. Innovation involves thinking differently, creatively and insightfully to have an impact on social and economic values and development. People, cultures, diversity, the overall ecosystem and the subsequent opportunities all drive innovation. Prime Minister Manmohan Singh, along with many others, including myself, understood that without innovation, India would simply be left behind. To continue the Indian growth story we would have to build an innovative nation. That is why the Indian government declared 2010–20 as the 'Decade of Innovation'.

India today is in the midst of the most exciting—and the most challenging—of times. The forces of technology, modernization and urbanization, coupled with the unique demographic dividend, are all shaping the future course of the country and paving the way for unprecedented development. However, as India moves on this trajectory of development and growth, people need to be mindful of creating a society that is inclusive and equitable. India has a huge reservoir of unmet needs in critical areas such as health, housing, education, energy, agriculture and transport, which is depriving a large section of the population of opportunities that could transform their futures for the better.

It is in this context that innovation is critical in India. Innovations that can offer solutions to existing problems where conventional approaches have failed to deliver results hold the key to India's development. Young people in India are tearing down the narrow domestic walls of religion, region, language, caste and gender that confine them. Government policies should be imbued with a spirit of innovation so that the creativity of a billion people can be unleashed.

India has had a long and proud history and heritage in the field of innovations related to mathematics, architecture, materials, astronomy, art, and so on. There are countless success stories recorded in agriculture, space, telecom, IT, energy, health and other innovations following Independence in 1947. There are many innovations-related initiatives to be seen at the National Innovation Foundation, Honey Bee Networks, government-run science laboratories, universities, independent institutions and businesses. India produces some of the world's great scientists, technologists and business entrepreneurs. It invests substantial resources in science and technology, and has some great laboratories and minds in the field of agriculture, medicine, space, energy, chemistry, biotechnology, nanotechnology, physics, mathematics, and so on. But the nation as a whole is very far from having a culture that values or nurtures innovation. Innovations are not used to solve the day-to-day problems of the people at large. At the same time people have begun inventing at all levels in the form of quick-fix workarounds known as *jugaad*s, what we in the technology industry might call 'a hack'.

But jugaads do not scale up or sustain. On the contrary, the ingrained Indian way of looking at life is hierarchical, deferential and tradition-ridden—as I know from long, hard personal experiences. I have been fighting against that mindset for decades now, from the first moment I embarked on the C-DOT journey. Nothing in the Indian environment is more challenging or exasperating than trying to change the viewpoints of people and get them to innovate. 'In India,' I had taken to saying in my speeches, 'we have a 19th-century mindset, 20th-century processes and 21st-century needs.'

So arises the great question: How does one go about changing such an ingrained national culture and psychology? How do you turn a country that is resistant to change into one that innovates as a matter of course, where innovation becomes part of its DNA?

Never in the history of India's government had anybody ever focused on a national agenda for innovation. But with Dr Manmohan Singh's declaration, innovation had entered the national conversation.

As the first step the prime minister appointed an adviser on innovation (with the rank of Cabinet minister) to drive the national innovation agenda. Simultaneously, we decided to set up a National Innovation Council, with about fifteen distinguished and well-accomplished leaders from all walks of life—businessmen, scientists, engineers, government people and academicians. The idea—and main objective—was to formulate a road map for what we wanted to do about innovations, keeping in mind the time frame of the year 2020, and create a framework for evolving a customized Indian model of innovation with a focus on inclusive growth, defining policy initiatives for the government, developing new attitudes and approaches, creating appropriate ecosystems, encouraging the Centre and the state governments to innovate, facilitating innovations at small- and medium-scale industries, encouraging innovations in public service delivery, identifying ways and means to scale and sustain innovations, encouraging research and development at universities and institutions, and encouraging new strategies, alternatives and globally competitive approaches.

In our first meeting the council discussed how we wanted to approach all of this. We knew we were in uncharted waters. Innovation in business is a common subject. A great deal has been written about it for business and industries. Management institutions focus on corporate innovations to enhance shareholder values. There are countless seminars, conferences and books on the subject; every business school teaches courses on it: How to design innovative products, how to translate innovations into business, with venture capital, private equity, patents, copyrights. But all that intellectual energy is focused on companies. There's little written about how to build an innovative nation and promote innovation in the context of a country.

Therefore, our challenge was unique. Our first heavy realization was that in a nation of 1.3 billion, it isn't possible for fifteen people to do much. A national innovation strategy had to be exactly that—national. It had to reach down into the grass roots and filter through the national core. Our job was to be cheerleaders, mainly. If we could put innovation on everyone's agendas, people would innovate, because at the end of the day governments don't innovate, nor do companies—individuals innovate.

How, then, to devise a strategy that would percolate down and energize as many people as possible? In a way, this was similar to the task the Knowledge Commission faced when we asked ourselves: What are the components of knowledge, and how can we best disseminate and activate them? My first approach to that was to break the subject down into five parts, into a 'knowledge pentagon', if you will. That made the issue manageable.

That approach appealed to me conceptually. So now I asked: What are the five most important things that matter in innovation?

The first point was that we needed to look at innovation as a platform. Innovation is not just about what happens in the laboratories. Innovation is required in products, processes, policies, plans and programmes. Innovation is a means of creating growth across many sectors—government, education, health, science, technology, business—nearly every activity that contributes to nation-building. Innovation is about changing mindsets, organizations, business management models, distribution, delivery, and a lot more. Innovation also requires the right human capital, government policies, risk capital, measurements, tools, market forces and business models.

The Internet has added a whole new dimension to innovations. It has changed almost everything related to human activities. It has impacted how we work, entertain, educate and socialize. It has far-reaching implications on businesses, products, services, distribution, delivery, finance, governance, and so on. In fact, the recent innovation drive has a lot to do with the way the Web has rendered the old ways of doing things obsolete. Due to the all-pervasiveness of wireless technologies and smartphones, people's lifestyles are changing rapidly on account of new technology and tools. Young people, especially, are embracing every new change to do more and more new things we had never imagined possible before.

The second corner of the pentagon was inclusivity. I was determined to make Indian growth inclusive. Everywhere else people were concerned about GDP, per capita income, stock indexes and other measures of wealth. But our job was not to create more millionaires, it was to lift millions out of poverty. So we said: Let's focus on innovations for the bottom of the economic pyramid. The top portion of the pyramid can take care of itself. The elite, educated and culturally advantaged have the talent and the money, they'll figure it out.

The third point was that innovation didn't happen in a vacuum, it took place in an ecosystem that fostered it. India's ecosystem for innovation was sparse. We had to find ways to build it further, to encourage venture capital and private equity, and strengthen patent-, copyright- and trademark-related protection. We needed to encourage universities to teach the subject of innovation. We needed to change business laws and tax regimes to make it easier for entrepreneurs to flourish. We needed to increase incentives and awards to encourage and reward inventors.

Fourth, we wanted to properly define some of the key elements of sustainable, affordable innovation. We wanted innovation in products that were durable rather than disposable. We wanted to look as far as possible to natural, renewable resources. We wanted to preserve customs and traditions that provided stability for local populations. We wanted to sustain the awareness of local ecosystems, a particular concern for India, keeping in mind its wild diversity of climatic, geographical and cultural–linguistic zones.

Fifth, we had to consider the possibilities of discourse. We needed to create a nationwide conversation on innovation. We needed to challenge old inefficiencies of the system and debate and discuss new possibilities for change and growth. We needed to question the status quo and, as best we could, inject that habit of creative thought into the national psyche. When one questions, i.e., when a discussion is opened up; it motivates people to think differently.

So we came up with these five basic ideas: innovation as a platform; inclusive innovation; the innovative ecosystem; innovation drivers; and the discourse on innovation. We collectively believed that there were substantial low-hanging innovation opportunities related to young local talent, increased collaborations, organizational flexibility, a knowledge network, global markets and the Indian growth trajectory. Recent successes in the ICT, pharma and auto fields had given India the recognition and ensuing confidence to build a sustainable innovation culture. We also believed that the five-pronged approach would foster innovations by democratizing information, identifying and empowering domain experts, ensuring public participation, improving ecosystems and launching a national conversation on innovation.

Once we had defined our priorities it was clear that we needed people at the state level and at the sectorial level to galvanize innovations in their respective jurisdictions. With that in mind I wrote a letter on behalf of the National Innovation Council to all the chief ministers of all twenty-eight states, which went something on the lines of: 'Dear Chief Minister: The government has established a National Innovation Council with the following objectives. I encourage you to set up a similar council to operate in your state.'

Each of our states had its own core competence—say, for example, in the area of forests, agriculture, mining, high tech, or big business—so each state needed to look at innovation in terms of its own environment and ecosystem. We indicated the requirement that state councils should not consist entirely of government officials, that they should include businessmen, scientists, engineers, women, minorities, NGOs, civil society, minorities, and others. We stipulated that they meet regularly, create funds, give awards, provide incentives, facilitate entrepreneurs and boost morale in every way they could think of. It was also prescribed that they map opportunities for innovations in the state, organize risk capital, identify talent, encourage local colleges and universities, work with industry groups and build the right innovation ecosystem.

That was in 2010. It took three years for all the states to set up their own innovation councils. They were resistant to the idea and were full of questions. What was it? How was it supposed to work? Why did they need it? But, eventually, each state set up a council that began thinking about how to propagate the idea of innovation in its own region.

At the same time, we decided to set up sectorial innovation councils focused on specific fields: Biodiversity, nanotechnology, materials, energy, wireless, textiles, pharmaceuticals, leather, diamonds, and so on, with domain experts taking the lead and ultimately helping us create a blueprint for innovation in their areas. We didn't know these fields, but the experts did. Our job was to encourage and enthuse them.

We set up thirty state- and territory-level councils and fifty sectorial councils. Now we had about 2000 people thinking and talking innovation—in addition to the university professors, technologists and business persons engaged with innovation in the normal course of their own pursuits.

As we got deeper into our endeavour, I found myself thinking increasingly about industrial clusters. For all sorts of historical and geographical reasons, specialized crafts and industries had developed in particular locales. Moradabad had 400,000 brassware workers; Surat had half a million people working and dealing in diamonds; Chennai had 200,000 in leather; Ahmedabad, 300,000 in pharmaceuticals; Agarthala, 250,000 in bamboo. On examination it turned out that India had 200 separate major clusters around the country.

Very few technology entrepreneurs were associated with any of these clusters, and very few of them, if any, had large companies. Most of the enterprises were small, traditional operations. Innovation was not part of their outlook. They had no financial resources, no access to loans; few workers had more than basic levels of education. Yet, they needed to innovate.

We decided to go into seven clusters to foster innovation. These included the auto-parts cluster in Haryana, life sciences in Gujarat, Ayurveda and furniture in Kerala, brassware in Uttar Pradesh, bamboo in Tripura and food processing in Tamil Nadu. We would take all factors into account and see what worked and what didn't—we were looking to develop a model that we could take to other clusters.

One of the seven we chose was the brassware cluster in Moradabad. The manufacturers are centred in a district packed densely with small workshops and home-smelting furnaces. As we began talking with the artisans and assessing their operations, the very first thing we learned was that they were all in it only for themselves. They liked the idea that we might be able to help them, but they didn't want the guy next door to have access to whatever it was we might be offering.

We told them that that mindset wasn't going to work, that we had come to help the entire cluster, not separate individuals. 'The first thing you have to do,' we said, 'is form an association. If you don't do that, we won't get involved. If you want to take advantage of the government's advice, money and know-how, you need to form an association. That's the only way we're going to work with you.'

That was a big exercise in trust for them. They had never done anything like that before; they had always looked suspiciously at the idea of collaborating with their neighbours—whom they viewed as their competitors. But they wanted us there, so they did form an association and set up a small office. Once they had done that we asked them, 'What is your main challenge?'

Some said they needed loans, lower prices for materials—standard stuff. To help them think outside the box, we sent in a number of scientists to teach them about innovation. We got the Tata group to contribute videotaped courses on innovation. Then we linked the association up with the local university and national laboratory to further their instruction and guidance avenues.

The Indian government was spending billions on university R & D each year. But the brassware makers were not benefiting from a single rupee of the corpus. There was no connection. The R & D scientists didn't even know that these brassware guys existed, let alone what their problems were. They were all off pursuing their esoteric research and presenting papers at international conferences.

So what we did was get everybody together.

Almost immediately we discovered that the brassware people had two major problems. The first was that the kind of furnace they all used had been designed nearly seventy years ago and was dated. Among other inadequacies, one major issue was that it didn't support vents. Smelting brass and other metals produced dense fumes loaded with toxins, which meant that physical deformities like crippling and fatal lung problems were common. Nobody had given any thought to the possibility of using a modern furnace.

When we went to the industrial engineers about this they said, 'Of course, we can do it, but no one ever asked us to.' So they redesigned the furnace, and we introduced the new model to the brassware workers. They were thrilled. With the new furnaces, productivity doubled. The smoke was gone, and everybody wanted the new furnace. So we decided to set up a company to build them, and we tied up with local banks to fund it.

The second problem that was voiced by the workers in the Moradabad cluster was that every finished piece of brassware needed polishing, which took half an hour or more—precious time wasted. It was a common sight to see some kid sitting around in the workshops, polishing brassware. When we asked the metallurgists if they might be able to come up with some kind of liquid to wipe the brassware for it to get a sheen rather than vigorously polishing it, they went straight to work and came up with a solution—literally. The brassware makers thought it was magic. It wasn't magic, it was simply basic innovation.

We had planted the seeds of change. Now, the brassware people have begun to think differently. Instead of being caged by the need to go about their work exactly as they had always done, they are looking at it with new eyes. They're looking for greater efficiencies and new products; they even want a peek at what the Chinese are doing. Ultimately, their association will become a marketing force to be reckoned with—it will take them global.

Agartala, the capital of the North Eastern state of Tripura, is home to the bamboo cluster. When we looked at it we learned that the bamboo industry there was losing jobs at an alarming rate to the Chinese bamboo market. Our analysis indicated that within five years a quarter of a million local bamboo jobs would simply be wiped out.

It didn't take long for our science team to discover what the issue was. Indian bamboo is not straight, it has knots. When you cut it, 40 to 50 per cent of it goes to waste. We sent in plant tissue culture experts to look into this and, happily, they were able to engineer the bamboo growth patterns so as to eliminate the knots altogether. The biotechnology for this was readily available, but nobody had thought in that direction.

Another problem was that the bamboo artisans' cutting equipment was just as antiquated as the brassware workers' furnaces had been. But that was what generations of bamboo workers had used, so that was what they had continued to use, as if it were a simple fact of life.

It was not a huge challenge for our engineers to redesign the cutting blades to make them significantly more efficient—a simple but crucial innovation.

Additionally, we found that a large number of the bamboo workers were wholly engaged in making incense sticks, a product with worldwide potential. Several hundreds of thousands of people make these sticks, and cutting sticks is their sole activity. The sticks are then sent to large manufacturers who coat them with incense and sell them for five times the price.

We told the scientists to figure out what incense application was all about and teach these poor artisans to put their own incense on the sticks, so they could move up the value chain. The bamboo artisans had simply not thought of this possibility. They understood their work to be just cutting sticks and selling them, and nothing else. Considering different options, possibilities and approaches just didn't enter their thinking process. We were essentially vertically integrating their services.

Big companies operate in a competitive arena and innovate. They understand that they have to, so the concept of innovation is part of their business culture and planning. But our work was dedicated to the poor person languishing at the bottom of the pyramid—the bamboo artisan or brassware worker or furniture maker or potter—who knows only what he has seen and has little clue about anything beyond his immediate work environment.

For us, inclusive innovation is the key. We want to go into areas where there's a craftsperson—someone making pottery or jewellery or painted tiles—and see how we can improve his livelihood with technology, to increase his or her income. The rich man is doing it anyhow, being globally competitive and selling for export. But, often, he's exactly the person who is keeping the traditional worker poor, because he's making the margin on the traditional person or small manufacturer's product. Meanwhile, the scientists and technologists are working for the rich, and nobody's paying attention to the poor.

Our model for inclusive innovation included creating local industry associations which had the ability to leverage loans, create economies of scale, and look for industry-wide initiatives that could spur growth. With our help, these local associations forged collaborations and partnerships with regional universities and R & D facilities, which resulted in advances in production, management and marketing.

Our cluster model, led by Samir Mitra from Silicon Valley, showed in a quick two years that with minimal incremental investment, innovation is possible in a collaborative context. We noted that the brassware and bamboo workers' incomes doubled; mango growers, who, not long ago, could only ship by air and sell regionally, because of the fruit's short shelf-life, found, with the help of food-technology research, that they could extend mango-ripening time enough to ship by sea and reach untapped markets in Europe, thus doubling the prices formerly received by farmers.

Design is an important part of the national innovation ecosystem, but India has very few design schools. The country's foremost National Institute of Design in Ahmedabad has produced some excellent designers. However, for a nation of 1.3 billion people we perhaps need at least a hundred new design colleges. China, in recent years, has set up several hundred new design colleges to meet the growing demand for design in its various sectors. With commitment to the goal of catalysing innovation in design, we decided to launch a programme to build twenty new design colleges in India. We invited private industry persons and experts for consultations, and collaborated with the human resource development ministry, IITs, and others, to prepare a blueprint for the way ahead. Rather than spending more money on acquiring land and buildings, we agreed to use existing institutional assets, with a focus on content and software. We also proposed to create special design colleges for health, agriculture, education and government. Today, design is not just about the products. It is mainly about processes, governance, organization, business models, and so on. The plan to build twenty new design colleges is under way and needs a champion to expedite it. One should never underestimate the power of design. It is the key to India's future growth and prosperity as much as anything else.

We at the National Innovation Council decided to create state and sectorial councils, twenty new design colleges and an innovation portal to improve the innovation ecosystem, launch funds, improve the working of industrial and university clusters, enhance training, provide incentives like scholarships and awards, establish innovation centres at national science centres, encourage innovations in schools, increase outreach programmes, enhance international collaborations, work closely with science and technology and other ministries and, ultimately, prepare multiple road-maps and get multiple institutions involved in the equation. We also worked with the external affairs ministry to begin discussions on innovation as an instrument of foreign policy. In furtherance of our plans we addressed a group of ambassadors from Africa, the Middle East and Latin America.

Unfortunately, there are no quick fixes. It is only a combination of hard work done by a large number of people for a long time to make an impact. Innovation is a process and a movement which has to be kept alive to transform the country. Innovation requires us to look forwards into the future and not backwards into our past. Innovation is about changing the status quo. Innovation is progress and prosperity. Innovation is a mindset that has to be embedded into our national DNA.

~

There is a time to do things the right way and there is a time to move on to do the right kind of things. When I was young it was important to me to do things right. This required domain expertise, discipline, attention to detail and diligence. However, having done several things right with confidence and comfort later on in life, I felt it was prudent to move on to doing the right things.

I have, maybe not so coincidentally, been involved in other areas of India's national life, associated in one way or the other with connectivity and nation-building. During the Manmohan Singh government I had an opportunity to work on a variety of challenging projects. I chaired committees to modernize India's railways, develop the smart-grid system, improve public broadcasting and define mobile payment. I also got involved in other initiatives related to electronic hardware manufacturing, 3G spectrum, semiconductor foundry, BSNL restructuring, innovations in urbanization, health information network, electronic health records, and so on. I also helped build national information portals on water, environment, energy, health, biodiversity, and legendary leaders Gandhi and Maulana Azad. My team of young people and I initiated several new ways of using social media—we held Twitter press conferences, hosted hackathons and held live talks on Google Hangouts, including other initiatives—to spread our message and the Planning Commission programmes to the youth. At my age, multitasking is essential to plant more seeds for the right things to do and, at the same time, to encourage and empower young talent to do it right.

Railways

Modernizing the railways, and the notoriously unreliable power system, in particular, were massive challenges that had, and still continue to have, the potential to bring prodigious benefits to India's economy. We estimated, for example, that the modernization of the railways would add 1.5–2 per cent to India's GDP.

India's railway network is the third largest in the world. We have 7000 stations, 131,000 railway bridges, 9000 locomotives, 51,000 passenger coaches, 2 lakh freight cars, and railway tracks running into 64,000 kilometres. We operate 19,000 trains every day—12,000 passenger trains and 7000 freight trains. The system transports 23 million people daily—translating to 7.2 billion passengers every year. The railways employ 1.4 million people. And they do 30 billion dollars a year in business.

Dinesh Trivedi, a forward-thinking railways minister, and a personal family friend, established two committees on railways: One to modernize, another to focus on safety. I was asked to help modernize the railways by chairing a committee comprising a distinguished group of members including Deepak Parekh, Maya Verma, Rajiv Lall, Vinayak Chatterjee, G. Raghuram and Ranjan Jain. Over a period of nine months of intensive work, our committee developed a modernization plan that addressed core assets, new revenue models, projects, enablers and resource mobilization. In particular, we focused on fifteen key areas related to tracks, bridges, engines, signalling, stations, terminals, public/private partnership, land, dedicated freight corridors, ICT, indigenous development, safety, funding, human resources and organization. Over a hundred railway professionals participated in the discussions and the working groups. Our final report provided a detailed road-map to modernize the Indian railways. To accomplish this we called for an investment of 100 billion dollars over five years, with another tranche of 100 billion to come later.

In order to raise sums of this magnitude our financial plans included creating public/private partnerships for the development of the huge swathes of highly valuable land owned by the railways, including the big city railway stations sitting on parcels worth several million plus an acre. Land could be leased or sold for apartments, office buildings, shopping centres, and so on. Infrastructure facilities such as the railway ministry's proprietary networks of hospitals and housing colonies could be opened to the public. The bulk of the costs, we believed, could be covered by monetizing assets the railways owned.

We submitted our report to the minister and he presented it to Parliament. We did a lot of lobbying within the government—the Planning Commission, the prime minister's office and even other departments, together with the minister. Everything looked good. But our plan had recommended a small fare-increase to encourage public support, which became an explosive political issue.

When Mr Trivedi announced the fare increase, the head of his political party, Mamata Banerjee, took serious objection. I have known Ms Banerjee for over thirty years. I personally respect her a great deal and have enjoyed a good personal equation with her. My wife and I have visited her modest home in Kolkata, where she has showered us with gifts, love and affection. I had prepared a plan for her to modernize West Bengal after she became chief minister. I had also attended her swearing-in ceremony as chief minister, a position she took after thirty years of communist rule in West Bengal. I thought she would totally support our plan to modernize the railways. Unfortunately, this small issue of the fare hike became a major political football. Mr Trivedi was removed rather unceremoniously from his position as minister of railways. Even the prime minister and his Cabinet colleagues did not come to his rescue. As a result, our well-thought-out plan got sidetracked. This particular issue could have been resolved by either the prime minister and/or the chief minister simply meeting with the railway minister and the committee and discussing the issues. Sadly, however, hierarchical structures and coalition government politics do not encourage these kinds of initiatives essential for problem-solving.

Smart Grid

As electronics and IT have become more prominent and more affordable, power-grid experts the world over have been looking at using IT to control power transmission, an approach they have christened the 'smart grid'. As of the time of writing this book, this idea was still new. Along with the smart grid has come the prospect of 'smart meters'—home meters that can control home usage in various ways. For the last ten years people everywhere have been experimenting with these things. To further explore this area, the government set up a task force on the smart grid in India, and I was asked to chair it.

India's grid is notoriously unreliable, facing huge shortages of power. We import almost all our oil, and our domestic gas supplies are severely limited. As a result the focus has been on hydropower and coal. Nuclear power plants and additional nuclear figures are in the pipeline, but there has always been strong resistance to using nuclear energy, so growth in the area is thus unpredictable. Since our hydro capacity is also limited, coal is the primary fuel for power generation. India has large coal reserves, but the quality of Indian coal is not good, and the pollution caused from burning it is a major problem.

In our first committee meeting I realized that everybody was looking to the West for solutions. But in fact the West's problems are very different from ours. A major challenge for us, for example, is that around 40 per cent of our power is stolen. People tap the lines. They simply run their own wires and steal power for their own water pumps and personal use. They tamper with their meters—electromechanical meters can be manipulated fairly easily.

To that end, we set up design teams, wrote new meter specifications and produced prototypes. I also emphasized that there were lessons to be learnt for the power industry from telecom on matters of deregulation, decentralization, privatization, distributed energy, micro grid, DC power, multiple sources and affordability. All the players reached consensus on this point. But, again, there was no management will to go ahead and do what was required. But the work is ongoing, still.

Public Broadcasting

Prasar Bharati, translating literally to 'Broadcast India', has two arms—television and radio—with nationwide reach, almost 40,000 workers, twenty-one television channels and 326 radio stations. Its reach is vast, but the programming content is poor and few people tune in. Instead, the audience chooses to watch private television channels. It is unfortunate that the government spends billions and still draws a small audience. At one time the programming served a valuable purpose: Farmers could get information on fertilizers and seeds, and dairy producers could learn about forage (or fodder) and the relevant equipment to use. But publicizing that kind of news has been superseded in a dozen ways for years. Prasar Bharati's programming has been meandering, aimless and irrelevant.

To try and turn this around, the government established a committee comprising seven distinguished experts in broadcasting and related areas, with yours truly as chairman. Our goal was to help modernize the public broadcaster and make it relevant. What should Prasar Bharati actually do? Why does India need it?

We spent almost a year on this project. We studied Chinese broadcasting, the BBC, the PBS. Based on everything we learned from other models we reached a conclusion: India *does* need a public broadcaster. But it needs to be a public broadcaster, not a government broadcaster. Instead of serving as a forum to publicize the government's agenda, broadcasting needed to address public interest in ways that would interest the public and help in the nation-building processes and programmes.

After several rounds of discussions, we decided to focus on eight areas: Organization, administration, funding, human resources, technology, content, social networking and globalization. Our report, submitted at the beginning of 2014, addressed all these points as well as other issues—the broadcaster's workforce, its equipment needs, and its potential to capitalize on assets and create public/private partnerships. Over 100 professional experts from the government, the private sector and the media from all over the country worked on preparing the content of the final report. The report is now with the government at the implementation stage. However, like many other reports in the past, it might also collect dust seeing that no one so far has had the courage to bring about generational changes to reform the system at multiple levels.

Mobile Payments

The mobile wallet is a disruptive technology. With large numbers of people below the poverty line, India is a prime example of a nation that will benefit dramatically from the introduction of mobile money. With that understanding, in 2012 the finance ministry asked me to establish a national committee on mobile payment. However, with the change in the government the work in this area sadly ceased.

Semiconductor Foundry

India had a semiconductor fabrication ('fab') facility in Chandigarh that burned down in the late 1980s and left a big void in the local electronic hardware manufacturing capabilities. For the last three decades, India has been importing semiconductor components from the global market. Today, it is very expensive to build semiconductor fabs with state-of-the-art technologies. It is estimated that it may require anywhere from 7–10 billion dollars to build a semiconductor fab. Normally, it may not make business and financial sense to invest that kind of money while global foundries have excess manufacturing capacities. However, for strategic reasons it makes sense. A large number of fab-less foundries and people who design very large-scale integrated circuits (VLSI) are well established in Bangalore, Hyderabad, Pune and other places to serve global markets.

Knowing the strategic importance of having a semiconductor fab in India, Dr V. Krishnamurthy and I went to see the prime minister. He agreed to our proposal, and we put together a team to explore the possibility of inviting and selecting the right partners to develop local foundries for commercial markets. It took us almost three years to put together a detailed recommendation for the Cabinet. In the process we had to understand the existing market conditions, invite consultants to perform various studies, meet with international players, set up evaluation criteria, invite bids, study various proposals, analyse investments, technology, manpower, markets, and a whole lot more. In the end we recommended that the government establish two private-sector-based semiconductor fabs to meet the growing demand in the country. The Cabinet approved the proposal and the ministry is currently in the process of implementing the plans.

Electronic Hardware Manufacturing

Presently, India imports over 100 billion dollars' worth of electronic hardware every year. India also exports 120 billion dollars' worth of software and related services. It is believed that at the present rate the electronics-hardware import bill could reach about 400 billion dollars a year in the near future. This would be an amount higher than India's import of oil. A country of 1.3 billion people cannot ignore the manufacturing of electronic hardware. Dr V. Krishnamurthy and I once again went to the prime minister with this concern. He listened to us carefully and suggested that we further examine this challenge and come back to him with a plan.

The key to electronic-hardware manufacturing is not just cheap labour but a real ecosystem coupled with semiconductor chips, embedded software, testing, real value addition and incentives to be globally competitive. Dr Krishnamurthy and I spent a fair amount of time, along with able support from the Planning Commission, the secretary of electronics, and others, to put together a comprehensive plan to increase local production and get foreign capital for manufacturing in India. Unfortunately, we had little success in attracting big international players to look at India for local manufacturing—partly because of complicated government processes and the lack of logistics. Once I had a meeting in Silicon Valley with several leading hardware manufacturers; one of the leaders openly told me that he is willing to move most of his production from China to India, provided we assure him of some logistical support. He said it would be cheaper for him to produce products in India for export to the Middle East and Africa. Unfortunately, the kind of support he expects is just not available in India. This includes the areas of space, water, electricity, access to ports, railways, roads, trains, manpower, tax holidays, and a lot more.

3G

India had been preparing to auction 3G spectrum for mobile-phone operators for over two years. The defence department had used a part of the spectrum for strategic activities, and the plan was to get them to vacate the spectrum for auction. One fine morning I received a call from the Cabinet secretary that the prime minister would like me to help review this situation. Immediately, a highly qualified joint secretary from the Cabinet secretariat came to meet me at the lobby of the hotel where I was giving a speech. Then he came to my office to brief me with all the relevant files and material.

I suggested we schedule a meeting with all the concerned parties: the Telecom Commission, BSNL, Wireless Adviser, the telecom regulatory authority, the army, navy, air force, the prime minister's office, the Cabinet secretary, the department of electronics—in all over thirty people. The meeting was held in the boardroom of the Telecom Commission. As part of my opening remarks, I said that this was an important issue for the government and that as domain experts we could not pass on this decision-making to a group of ministers; we needed to give them firm answers along with various trade-offs to move forward. I said, 'In the next three hours we would need to arrive at our final recommendations.'

After all the presentations, I led the discussion to request the defence department to vacate the wireless spectrum in favour of the fibre-optics network. We had already built the National Knowledge Network, and we could similarly quickly build a dedicated fibre network for the defence department to meet their strategic needs. Everyone thought it was a good idea, provided the government would be willing to allocate additional capital to build a dedicated fibre network. However, the concern was: Can we get approval from the finance minister? I assumed responsibility for this aspect. That very evening I went to the then finance minister, Mr Pranab Mukherjee. He listened to me carefully, understood the trade-offs and immediately agreed, in principle, to proceed.

BSNL

Bharat Sanchar Nigam Limited was the largest government-owned telecom operator that had been valued in the past at 70 billion dollars, but was now bleeding freely. It needed fresh capital from the government to survive and sustain itself. The prime minister was very concerned about this and called a meeting of almost fifteen people including ministers, secretaries, Cabinet secretaries, principal secretaries, and others. After the presentation, the prime minister asked me to offer my comments. I was very critical of the situation and basically disagreed with what the ministry had said. I felt the state of affairs was very serious and that the funding requested by the ministry would not fix the problem. It required a new strategy and a new approach. After a round of discussions, the prime minister asked me to lead a committee comprising well-known banker Deepak Parekh and the secretary of telecom P.J. Thomas, and to give him a report on BSNL in thirty days' time.

In 2009, BSNL was the seventh-largest telecommunications company in the world, providing a comprehensive range of telecom services in India. It had an equity capital of Rs 12,000 crore, net assets worth Rs 88,000 crore and a turnover of Rs 35,000 crore. Further, the company catered to 90 million customers, counted 300,000 employees on its rolls, boasted 750,000 kilometres of optical fibre, a network of 40,000 towers, extensive urban coverage (to the exclusion of Mumbai and Delhi), unparalleled rural coverage, and many other unique assets and capabilities that offer significant potential for growth, revenue generation, value unlocking and social relevance.

This wholly owned government enterprise was under severe pressure and was making losses for the first time in its history due to increased competition, a declining fixed-line market, antiquated processes and procedural bottlenecks, especially related to the purchase of equipment, a bureaucratic- and government-dependent decision-making system, a lack of collaborative actions, a large workforce, a profusion of regulatory changes, operational inefficiencies, and other internal and external challenges.

There are several other public-sector companies suffering a similar fate. Many companies do not even have a CEO appointed for many months. In many of these cases the problems are known, the challenges are clear and the solutions are suggested by many qualified people. However, there is a lack of political will and adequate leadership to take the system head-on to implement all these massive reforms. Unfortunately, our recommendations could not be implemented because no one—including the BSNL board—wanted to rock the boat. Status quo is comfortable and preferred. It is a popular notion that change is difficult and must be avoided.

Urbanization

To promote innovations in urbanization, a meeting was organized by the National Innovation Council in collaboration with the urban development ministry, headed then by Mr Kamal Nath, at Vigyan Bhawan in Delhi. Several hundred mayors, municipality commissioners, officers and other local political leaders from all over the country representing cities participated. It is estimated that over 600 million people in India will move to an urban area by 2030. This will increase the workforce in urban areas by 270 million and lead to the creation of 70 per cent of new jobs in Indian cities. A staggering 90 million urban households will be a part of the middle class by 2030, and seventy cities will have a population of more than 1 million. Over 1.2 trillion dollars will be required to meet projected demands in Indian cities. With this kind of growth and potential opportunities it is important to focus on innovations in urban development.

At the conference, presentations were made on water, sanitation, energy, employment, education, health, transport, security and other relevant urban challenges. However, the key was to essentially focus on organizational challenges related to the autonomy of the mayors and elected officers in the cities. Indian mayors are essentially not empowered to have the kind of autonomy and flexibility typically needed to run their cities. Hardly anyone knows about the mayors of the leading cities in India. Existing political structures have not given the required (or deserved) leeway and power to mayors of big cities, as a result of which, cities do not get to effectively implement growth plans. This issue was highlighted by almost all the mayors present. The conference concluded with a set of recommendations being drawn up. Unfortunately, implementing a reform like this would require a fair amount of discussion and dialogue in Parliament in order to pass the relevant bills and make new laws.

This is an example of a case where we know what needs to be done, but it just doesn't get done because of conflicting priorities, vested interests, complex procedures, and the lack of appropriate champions and domain experts to drive change. In most cases, the organizational architecture inherited at the time of Independence, and further complicated and weakened by vested interests, is not in tune with the developmental needs at all.

Portals

Recognizing that the Internet constitutes a powerful and democratic source of information and knowledge, the National Knowledge Commission decided to create a series of portals in key sectors such as water, energy, environment, biodiversity, education, health, and so on.

These Web portals are designed to become a decisive tool in a popular movement in support of the right to information, transparency, accountability, decentralization and people's participation. The idea was to provide portals as a single point of access for all consolidated information, applications and resources on the sector, to cater to a wide spectrum of users, from citizens to entrepreneurs, small-scale industries, students, professionals, researchers and local practitioners.

While the government is a key partner in the initial set-up, all portals are managed by a consortium, with adequate representation from a wide range of stakeholders from various sectors including NGOs, advocacy groups, international bodies, government departments, the private sector, R & D institutions, universities, etc. This will ensure that the portal remains a dynamic repository of information from multiple sources to aggregate content. A collaborative model is adopted for portals, so that all the stakeholders participate in sharing and discussions in a rich and meaningful way, such that information cannot be monopolized by one group. Portals are designed to have greater community ownership in order to ensure sustainability and success.

~

India Forum

The India Forum, established in 1966, was my first non-profit activity. It began as a discussion group in Chicago to educate and enlighten me and my close friends about ourselves, our society, and issues related to national and international developments.

During the Technology Mission activities in the mid-1980s, I had an opportunity to work with a large number of NGO organizations and leaders from all over India. Some of my friends, like Sanjit (Bunker) Roy, Aruna Roy, Hiremath, Ravi Chopra, and many others, left behind their lucrative careers to work for the public good in India. Over the last three decades, I have been personally engaged in various NGO activities.

The Institute of Trans-Disciplinary Health Sciences & Technology

In India we have around 6500 medicinal botanicals that are unique to the Indian climate. I had a knowledge of medicinal plants because of my mother. She delivered eight kids at home in a tribal area of Orissa, where there were no doctors, hospitals, nurses, pharmacies, electricity or running water. All eight (out of eight) children turned out to be mentally and physically healthy. My mother must have done *something* right. I remember her grinding plants and leaves for coughs and colds. When Darshan Shankar said in 1988 that no one had documented Indian herbal plants, I thought it would be a good idea to create a computerized database of all the medicinal plants of India, in order to preserve Indian medical heritage.

Darshan and I decided to start a non-profit foundation called the Foundation for the Revitalization of Local Health Traditions (FRLHT), in Bangalore, to document India's medicinal plants.

We launched the foundation but quickly realized that nobody had any interest in it. Nobody in India would give us money—not the government and not even the private companies. We were widely ignored. Finally, we received some initial seed capital from the Danish International Development Agency (DANIDA), under the foreign affairs ministry of Denmark, so we were able to at least get off the ground.

That was twenty-five years ago. Now, the institute has a 17-acre campus in Bangalore, around 300 full-time workers, physicians, biomedical scientists, botanists, ecologists, foresters, Sanskrit scholars, computer professionals, gardeners, and others. We have documented most of India's medicinal plants and established the largest global conservation network for preserving their genetic pool. We have established 110 Medicinal Plant Conservation Areas (known as MPCAs), the size of each being around 200 hectares, in collaboration with forest departments across thirteen states. We have a computerized database on the medicinal botanicals and traditional pharmacology taken from medical texts written over the period ranging from 1500 BC to 1900 AD. We have undertaken scientific studies on phytochemistry and biological activity. We have established a 100-bed integrative hospital, with support from Ratan Tata, and we have recently launched the Institute of Trans-Disciplinary Health Sciences & Technology, exclusively for PhD studies in transdisciplinary medicine, which is also funded in part by the Tata group. Darshan Shankar is the institute's vice chancellor, while I serve as chancellor.

The India FoodBanking Network

The idea for this foundation came about when I was on the board of the Global FoodBanking Network (GFN), which is based in Chicago. GFN has a presence in about thirty countries and feeds approximately 40 million people.

The idea of the India FoodBanking Network (IFBN) is to develop and support community efforts to take on the responsibility of collecting food, storing it and distributing it to the needy in local communities. India produced its highest-ever amount of food grain: 264 million tons in 2013–14. At the same time India also had 200 million hungry people. How could this be allowed?

Based on this harrowing fact, we decided to launch a series of food banks in India. This was a new idea for the country. In India, most feeding programmes are either run by governments—for feeding children—or by temples, gurdwaras, churches and mosques (to feed their own and sometimes the public). But the larger communities themselves have never taken on the responsibility for feeding the hungry around them, irrespective of who they are.

I worked first with the Delhi government and we established a food bank in the city. Subsequently, food banks opened in Gurgaon, Noida, Ghaziabad, Kolkata and Bangalore. Now, the IFBN has partnered with the Rotary Clubs in India to organize food drives in over ten cities all over the country. In collaboration with Britannia, the food-products corporation, Rotarians conducted several food drives to feed the hungry, the needy and underprivileged in their respective localities. This exemplary participation of the existing infrastructure of Rotary Clubs, corporate support by Britannia as well as the network support provided by IFBN, shows that hunger elimination is a collaborative effort and can be achieved in our lifetime with existing resources in hand.

My dream is to make sure that all 640 districts in India have a food bank, so that the people of the district will take the initiative and the responsibility of feeding their hungry. My ultimate goal is to eliminate hunger in India through the food-banking programme by 2025. The IFBN is fortunate to have the support of Cargill, Reliance, DLF, Britannia, the Muthoot Group and many other institutions and individuals. This effort is led by Mrs Vandana Singh as CEO.

People for Global Transformation

People for Global Transformation is an international interdisciplinary working group which brings together about twenty global leaders, focuses on the changing geopolitical equations of the time, and deliberates and takes action on the transformative potential of technology. The idea has its origins in a friend in Paris, Mr Hubert Védrine, who had been chief of staff to French President François Mitterrand, and was the French foreign affairs minister under Jacques Chirac. Hubert Védrine and I both saw a pressing need to develop a non-governmental forum for disruptive thinking on issues such as governance, health, technology, education and urbanization, to name a few.

We decided to bring together a select group of global thinkers across several domains, including former Japanese prime minister, Yukio Hatoyama; former Finnish prime minister, Esko Aho; Columbia University's Saskia Sassen; former UN deputy Secretary General, Louise Fréchette; and former Cabinet minister of South Africa Jay Naidoo. The group meets once a year, in France and India, alternately. Our first meeting was in Mumbai in 2012 and was made possible with generous support from the Reliance Foundation. Currently, our work focuses mainly on urbanization. We intend to set up pilot projects in a few carefully selected cities around the world.

The Global Knowledge Initiative

In 2009, Nina Fedoroff and I founded the Global Knowledge Initiative (GKI), a non-profit based in Washington DC. Nina is a world-renowned bioscience investigator specializing in genetically modified seeds. She is the former president-elect of the American Association for the Advancement of Science, winner of the National Medal of Science (which is the highest award for lifetime achievement in scientific research in the United States) and is also a former science adviser to two former Secretaries of State—Condoleezza Rice and Hillary Clinton. GKI is led by Sara Farley, who is its chief operating officer.

GKI's mission is to solve challenges facing the world's poorest and most vulnerable populations by building problem-solving networks that leverage best-in-class research, scientific expertise and various technologies. Our underlying thinking in founding GKI was that the foremost challenges of today—mitigating climate change, ensuring energy security, reducing food loss—are all complex and multisectoral, and thwart the efforts of single actors. In resource-constrained economies like those seen in many developing countries, the challenges of connecting to the required expertise and resources are often magnified, limiting paths towards solutions. Creating lasting solutions to these and other global problems requires the collective work of many problem-solvers who pursue common goals and bring to the fore their varied perspectives, resources and areas of expertise with regard to these goals. With that in mind, we established a team in Washington to develop programmes that support and create networks and have the capacity to solve concrete problems collaboratively on a global scale. GKI's programmes have engaged problem-solvers on a worldwide scale—policymakers, entrepreneurs, students, community leaders—from fifty countries to date.

Action India

About twenty years ago, a group of friends and I had a big meeting at the Gandhi ashram in Sabarmati, Ahmedabad, on what we could do to initiate action in India, instead of having mere conversations about actions. Subsequently, we founded Action India to hasten the development in India, and create a human and material resource base and a climate for innovation through consensus and public dialogue. We fund a few small programmes to encourage the youth in Indian developmental activities.

Action for India

The mission of Action for India (AFI), run by Sanjay Kadaveru, is to help social innovators in India overcome barriers to scale up and achieve greater impact at the bottom of the economic pyramid. AFI connects social innovators, mentors, investors and government officers to network for productivity and efficiency. AFI is headquartered in New Delhi, with a chapter in Silicon Valley. We hold a yearly conference bringing together about 300 delegates. We select the top ten social entrepreneurs and give them awards, and connect them with funding agencies as well as provide other support. AFI has been supported by the Deshpande Foundation and other donors.

Scientika

Scientika's goal is to promote policies and programmes related to knowledge and urban development in Mexico. It has published and printed half a million copies of books on Mexico City. A group of young professionals work on this initiative under the leadership of Javier Jileta, a young Mexican economist.

United Nations Broadband Commission

Affordable high-speed broadband connectivity to the Internet is a foundation stone of modern society. As in the case of the Industrial Revolution, the digital and broadband revolution will create both winners and losers. The UN Broadband Commission aims to help everyone benefit from the advantages offered by broadband. The commission meets twice a year and has about fifty commissioners from all over the world. In 2010, I joined as a founding commissioner. The commission has five global advocacy targets which include the issues of universal policy, making broadband affordable, connecting homes to the Internet, individual Internet usage and gender equality in broadband. To date, the commission's initiatives have included several major reports that were presented to UN Secretary-General Mr Ban Ki-moon during the commission's annual meetings.

ITU's m-Powering Development Initiative

With mobile subscribers approaching 7 billion in number, it is clear that mobile communication will become a universal tool with benefits far beyond voice and text as originally envisaged. With such powerful technology available in most rural and remote areas, and such unprecedented computing power in the palm of our hands, it is imperative to harness this technology for appropriate use in the areas of health, education, agriculture, commerce, sport, banking, and so on, to achieve sustainable development. The m-Powering Development Initiative aims to extend the benefits of mobile technology to all strata of society, in order to build a truly inclusive society, with special focus on remote rural and underserved areas. It is expected that this initiative will add to GDP growth and create employment opportunities too. I chair this initiative of the International Telecommunication Union, and another thirty distinguished members from all over the world make up the rest of the group.

The World Wide Web Foundation

This organization was established in 2009 by the English computer scientist best known as the inventor of the World Wide Web, Sir Tim Berners-Lee, to tackle the fundamental obstacles to realizing his vision of an open Web—which is available, usable and valuable for everyone. The Web is the most powerful tool for communication in the history of humanity, creating the potential for all people to participate in building a more peaceful and equitable world. The World Wide Web Foundation seeks to establish the open Web for the global public good and as a basic right, ensuring that everyone can access and use it freely. A registered charity in Switzerland and the US, the foundation has offices in Washington DC, Geneva and Cape Town. I serve as a director of this foundation.

Having lived in Chicago for almost fifty years, I have been active in the past with various community activities. For almost ten years, I had the honour of serving on the board of trustees at the Illinois Institute of Technology (IIT), where I studied in the mid-1960s. I am also on the board at the Institute of Design, the world's largest postgraduate college in the field of design. I also worked with IIT to bring its online education programme to India over ten years ago. Now, IIT teaches students in over five major cities, with over 100 people graduating every year in India. For almost five years I served on the board of the Chicago Humanities Festival, an almost three-week-long series of lectures, concerts and films designed to create opportunities for people to explore the arts. Since 1990, the festival has promoted humanities as a vital and vibrant ingredient of daily life, and the event now takes place at more than thirty venues across the city, involving more than forty partner institutions, hundreds of volunteers and attracting over 50,000 people.

~

I have had the opportunity to innovate all my life. Most of my personal work is all about disruptive innovations. I first started with digital switching in 1966, which ultimately changed and modernized telephone systems all over the world. C-DOT, in 1984, was disruptive because of the focus on the indigenous Indian model of development and rural communication. My electronic diary—invented in 1973 and patented in 1975—was the first electronic handheld device ever conceived and produced in large quantities globally. Then the mobile wallet that I invented in 1994 was a pioneering work in the mobile-payment system of the future. In the process I made lots of mistakes and failed several times, but, ultimately, I learned to appreciate the romance of innovation and innovating. I have over 100 international patents and have made millions of dollars building innovative companies. Even as a seventy-three-year-old man, I still keep inventing, filing more patents, and seeing new opportunities to design products and change the world. My understanding and commitment to innovation comes from these real-life experiences. I firmly believe that India has reached its tipping point. She must focus on innovations to bring about generational transformation. We have seen that old systems do not work. And old mindsets must change. The young must demand change, and they *must* innovate to build the new dynamic, diverse and democratic India that the world needs.

I have been fortunate enough in this regard to have been born an Indian. India is a land of extremes, wildly diverse in almost every dimension of its life, a land of mountains, jungles, forests and deserts, of floods and droughts, a grand melange of peoples and languages—it is in so many ways a chaos and confusion of humanity, of differences, disunity and disconnection.

I was equally fortunate to have travelled to America, where, by simple chance, I found myself engaged with the technology of telecommunication, which is at the foundation of the art and science of connecting people. I immersed myself in a nation that needed connectivity as its lifeblood and, as luck had it, connectivity became my domain of expertise.

In America, too, I found myself in a place where the status quo was barely tolerated, where problems existed not to be endured but to be solved, where life seemed charged with possibility and the will to fix, innovate and change things for the better. The America I found was, like India, a place of diversity, but a place where people weren't controlled by narrow distinctions or parochialism. America revealed to me a different way of thinking about the world.

Perhaps not so strangely, the great figures of modern Indian history, the founders and shapers of Indian society, have almost all come from the outside in one way or another—Mahatma Gandhi, Jawaharlal Nehru, Sardar Patel, and B.R. Ambedkar, who wrote the Indian Constitution; this illustrious list also includes also the giants of industry: Tata, Ambani, Birla, Bajaj and Premji; and of agriculture, like my legendary colleague Verghese Kurien.

All of these legends lived and studied abroad. As a result they were able to see India from the outside as well as from within. To truly understand and appreciate India, it can be essential to have the ability to view it from an outsider's perspective. When you've been in India for a long time, it's easy to get sucked in by the day-to-day demands—the survival issues, the prevailing (and sometimes retrogressive) attitudes and habits of traditional mindsets. When you're in India you can so easily get trapped in the confines of family and caste and region and personal rivalries, where each state has its own history, culture, language, art, food, customs and festivals. It's hard to get away from all that. But when you go outside you see all of India, in its entirety, its diversity, its complexity and vastness—you see the big picture.

Our leaders brought with them, from the world beyond, different perspectives on the nation's problems. But they did not blindly import Western models of government or business. They saw, each one of them, that we needed to think differently, yes, but, most importantly, they saw that what we build ourselves had to be by and for India. It had to serve our particular needs while embracing the best of our national characteristics. I have felt exactly that way about connectivity. We had to fit it into the Indian landscape and make it serve Indian needs.

But India's immeasurable diversity also means that we, as Indians, are, in a sense, a model for the world—immensely diverse, replete with distinct cultures, languages, colours and ethnicities. This being an organic truth, what we do in our country has particular significance for the rest of mankind. Our story, India's story, radiates meaning. It is of consequence. I find great pride—and great hope—in knowing this after a life spent in technology.

16

At the Crossroads

The government, under the leadership of Prime Minister Manmohan Singh and Congress president Sonia Gandhi, had been in power in India for about ten years, from 2004–14. The next phase of elections were around the corner. Their government had done well in the last two innings. The economy had grown at around 8 per cent on an average for eight out of ten years. However, the last two years had been difficult, illustrated by the downturn in the economy and the changing business climate. As a result, the public perception and approval quickly changed to overall negativity, with the public focusing on the problematic issues of corruption, weak leadership, incumbency and dynasty rule.

Taking advantage of the situation, the Opposition started an early campaign with a focus on American-style presidential elections—personal attacks, corruption charges and the usual promises for a better future. Finally, in 2014, the people of India voted the BJP government led by Mr Narendra Modi, former Gujarat chief minister, to power. It was time for me to resign. It was also time for someone else to come in and pick up from where we had left off. I called my team in Delhi and told them to wind up our office at the Planning Commission and to close up my home at 11 Safdarjung Road in Delhi. After a few weeks, I visited the Cabinet secretary and the principal secretary in the prime minister's office to brief them on my concerns related to the follow-up on some of the initiatives we had launched.

After ten years, I had, once again, more time for my family and personal life. It was time to review, reflect and redefine my work so far, and plan for the future. That started me thinking about being at the crossroads.

What does it mean to be at the crossroads? I am at the crossroads between public and private life. India is at the crossroads between inclusion and exclusion, with potential for unprecedented sustainable growth through innovations in processes and platforms. The world is at the crossroads between the old economic model based on consumption and the new economic model based on technology and the Internet. Now, it was time for me to think about my legacy, my India and my world. What kind of a world have I inherited, and what kind of a world will my generation leave behind for our children?

I inherited a simple, clean and poor world. We will be leaving behind a complex, polluted and rich one. Today's generation has everything at their fingertips. In this complicated and noisy world we are all more focused on material gains and less on personal growth. Everyone today is focused on the American model of consumption, which is not scalable, sustainable, desirable or workable in many parts of the developing world where hunger, poverty and unemployment are the real challenges. We need a new model of development. We have spent a great deal of time and investment in building Six Sigma–quality products, but we have hardly made the required investments in building Six Sigma–quality people. These are some of the complex issues we face today.

The World

The great American secretary of state Dean Acheson wrote a memoir entitled, *Present at the Creation: My Years in the State Department*, in which he referred to being present at the creation of the post–World War II world. The image he painted was that after the mind-numbing destruction of the war, a world came into being that was altogether different from the world that had preceded the war.

That emerging world was shaped by the onslaught of new historical forces. The world was now bipolar—a Western democratic bloc and an Eastern totalitarian bloc. The Western bloc was dynamic, characterized by free markets and elections, and the rule of law. With its economic machine racing, the Western bloc left the Eastern bloc behind in a cloud of dust. The dominant giant and leader of the Western bloc, the United States of America, emerged as the most powerful nation on earth; it was challenged militarily by the Soviet Union, but was unmatched in its economic might.

At the same time, the colonial empires of the pre–World War II world were fast dissolving. In Africa, the Middle East and Asia, the former powers were retreating, fighting doomed rearguard actions or simply pulling up stakes and departing, in the face of epic independence movements. Mahatma Gandhi had learned his lessons and found his courage in Africa, and he then returned and fought for the freedom of India. By the middle of the 20th century it had become amply clear that the world was being decolonized. The process was under way and was irreversible.

While these historic political and economic realignments coalesced and the new world took shape, another event occurred in Murray Hill, New Jersey, that was to change human history in even more profound and comprehensive ways. There, in 1947, at the Bell Laboratories, William Shockley, John Bardeen and Walter Brattain created the world's first working transistor, or semiconductor.

Before long the transistor was making an impact on a variety of commercial products, beginning with radios, then televisions and tape recorders. But in the course of time, especially after the development of the microprocessor in the early 1970s, the technology generated by transistors would begin to impact almost every aspect of human life.

Meanwhile, the United States and its allies were creating a panoply of institutions intended to strengthen, sustain and stabilize the economic and political systems that informed the new world, notably: the North Atlantic Treaty Organization; the UN; the World Intellectual Property Organization; the World Trade Organization; the World Health Organization; the United Nations Educational, Scientific, and Cultural

Organization; the United Nations Children's Fund; the International Telecommunications Union; the World Bank; and the International Monetary Fund. These post-war institutions have been with us ever since, helping shape international relations and projects ranging from economic development to humanitarian aid.

For the past half-century and more the United States has not only been the global economic leader but the very 'seedbed' and cradle of innovation and technological progress. For fifty years America has been unchallenged as the world's creative engine to the extent that it can be safely said that major innovations have come only from America and nowhere else. In my opinion, nobody else has invented anything substantial in the last fifty years. Nobody! I'm talking about the big inventions and discoveries—semiconductors, microchips, DNA, genetics, biotech, nanotech, laser, material research, venture capital— practically everything has come from the US.

This is the case because the US has invested hugely in defence, advances from which ripple out continuously into the civilian sphere. In addition, the country is blessed with a world-leading research-based education infrastructure—MIT, Stanford, Caltech, Harvard, and others. Technologies and research coming out of the US and these institutions have helped increased longevity, decreased infant mortality, improved communication, transportation and energy supply, and substantially enhanced the quality of life the world over. At the same time technology has still not been able to address the challenges related to poverty, hunger, terrorism, environmental blunders, deforestation and climate change.

Over time, transistors made satellites possible, upgraded TV and telecom, and began to tie people together in a way the world had not known before. As these events were unfurling, the rest of the world was witness to what was going on in the West. The Berlin Wall had gone up as a cruel physical barrier, keeping East Germans from fleeing to West Germany. But everybody on the eastern side could see what life was like in West Germany. The physical wall had no meaning—and that was because of transistors, because it became so cheap to own TVs and radios. If it had been the vacuum tube days, radios and televisions would never have proliferated the local markets the way they did even behind the Iron Curtain.

The result was that people in the Soviet could begin to *see* the benefits of information, communication, democracy, and the modern consumer culture that went with these things. As a consequence, in many places, people came to feel that communism as a concept was just not workable. In Poland and elsewhere, communism had crumbled with startling rapidity. The Berlin Wall, the symbol of Cold War confrontation, was torn down. People saw a unipolar world forming, with the US as champion and leader of the band of nations.

At the same time the European Union was being organized. With Europe concretely becoming a more singular entity riding on America's coat-tails, the world's direction and destiny seemed unmistakable. A leading geopolitical thinker, Francis Fukuyama, labelled the phenomena 'The End of History'.

Then came the shock of September 9/11. When that catastrophic event happened, everything changed. America, the exuberant leader of an exuberant world economic and political order, turned its attention solely to defending itself. Very large investments were being channelled towards security instead of growth. America was on the defensive. And as its ascendancy slipped, the rise of other economic power-centres—India and China in particular—gathered momentum.

Both nations were transforming their economies. India's economy had been socialist, command-driven and largely closed, business-wise, to outsiders since Independence. China's economy had suffered the traumas of hard-core Maoist communism. But by the early 1980s China, under Deng Xiaoping, was well on the way to divorcing itself from its economic ideology and embracing private enterprise. In India, the economic liberalization envisioned by Rajiv Gandhi was realized under Prime Ministers Narashimha Rao and Manmohan Singh. With their newly reformed economic structures, India as well as China emerged as free-market dynamos. Other smaller states, the Asian tigers and others, and EU countries also were coming into their own. The jigsaw of the world power dynamics had shifted. No longer were we in a bipolar—or unipolar—world. Now, the world enjoyed multiple power-centres.

Today, we are seeing a reconfiguration of the international order. This tectonic geopolitical shift is happening at the same time that a technological revolution is transforming the way we live our lives. The transistor, born in 1947, has given birth to technologies that were unimaginable only a few years ago—including compact, light-as-air computers, thousands of times more powerful than the early models that took up large rooms; smartphones; tablets; high-speed networks; virtual reality; 3D printing; and the Internet.

The Web has created a new world. We see this every day, but because we are in the middle of it, we have a hard time grasping just how amazingly and thoroughly it is remaking our lives. I personally believe the Internet is a bigger event than World War II, in terms of its disruptive power; it is bigger even than the atomic bomb. It is, very simply, changing how we do what we do, and how we are what we are. We are viewing the new possibilities one piece at a time, activities done wirelessly—shopping, reading books, getting our news, driving our cars, banking, communicating with friends, family and business associates, shipping goods, looking for lovers and life partners, collaborating with colleagues, getting entertained, and joining vast communities of people with similar interests or commitments. In the process, commerce and finance have changed, and healthcare, relationships and education are all changing—right before our eyes. And all this, and more, is happening at an ever-quickening pace.

Technology has given us the ability to digest, analyse and manipulate massive quantities of data, which has led to discoveries in biomedicine, nanotechnology, and materials and other sciences. Materials science, together with bioscience, has enabled us to grow and implant human organs, relatively simple parts now, but more complex organs in the foreseeable future. GPS and advanced sensors have made it possible to design self-driving cars. Google has done it. Volvo prototypes are on the test tracks. Punch in '500 Sunset Boulevard, Los Angeles' into your on-board computer, then sit back and read your paper or take a nap, while the car takes you to your destination.

Also, the car that's driving you may be small and light, merely a comfortable cubicle, because nanotechnology will gift us materials that are massively strong and totally resistant to crashes. Today, to transport a 200-pound body you would need a 2000-pound car. Tomorrow, you'll only need a 200-pound car. The car will be a different concept, as will the surface it will be driving on. Nanotechnology has the potential to make new roads, where you will be able to just lay down a thin sheet of metal, and that's it.

So, we'll build roads differently, we'll build cars differently, we'll build homes differently. We'll solve transportation problems differently. At the same time, we may even delight in the possibility of pre-lit trees, underground refineries, distributed direct-current unlimited power, capsules to cut calories, liquid to permanently colour your hair, customized drones, hypersonic travel, smart cities, and a whole lot more. All of these will change completely the people, the places and the world we know today by the time the next generation comes around or the one after that.

These are not tall claims or some futuristic pie-in-the-sky predictions. These are developments that are under way and sure to be accomplished in some form in the reasonable future. This is not about modifying what we do now. It is about leapfrogging into systems that are completely new. It is about wearable computers, smart cities and personalized medical care based on our genetic read-outs; it is about unlimited energy, hypersonic travel, and fabricating, through a 3D printer, replacement body parts like hearts and lungs from one's own tissue cells.

∼

In the same vein, I often talk about higher education, an area long overdue, even now, for a radical upheaval.

Today, teachers are doing what they have done for millennia; they create or master content, then they come to class and deliver said content. But, in fact, we don't need teachers any more to create or deliver content to teach students. We already have content created by the most accomplished professors and most effective teachers in the world. Everything is already online—MIT OpenCourseWare, edX from Harvard, and the universities of Berkeley, Stanford, Oxford, and the Indian Institutes of Technology and the Indian Institutes of Management (IIMs), the world's best professors from the world's top universities. Video lectures, interactive courses and entire curricula are available on the net, at the push of a button.

I'm not talking here about distance learning, which shouldn't be confused with the idea of education on the Internet. There's no reason why four or eight kids can't meet at a coffee shop, a train station, a bus stop, a shopping mall, a library, or in someone's house, and have a class and sit down and study. The students start listening to a lecture by Professor Joseph Stiglitz, Professor Francis Fukuyama or Professor Richard Dawkins at eight o'clock, a scheduled class. They listen from eight to nine. Then there's discussion they conduct amongst themselves. (It has been proven that kids learn more from each other than from a teacher.) Then they bring into the discussion someone who's already passed that course. The person can join, on Google Hangouts, the other groups studying the subject. Help arrives in the form of a teaching assistant. A professor's visit is scheduled once a semester. The faculty doesn't need to be present in the classroom, in person, every day or three days a week. But it's stimulating for the students to see and listen to their guru in person on occasion. Students can write papers and get feedback in conferences scheduled at everyone's convenience; they can take online exams to demonstrate their competence in the subject. These tools are already available, and they are becoming more powerful with every passing day.

In this kind of learning environment, teachers aren't needed to convey content. They're needed, instead, as mentors, to guide students regarding what to study, which courses to take, which professors are best, how to find resources and do research, and how to make the most effective, most successful use of what they have learned.

Of course, we haven't been able to achieve this ideal today. Instead of training people to be mentors, we're training them to be teachers in the old-fashioned sense in order to impart knowledge in obsolete environments as per obsolete methods—with x number of students per class, old grading systems and stiff, archaic concepts of teacher–student relationships.

All that has to go. But India is not letting it go. Teachers are the biggest bottlenecks, not just in the United States, but in our country too and all over. 'Oh,' they say, 'you cannot make changes like that.'

I say, yes, you can make changes like that. Why should it take four years to get a degree? Who decided so? Why must I accept the teachers I'm given instead of looking to see which of the world's best minds are available and choosing them for imparting guidance myself? For instance, if I needed surgery, I would look for the most competent surgeon; why should I not be able to do that with my professors too? My life may be at stake with my surgery, but my future is at stake with my education. The current structure is caving in, but we're conditioned to accept it as it comes. But technology is breaking those structures. Earlier, it wasn't possible to think about breaking the structure. Today, I have the tools to do it.

Technological innovation has given us a roadway to an educational model (or models) better—and far cheaper—by many degrees than what we have now. But taking advantage of the situation requires a radical restructuring of our educational institutions. We must recognize and accept the fact that our customer is the student. We must meet their requirements especially with regard to learning models, learning methods and learning habits. These things have changed completely in the last two decades. Today, to truly learn, all you really need are motivation, time and content—nothing else.

The same is true of our other major institutions too. The conclusion of World War II placed us in a new world. We are, today, facing another new world, and we are again at the crossroads. We too are present at a creation, composed of fundamental economic and political realignments and historic technological interventions. Just like after World War II, when new institutions were needed, we must now scrap our obsolete institutions and build new ones so that we can respond to our new reality.

We can fully recognize, a decade and a half into the 21st century, that our post–World War II institutions have outlived their utility. Nobody, though, wants to accept that and act on it. We see the crises, one after another: Market crash, financial crash, the housing bubble, unemployment, environmental degradation, EU problems. And we hear people saying, 'How do I fix this crisis?' as opposed to saying, 'These are not isolated crises at all; they are due to a barrage of events that are changing the world.' There is a crisis today, because the future is catching up with us, and fast. We have borderless technologies driving our future, but at the same time we have people mindful of borders and parochial outlooks deciding our futures. How is that possible, or fair?

At G8 meetings, everybody wants to go back to what the world used to be. They still want their national federal reserves. They still want to pump money in to straighten their banks out, to fix student loans, to fix their mortgage crises. Nobody seems to be saying, 'Wait a minute, these things cannot be fixed in today's world the way we are trying to fix it. We have to create a whole new set of institutions.'

The classic example I always give in this regard is of intellectual property (IP). Everybody talks about global markets and free markets. But nobody remembers that the IP organization is based on national views. So you have an international market, but national IP regimes.

If I have a patentable idea, I have to apply in the US or India, then in France, Germany, China, Russia—wherever. And everybody wants a translation in their respective local language, and then they get to decide for themselves whether my invention is patentable or not. This is opposed to the open approach of saying that since we are a global community, there should be a global patent regime. We should have a global court where you apply for a patent, then either it is issued or it is not, applicable in every jurisdiction. Something cannot be an invention in America and not an invention in China—or half an invention in Japan.

The new reality, that has not yet sunk in, is that IP has to be one, the financial system has to be one. Environmental laws have to be standardized—your air and my air are not two separate entities. As we are connected in the world, and as we are really and truly a global village, we must create systems and platforms across the board that are applicable to everybody. The need of the hour is a global federal reserve and a global patent court.

I'd even go so far as to say that we need a framework for a global constitution, a global currency, new global institutions, new economics, new jobs, new measurements—and a common global minimum agenda. We also need an international call to action to meet the needs of the 21st century. This framework is timely because the Internet has changed everything and simply levelled the world. The Web challenge, today, is not to keep doing the same things we do now, but to do new things that we have never done before. This will require new methods, new models and a whole different global mindset.

We're clear as a world community that democracy is what people want—Human values. Freedom of speech. Basic human rights. Freedom for women. Quality of life. Happiness. Fulfilment. Freedom of choice. A free-market economy. Development is no longer about more consumer goods and growth for a few. Development is about being democratized. It is more about inclusion, equity, employment and prosperity for all. For the first time in human history we now have technologies to solve problems related to poverty, the environment, employment, education and health for every citizen of the world. However, it will require new global organizational architecture that will have the ability to cut across national boundaries and deliver a new model of development. All of these ideas and values are becoming universal, and it is the world that embraces these ideas and values which is at the crossroads. That is the world that needs to make a choice—whether to sustain itself and grow, or to allow the cracks forming in the structure of civilized life to widen and undermine a future that needs to be committed to the greatness and essential decency of the human race?

India

India is a nation that combines ancient civilization with thousands of years of ups and downs, material prosperity, social and political conflicts, agricultural achievements, examples of excellence, struggle for development and substantial poverty. India has given the world major religions, unprecedented knowledge in astronomy, medicine, mathematics and materials science, and the concept of zero. This India of yore has changed substantially in the last fifty years and is at a turning point in her history.

In order to understand why India is in such a position, one has to first go back in time. In 1760, India was the largest economy in the world, constituting 27 per cent of all global economic activity. India was at the very centre of the vast Indian Ocean trade, which for centuries dwarfed that of Europe. India was a land of gold, spices, fine jewels, textiles, furnishings and processed goods of all sorts, the essential link between the riches of the East, Persia and the Arab world. India had some of the best universities in the world over a thousand years ago—the Nalanda and the Takshashila. People from all over the world, including China, came here to study. India was also a very innovative country in terms of metallurgy, astronomy, architecture, art and crafts. India invented the concept of zero and contributed a great deal to modern mathematics. India's diversity has been a fertile ground for Indian innovations.

Then came the gloom of colonization—the British Raj. Systematically, the Indian economy declined from 27 per cent to 2 per cent. British foreign policies smothered India's foreign trade. Domestic industries were either stifled or exploited for England's benefit. There was little or no industrial development. Agriculture declined, creating recurrent famines as population growth accelerated.

As a result, at the time of Independence in 1947, India was more or less bereft of industrial and trading resources, left with a population that was, to an unfortunate degree, malnourished and illiterate.

The nearly 200 years of British colonization had also magnified India's own historical closeness to caste and class hierarchy. When the last British colonials departed through the Gateway of India, they left behind a people largely unequipped, either psychologically or in terms of resources, to face the challenges of the modern world.

So the Herculean challenge for this India of 1947 was to rebuild itself, or rather, build itself from the ground up. But India's founding fathers had a vision for how to make this a reality. They—Gandhi, Nehru, Patel, Menon, Ambedkar, Shastri, Azad, Prasad, and their worthy colleagues—were committed to the ideal of a secular, democratic, open and inclusive society, and they built India's new political institutions around those principles. In a land with very little basic infrastructure, they faced, head-on, the burning need for roads, power, steel, concrete, railway stations and housing. To meet such monumental challenges they needed engineers and scientists, and they dedicated their educational resources to institutions of higher learning which could train students in those areas—a case in point being the now-world-renowned IITs and IIMs.

For their economic model, the founders focused on the Soviet Union, with appealed to them with its gigantic industrial projects, its public-sector ideology, and what seemed to be its fundamental antipathy to economic disparities. In point of fact, the Soviet public-sector model was as much a necessity as it was a choice. After the British withdrew, there was, in essence, no Indian private sector to turn to. There was no private industry at all. There was no private investment money and no banks with adequate capital. Looking back on that period, many commentators now say that the founding fathers made a mistake—they should have taken the path of private free enterprise. But in fact there was no private path to take. Nobody had the know-how, nobody possessed the technology, and absolutely nobody had the money. Only the government could make the investments, only the government could hire the necessary talent.

As the economy sputtered slowly into life, India's political democracy took root. This, too, was an often-painful exercise; but over the years the ideas of elections and the rule of law had implanted themselves in India's sociocultural DNA. Along the way there has been utterly regrettable violence—Mahatma Gandhi, Indira Gandhi and Rajiv Gandhi were assassinated—but there has never been large-scale political upheaval. India's transition from an exploited colony to a functioning democracy has enjoyed a relatively stable, undisturbed passage.

In the sixty or so years since Independence, India's government-sponsored accomplishments in significant areas have been remarkable, most of them spurred on by technology. At one time, it was believed that India was a train wreck, a country with out-of-control population growth that would never be able to feed itself. But, today, India not only produces enough to feed its 1.3 billion people, it has surplus food grain. At the same time, unfortunately, and in bitter irony, India also has the largest number of people who go hungry in any nation—a shocking 200 million. The technology to produce food was mastered, but the technology of distribution and logistics has not managed to fulfil the need.

India benefited from USAID and other sources of relief at crucial times, but food production went up primarily because Nehru and the others brought back from foreign shores Indian scientists who engineered a green revolution *here*. In 2014, India produced the largest amount of food grain in its history. Milk production also hit record levels with interventions by Dr Kurien, father of the 'white revolution' that made India the world's largest dairy producer.

The second technology success story is to do with atomic energy. Dr Homi Bhabha was an atomic-energy genius who initiated a massive nuclear energy infrastructure that now employs thousands of scientists and engineers, working on cutting-edge reactors, isotope research for medicine and agriculture, metallurgy, materials science, quantum physics—spanning the entire gamut of nuclear-related activities.

Space is another area that has seen significant Indian achievement. India has been launching satellites since 1975, and has developed its own sophisticated delivery systems that operate at one-fifth to one-tenth of the costs elsewhere in the world. The recent Indian foray into the great unknown, the Mars Orbiter Mission, or 'Mangalyaan', launched in 2014, is an excellent example of Indian capabilities in space. Much of our space technology is now being used for agriculture, remote sensing and other geospatial projects.

The field of telecom and IT, too, has been a success story. I have seen much of that through, but only with the help of close governmental cooperation, and a lot of young Indian talent, coming largely out of the Indian Institute of Technology–system system of universities established early in the country's modern history. There were other key areas like power, transport, roads and education which also received attention and resources for development.

The government's emphasis on these areas, though, meant that other dimensions of India's national life had not received adequate attention. The founding fathers, for example, had invested heavily in higher education, but had, to a large extent, neglected primary education. Industrial development was high on their agenda, leaving rural development behind.

There was no comprehensive approach to the problems of female illiteracy and infant mortality. As a result, the population shot up. If our nation's founders had focused on these two earlier, the population would probably have been capped at 700 or 800 million. In those places where female literacy is going up and infant mortality is going down, population growth has been managed. Kerala is the classic example of human development, a state where the population growth rate is declining.

The application of technological advances in the fields of agriculture, space, atomic energy and telecommunications definitely galvanized those areas during the time that India's economy was socialist and largely closed to the outside world. But in 1991 the government decided to liberalize the economy with a systematic programme of deregulation and privatization, imposing a tax-reform regime and opening the country up to foreign investment. As a result, money flowed in, domestic manufacturing, the service sector and commerce, in general, took off, and India began growing at 8 or 9 per cent, a momentum that persisted for well over a decade.

Indian economic activity is shackled by procedures that hamper not only business growth but one's personal life as well. The fact is that almost all of India's administrative and legal processes are obsolete, many of them straight out of the 19th century, left behind by the British Raj, complicated by India's own penchant for bureaucracy and, to add to the mess, now undergoing computerization.

How do you get your birth certificate or land deeds, or get your child admitted to school? How do you start a company, or close a company? All of these procedures are based on convoluted, archaic application forms and other superfluous technicalities. To start a company one has to fill out so many forms and get so many permissions that potential entrepreneurs are overwhelmed and thus discouraged. In these circumstances, it's hard to understand why anybody would want to start a business. And to add to the travesty of affairs, to close a company is almost impossible. The existing labour laws are relics that inhibit business and enterprise to the vast detriment of the workers as well as employers.

India is at the crossroads today, because India has reached the tipping point for expansion, excellence and equity. India has huge potential because of young talent and technology possibilities. However, India has three fundamental challenges today. First is the problem of disparity—between the rich and poor, the urban and rural, and the educated and uneducated. It is a case of Us and Them. This has to be reduced substantially by a commitment to inclusion and equity through democratization and decentralization. Second is the challenge of demography; there are a whopping 550 million below the age of twenty-five who need to be skilled, educated and empowered for employment. This is the workforce for the world. The third challenge is development—everything is happening in India, but perhaps not at the pace we want.

India is at the crossroads today, because there are fundamental challenges related to corruption, the black market, the status of women, security, employment, education, health, infrastructure, energy, governance, institutions and technological interventions to really bring about generational change. India needs major administrative, judicial and political reforms. I often say this: I feel that India has a 19th-century mindset, 20th-century processes and 21st-century needs. India must first begin to change the culture and mindsets and think big, with a logical and scientific approach to many of the developmental challenges in order to accelerate the process of modernization. Like in some successful businesses, India needs innovations in the areas of flat organizations, new work culture, environment and methods. India needs a large number of domain experts at various levels equipped with a missionary zeal to get things done on time. India needs a lot more energy and infrastructure to create millions of new jobs tomorrow. India also needs an Indian model of development, and traditional Indian values and wisdom for Indian solutions. India essentially needs change makers and change agents with courage and soul.

Now, India has a burgeoning talent pool, a result of the resources the founding fathers dedicated to the IITs and IIMs. India also has a large talent collective of non-resident Indians (NRIs) abroad who are very accomplished. There are about 25 million people of Indian origin living outside of India. They are in the Middle East, sending remittances in billions every year. They are in the US and Europe, running banks, industries, hospitals and universities. They are also in Silicon Valley, building state-of-the-art technologies. This brain bank is a brain gain and brain chain for India. India needs to capitalize substantially more on its youth and NRI talent through new incentives and flexibility shown by the government and industries. If young Indians and NRIs are successful abroad, then why not at home? What do they need?

Indian businesses have done very well after the nation underwent the process of market liberalization in 1991. In particular, the telecom, IT, pharma, auto, two-wheeler and consumer goods sectors are examples of local initiatives meeting local demand and growth. Not too long ago it used to take ten years to get a telephone connection, five years to get a scooter and three years to get a car. Now, everything is available on demand, instantly, and also boast of international-quality standards. In the process, India has increased its export of products and services and also built several Indian multinational companies with a presence in all the major global markets. Some of these companies are listed on global stock markets and valued in the multibillion-dollar range. Indians get respect for their talent, and India is recognized as a rising global power centre.

Similarly, India needs to focus on technology and talent in agriculture, food processing, water management, rural development and construction to create larger numbers of new jobs and ensure sustainable development through decentralization. It is believed that the modernization of the railways would add 1.5–2 per cent to the GDP, and that a revamping of the judiciary and the police would add the same amount as well. In fact, these are huge opportunities in the near future for growth which could be possible just by fine-tuning the system. However, this requires political will, national consensus, new organizational architecture and well-thought-out integrated plans for speedy implementation.

Technology is a great enabler. It generates growth and is a pathway to alleviating poverty. I usually say that technology is the great social leveller, second only to death. This isn't some exotic, urban, fancy, intimidating pseudo-philosophy. Technology is problem-solving—the root word is from Greek, *techne*, an art, a skill. Technology is the art or skill of solving problems. But technology needs the mechanisms and structures imposed by the government, the academia, the law and business life, which will allow it to flourish, run freely and unleash its power. And these are precisely the mechanisms today that grind and creak with the sclerosis of decrepitude and age.

India stands posed at the threshold of great change. Splendid technological interventions are in the offing, and we possess a large pool of young talent eager to exploit and build on the opportunities the world has to give. We have, today, the ability to bring about generational change. The question is: Will we or will we not squander this crucial moment away?

And what we do here is not simply an Indian affair. India's population is the youngest in the world, and it's getting younger, while the workforce of the other nations is ageing. Our young people will comprise the world's talent and upcoming workforce. India's needs are immense. But India's talent pool is deep and bountiful. The world is looking to India to find affordable, scalable and sustainable solutions for basic needs: Food, shelter, infrastructure, education and health. India's place in the game is to make sure that the talent is used properly to solve the problems of the poor. This is the Indian model, essential, because India is a democracy. It is the laboratory for the democratic world, the democratic world's potential engine for growth. But for this to come about, India itself must change. And for that, she has nowhere to look but within.

I remain very optimistic about India because of my faith in the strong Indian-family system, the young talent pool, the heady successes of the recent past—and the potential of the new technologies of the future. The image of India that the world is used to seeing, that of snake charmers, serpents and sadhus is fast changing to software, technology systems and service providers for the world. The stereotypical images of Indian poverty are metamorphosing into bright and optimistic images of a changed India characterized by education, performance, productivity, progress—and prosperity for all.

Myself

I realized that I am also at the crossroads, like my world and my India. Technology has changed everything, including me, and the potential for change is even bigger in the near future. Is it time for me to change too? Now that I am not going to be preoccupied with India, is it time to pay attention to the wishes of my family? I know that Anu wants me to spend more time at home, travel less, meet with family and friends, and focus on my health. Salil agrees with her and wants me to use my unique experience, exposure, and high-profile contacts in India and abroad to build a family fortune. He has been trained at MIT and Harvard to focus on financial returns and business success. He perhaps feels that I have wasted my time in India working for a rupee a year for over two decades. Maybe he feels that, instead, I should have used my talents to make billions like some of my friends in the IT and telecom industry. Father and son have an unspoken disagreement on our approaches to work and service. Salil once told me that he did not respect Gandhi as a role model because Gandhi ignored his family. Rajal, on the other hand, has appreciated my work in India and supported me in doing all that I want to do. But now she wants me to slow down, enjoy life and relax a bit more. How do I make all of them happy, and still be happy myself?

When I look at my life I see that my purpose has been to connect people, to network them. If I'm anything, I'm a network man. I've networked rural India through telephones. I've helped in taking technology to people. I've networked knowledge institutions through fibre optics. The point of connectivity, as I have understood it, is not simply to network people and institutions, it's to create an environment for innovation—which is what drives growth, and drives the economy and creates jobs. Connectivity and innovation change the world. They have done that in astonishing ways during my own lifetime. They will only increase the speed and breadth of change as we move forward.

My core has been centred around work and curiosity. I learned to work hard from my father, and cultivated perfection from my mother. To me, work is duty; it is my spirituality. I strongly believe that life has to be work-centric as opposed to pleasure—or even family-centric. Since I am a work-centric person, life's ups and downs do not bother me. I am hardly unhappy, distracted or depressed. I am never in a hurry to celebrate successes or be discouraged by failures. I always create my own work. I look forward to new work. Work could be of all kinds—building something, polishing shoes, cleaning, reading, painting, analysing, inventing—anything. I like to do multiple things in a timeshare mode. If one thing doesn't work, I go on to the next. There is never a dull moment in my life. My average day starts early in the morning with cleaning floors, and ends late at night with checking and responding to final emails. There is never a holiday for me, no Saturday, no Sunday. Work is my meditation. It never stops. Work makes me happy and content. Work helps me relax.

My motivation comes from within. To me, work is a journey where there are no destinations. The journey is about travelling. In the process, I meet interesting people, learn new things, experience new joys, cope with new sorrows, and life goes on. The journey always has some purpose. It has to create values, achieve results, solve problems, build things—and make the world a better place to live. I like to solve large, complex, multidimensional problems that have long-term implications. Basically, I am an engineer and a change agent who looks at input, output, delays, feedback, operation, multi-variables and responses. There is a pattern to this journey, because I drive it. I design my own destiny. I do not wait for someone to give me direction. There are too many interesting things to do in life. There is so much to change, learn, build and experience, so many good people to meet, and lots of love and affection to share.

The best course of action for me is to keep doing what I enjoy doing. Connecting, changing and working for as long as I am well and able. However, I do need to spend a little more time at home to write and paint, while focusing on my legacy.

17

Aria

It was a cold and snowy day in Chicago, not unusual by any means, and I knew this from my more than forty-five years spent living here. What I didn't know at the time was that this particular day would be like no other I had ever experienced in my life.

I was sitting in a meeting in our conference room at the office, when I noticed my phone vibrate. It was my daughter, Rajal, who was living in Los Angeles at the time. Her message was short, punctuated. *Dad.* It said. *She is here. And she is perfect.*

I dismissed the message at first, not sure what she was referring to. She is here? Who? Where?

I exited the meeting and called Rajal. 'Is everything all right?' I asked.

'Dad,' she said. I could tell from her voice that it was something important. 'It's Aria. Your granddaughter. She was born just a few minutes ago.'

I was rendered speechless, for what felt longer than just a few moments. 'She's here. But where?' My son, Salil, and his wife, Arpita, were living in San Francisco, so I was having trouble grasping the logistics of Rajal's call—perhaps because it was easier for my technical mind to focus on the logistical details than on the momentousness of the occasion.

'San Francisco, Dad. I flew here early this morning,' Rajal explained. 'Just in time.' Even though we were expecting the birth of our granddaughter to happen in the next two weeks, it was still difficult for me to comprehend that it had actually happened. My daughter-in-law had just given birth to the newest member of our family—the newest Pitroda. My own daughter had been around to see the miracle of life, and my son, who I had seen being born thirty-six years ago, was now a father himself.

I called Anu at once. 'Let's go.' It was all I needed to say. We were on the next flight from O'Hare to San Francisco, transferring swiftly to a taxi straight to the hospital to see Aria.

And that's when it happened.

I had heard the stories for years now—all my friends whose children had had children—the 'grandchildren stories'. The stories of how their lives had been irrevocably altered. I would politely listen and nod my head, and then preoccupy myself with the items on my to-do list, the next big challenge I had set for myself, work and service, and so on.

But when I held her—when I first put that child, less than a day old, in my arms—I, too, succumbed to that most natural feeling of being a grandfather. I never thought something like that would happen to a man like me.

It was a jolt. Her shock of black hair, her big eyes. It was in those eyes that I saw it. It was my past—my own parents, and their parents before them—but more than that, it was the future. It was Arpita and Salil and Rajal. For a split second I saw in her Salil's big eyes, Arpita's delicate features, Rajal's black hair and Anu's knowing, wise look. And the next minute, all these elements had diffused together to show me a beautiful little personality all of her own and complete in itself. I saw in her our family. I felt more love than I knew I had in me. I looked into her eyes and saw everything that will be—even when I may not be here to see it myself.

I looked at her, this tiny, newly arrived person with great intensity. I looked at those eyes again and again and I saw in them things

I never expected. Never in my life did I suspect that holding your own grandchild would be like nothing else you have ever felt before. My own genes. You can sense them. It is almost a tangible feeling. You see your grandchildren and you know. I tried to find words for it to verbalize what I was feeling. And all I could sum up and say was that I felt *connected*. Funny, I had worked all my life to connect people through telecom and IT, through work and values, across continents and cultures. I had used the word 'connectivity' a billion times. But this time was different. In one look, it was Aria that connected me to my own heart.

Aria's birth got me thinking. She was the fifth generation of my family that I had known personally. You don't ordinarily think about the different generations of your family, at least I never really had. But a grandchild does something to you—a grandchild summons the past generations up into your consciousness in a haze of memories.

I had known my grandfather, Kalyanji Pitroda, the Tikar farmer and blacksmith, my parents, of course, myself, Anu, Salil and Rajal, then Arpita—and now this baby, Aria. I was exactly in the middle of these generations, the link between them.

My grandfather could never in his life have imagined that I would be in San Francisco for the birth of his great-great-granddaughter. I'm sure he had never even heard of San Francisco. He wouldn't have known where it was or what it was. He had no clue about what would become of his family, where his family's lives would take them.

My grandfather knew me. I wasn't that different from him, I was a village kid from a place that hadn't fundamentally changed in a thousand years. Of course, I was able to go to school and then college. But even then, I still belonged to my grandfather, to his culture, to his roots. But whose culture was this baby going to belong to? Not mine. Even Salil and Rajal did not belong to my culture.

My father had been living with us in Chicago when Salil was born. What had he thought about his new grandson, born in America, a child who would be raised as an American? Did he wonder what this child would know of him, of his own life's journey, of his country? Had that entered his mind? Had it entered my mother's? Lying awake in bed that night I examined the history of our family over and over.

∽

It was a late night in Delhi in September 1985. I was eating dinner when I received a phone call. My father had fallen seriously ill in Chicago and I had been summoned. I boarded an Air India flight three hours after the call. After arriving in Chicago I went straight to the hospital, where my father had been placed in the intensive care unit. He had been a chain-smoker for over fifty years and was suffering from throat cancer. For the last two years, he had been on regular medication, and was trying radiation and chemotherapy. He had been at home under family care for most of the time. All of a sudden, he had experienced trouble breathing and had been admitted to the hospital. Now, with his wife, his children and his grandchildren by his side, he knew his time had come. Just before I had left for Delhi, my dad had held my hand and said, 'I want you to take care of the family, along with your brother Manek, when I am not around.' I could see the pain in his eyes.

The next morning, I got a call from one of our family friends Dr Vyas, who said, 'I am sorry to hear that your father passed away.' I was shocked. The hospital hadn't informed us yet.

To me, my father was a symbol of migration, enterprise and hard work. He had left his birthplace at an early age to migrate to Orissa, a thousand miles away, to find work. He had worked hard and raised a large family there. He had ensured that all his children received a good education and a better life than he had had. He worked tirelessly and never complained about it to any of us. He took his responsibilities very seriously and sacrificed a lot for the family. He built and was like a solid roof for all of us. And now, without him, it felt like we had no roof over our heads, no protector.

It was up to me to personally break the news to our family. First, I went to Manek, who lived a few miles south of my home in Downers Grove. He was having breakfast and was surprised to see me that early in the morning. I told him that I had been in the neighbourhood and had thought of stopping by. Once he finished his breakfast, I told him that our father had passed away last night. As expected, he burst into tears. After a while, we went to our younger brother, Pinu. Finally, all three of us came to my home to break the news to our mother, sisters and wives.

We asked everyone to assemble together in the living room. We brothers sat next to our mother, and told her gently what had happened. Immediately, the room was filled with screaming and crying. Our mother, in Gujarati tradition, took both her hands—decked with glass bangles—and, with great force, banged them on the table so they smashed into tiny pieces. Then she wiped her sindoor and bindi from her forehead in ritual recognition of the fact that her partner of over fifty years had left her and that she was now a widow. Seeing our mother do this shook us to our core and was quite a way to remind us of the end of an era in our family.

Finally, we went to the hospital to identify our father's body from the morgue and make arrangements for his cremation at a nearby cemetery. At the cremation, standing there with my family, I got to thinking more about death and how we all deal with our dead. We cremate, we bury, we leave the cadavers to vultures to deal with, but, ultimately, dead bodies disintegrate into dust and come full circle—it returns to the earth it came from. We collected my father's ashes so we could scatter them in the Ganga, as desired by our mother. A few months later, Manek, our mother, Anu and I went to Haridwar, where Manek performed all the necessary rituals. We dispersed my father's ashes in the Ganga and watched them float away and vanish into the water.

In India there's a custom meant to be followed after the death of a loved one that I hadn't heard of before. One is supposed to take a bit of bread dough and divide the dough into three little mounds. You then place these pieces on the ground near your house and say a special prayer. Crows, symbolizing one's long-dead ancestors, are meant to come and eat the dough.

'Ba,' I said to my mother, 'there are no crows here.'

'No,' she said, 'it always happens. Your ancestors come. The crows are our ancestors.'

Anu made the dough and we arranged it into little mounds. I've never been religious. I'm an engineer, a technologist. I have always joked that I outsourced religion and related matters to Anu. And so when the crows actually appeared and ate up the dough, I was astonished. It was our ancestors.

~

My mother was also with us when we lost her to liver cancer ten years or so after my father passed away. Anu took care of my mother as her health deteriorated, staying with her morning and night, bathing her, feeding her, comforting her.

It was a hot summer night in Chicago when my mother started throwing up blood from her mouth again. This was a frequent occurrence by this point, but she was brave and dealt with it as best she could. However, this time it was different. We called an ambulance and went to the hospital. My sisters had flown in from all over the country to be with our mother. I came home at 11 p.m. when her condition stabilized. At 2 a.m. I received a call that Ba had passed away while singing bhajans together with her four loving daughters.

Ba was cremated at the same cemetery as my father. At her funeral, I talked about how she had lived a colourful and fulfilling life, a life of discipline and order. She worked very hard all her life, raising eight children and managing an entire household single-handedly. When she died she had over twenty-five grandchildren and several great-grandchildren.

I viewed Ba as the architect of my life. My father was my role model for hard work, while my mother was everything else. When Ba died, I felt really lonely and helpless, as if the earth had moved beneath my feet. With her, an entire generation of traditional wisdom had been lost. I used to say to her that when she leaves us, the Pitroda-family pickle technology would be lost forever. She used to make over sixty different types of pickles—we used to have a special pickle room at home that she would fill with unique varieties of pickles for our circle of family and friends.

I thought of my parents, alive now only in the hearts and memories of those of us who knew them. When someone dies, the memories of how they talked, what they sounded like, how they acted, what they had done in their lives, who they had been, all of it vanishes along with them.

~

Looking at Aria, holding her, I thought, *I must leave her all my memories—for her, this newborn baby, so she would know how it came to be that a little Indian girl was born in California instead of in a tiny farming village perched on the edge of the Kutch salt desert.*

Eventually, Aria will want to know who her grandfather was. Where did he come from? Why did he come here? What did he do here? At some point in her life she will want to learn about her roots.

And I realized that what her father would probably tell her would be very different from what I would have to say. Salil—born, raised and educated in the United States—would naturally see things from his own perspective. But what about my perspective? Nobody else would have that once my generation and I were gone.

This got me started on my identity—who am I, what do I do, what do I stand for? I want Aria to know that we are Gujaratis. Our ancestors came from Africa, like everyone else's, and we settled in Kutch, Gujarat. Finally, they moved to the southern border of the Kutch desert to a small town called Tikar. I want her to know that we speak a language called Gujarati, and that people from this part of the world are known for their entrepreneurship and trading prowess. They are also known for their close family ties, simplicity, honesty, humility and hospitality. I want her to know that a large number of Gujaratis left their ancestors' homes to explore new frontiers and look for work in the Middle East, Africa, the UK and the US. My father came to Orissa from Tikar much the same way, looking for work, and settled there to raise a family of eight kids.

My brother Manek is in possession of a list of twenty-four generations of Aria's grandparents, collected from various village documents. Here is the family tree—Aria, Salil, Satyan (Sam), Gangaram, Kalyanji, Hirjee, Vela, Vashata, Vira, Lumbha, Mona, Varsha, Aala, Chottao, Dunger, Jiva, Aala, Vachha, Vasa, Karman, Samat, Jagmal, Naran, Lalji, Bhaga and Meghji.

I come from a very humble background. Born in a tiny tribal village in Orissa, I studied in Gujarat, came to the US to learn and stayed back to earn. In the US I married a Gujarati girl, started a family, built businesses, made some money and started dreaming big for India. I moved to India to improve telecom access, supported by the young dynamic Prime Minister Rajiv Gandhi, launched multiple national initiatives, had a heart attack, experienced the death of my friend and prime minister, Rajiv—and totally lost my heart.

My time in India had left me broken emotionally and financially. I had to come back to America to earn and piece my personal life back together. Once again, I built businesses, raised two great kids, took care of my parents, then returned to India a second time to continue dreaming big on knowledge, information infrastructure and innovation. In the process I battled cancer, had another heart surgery, and continued to enjoy working on both sides of the globe with loyalty and commitment to two great democratic countries, India and the United States of America.

Because of my early upbringing in a tribal area, I was very concerned about the development of the people at the bottom of the economic pyramid in India and elsewhere. I learned a great deal from the US, which empowered me to think big and dream big. I mentored and benefited from young talent and their energy. I have always been a man in a hurry, someone who knew that there was little time and too many things to do.

I did not take due care of my personal health and personal life. I never had a pension plan, retirement fund or life insurance policy. I never played golf, was never affiliated to any club, hardly attended any parties or weddings and hardly watched any TV or movies. However, I lived a simple, ethical, moral, content, fulfilling and happy private life.

As I have become older I have realized that my metaphorical roots lie in the ancient wisdom of India, deeply embedded in family values, communities, culture, democracy, duty, karma, simplicity and selfless sacrifice. My tree is made up of technology, information, energy, enthusiasm and motivation. And my fruits relate to new models of development with a focus on generational change in education, economy, management, leadership, institutions and infrastructure. Gandhi is my true inspiration. Like him, I also believe that true innovations happen when what you think, what you say and what you do interact with and are in true harmony with each other. Early in life I realized that building a nation is very different from building a company. Building a nation requires long-term commitment, patience, perseverance and hard work.

I have seen so much change in my life. I was born in a time of firsts—when the first nuclear chain reaction was established, the first atom bomb was manufactured and the first transistor was invented. In the course of my working life, I have seen it all. I have seen a lot of technology developments related to radio, television, telephones, computers, software, consumer goods, transport, health, energy, cloud computing, components, smartphones, and so on. I have seen change from and in all dimensions. I know that to build something new one has to kill something old.

But leaving behind the old is not that simple. We all have attachments, emotions and memories connected to our past, but we need to move on in order to build a new future. To survive in a constantly changing environment I had to continue to change and redefine myself. In the process I was inspired by Gandhi to strengthen my inner core and self, and my values, virtues, ethics, morals and character. Like Gandhi, I have maintained journals for the past fifty years of my life. They are lying in a big metal box in my home for Aria and the other grandchildren to explore in the future.

I want Aria to know that I was a loner. I never could fit into any box, club or society. I was not a businessman, politician, scientist, administrator, professor or activist. I was always an outsider, an interloper, a change agent, a catalyst, someone who believed in creating bypasses. In the process I inculcated unique multidimensional abilities to solve large, complex problems. I also built a network of connections and contacts with global leaders and champions. I want Aria to know that I lived in multiple countries, different cultures—and multiple realities—at the same time. I had lots of energy and focus, and learned to get things done against all the odds of the world stacked up against me.

Aria came into the world from privileged quarters; she has an influential grandfather, highly educated parents, wealth and a perch in the United States—the exact opposite of my early situation. Today, the technological possibilities are limitless. She is also lucky to be born in one of the most democratic, prosperous and innovative countries in the world. Her generation will bring forth more global equality and equity through giant strides in applications of information, biotechnology, nanotechnology, materials science, genetics, stem cell research, alternative energy, etc. It is even possible that her generation will live to be 200 years old. They will indeed be the new generation of global citizens with infinite multicultural possibilities. I hope that in spite of all the technological possibilities the fundamental human values will remain intact for her generation with a strong focus on the self, family, love, freedom, work, pleasure, and peace and prosperity for all. As a result, I strongly believe that Gandhi will be more relevant to her generation than ever before.

Anu and I were in San Francisco for a week with nothing else to do but pay attention to this little one that had come to us. We were all there—Arpita, Salil, Rajal, Anu, and Arpita's parents, Dr Hiralal Patel and Nilaben. We took turns staring at and holding Aria. We bought chocolate cigars, fancy wines and good food to celebrate. However, I was off in my own world, thinking, *What does this mean? And when all is said and done, what is next?* What is it that I could say to her? How would I explain things to her, tell her how it was. I wanted to build a bridge for her to travel back in time on whenever she was ready to do it.

Fifty years from now I could imagine her talking to the others, Rajal's kids, other Pitroda grandkids, her cousins, maybe even more of her siblings to come, sitting around and saying, 'Who was that guy, that old man? Who was that half-mad person who came here a hundred years ago and brought everyone with him? Who was he? What did he do? What were his values? What did he stand for?' And if I could explain it to her, I could explain it also to Salil and Rajal, loved *and* neglected by me during their own childhoods.

'He had two great kids,' Aria and the others might say. 'He had a good innings. He and his wife worked hard. He brought the family here. Took care of his own parents. Made millions in America. Then worked with Prime Minister Rajiv Gandhi to help modernize India through telecom and technology. In the process, he almost killed himself and went broke. However, he picked himself up from the financial floor, rebuilt his life in America and, once again, in spite of two more near-death experiences, he worked with Dr Manmohan Singh on modernizing India through improving knowledge, digitization and innovation.'

And maybe, at the end of the day, that is the sum of my life—my purpose.

My dear friend, the psychiatrist Prakash Desai, said something to me in his last days, when due to throat cancer he could barely utter a word or two at a time. Long ago, during the time of the India Forum, he had talked to us about what makes a person normal. We were in our late twenties then. 'Do you remember that?' I asked. He did. 'And what do you think now?' I asked. I would have loved to have heard him explain fully, but he was in too much discomfort and the strain was too much. 'Fulfilment,' he said. 'Love . . . work . . . fulfilment.'

Work, I understood. I don't know if I could have defined what 'fulfilment' meant to Aria. At the time this book goes to press, Aria is four. I have watched her grow. We have Skype conversations almost every day. We two are connected. And when all is said and done, Aria may well be the answer to my search for connectivity and my lifelong journey to connect a billion in India with telephones, technology, knowledge, information and innovations.